The Complete Photo Guide to

PERFECT FITTING

Creative Publishing international

First published in the United States of America by
Creative Publishing international, Inc., a member of Quayside Publishing Group
400 First Avenue North, Suite 300
Minneapolis, MN 55401
1-800-328-3895
www.creativepub.com

ISBN-13: 9781589236080

10 9 8 7 6 5 4 3

Library of Congress Cataloging-in-Publication Data

Veblen, Sarah.
  The complete photo guide to perfect fitting / Sarah Veblen.
    p. cm.
  ISBN-13: 978-1-58923-608-0 (pbk.)
  ISBN-10: 1-58923-608-4 (soft cover)
  1. Dressmaking–Pattern design–Pictorial works. 2. Clothing and dress measurements–Pictorial works. 3. Clothing and dress–Alteration–Pictorial works. I. Title.

TT520.V43 2012
646.4–dc23

                                            2011023810

Printed in China

Copy Editor: Catherine Broberg
Proofreader: Karen Ruth
Book and Cover Design: Kim Winscher
Page Layout: Danielle Smith
Illustrations: Bonnie Veblen
Photographs: Imagebroker/Alamy: 6 (top left); Interfoto/Alamy: 6 (top right); Chaloner Woods/Getty Images: 6 (bottom); Nina Leen/Getty Images: 24; Shutterstock.com: 45; Corinne MARCHETTI/Gamma-Rapho via Getty images: 193; Michael DeFilippi: all other photography

Dedication

To Charles Kleibacker,

for his life's work of keeping the craft alive.

And to Bonnie,

who was there for me every step of the way.

Acknowledgments

Heartfelt thanks to everyone

who helped in many different ways:

A Fabric Place
Michael Bearman
Rae Cumbie
Michael DeFilippi
Blondell Howard
Henrietta Jones
Tovah and Nick Kopan

Marcie Levendusky
Annie McCarty
Douglas Preston
Bob Ross and Lorraine Ferland
Elisabeth Stewart and family
Krista Veblen

The Complete Photo Guide to
PERFECT FITTING

**Creative Publishing
international**

CONTENTS

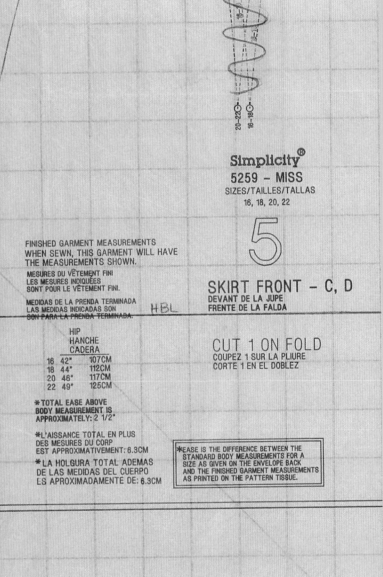

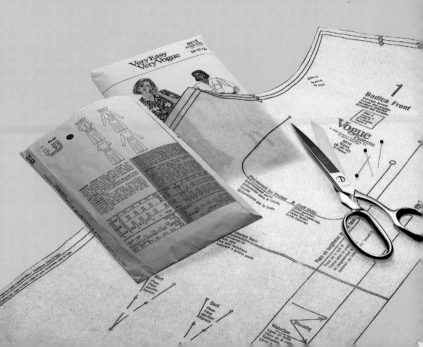

Introduction

There's an aura of beauty about a woman wearing clothes that fit her well, regardless of her figure and facial features. Her clothes create a sense of balance and proportion for her body, which is flattering to her and visually pleasing to others. She's definitely wearing her clothes, rather than her clothes wearing her.

Although styles change and clothing fads come and go, the hallmarks of well-fitting clothes remain the same:

- There are no unintended pulls or folds in the fabric.

- The fabric falls smoothly over the body.

- The garment is proportionate to the wearer's body.

- The cut of the garment is flattering.

When wearing clothes that fit, we not only present ourselves better, but we feel more comfortable. And when we feel at ease in our clothes, we think more clearly, interact with other people better, and approach the day's challenges and pleasures with a healthier attitude. There is no need to feel squirmy in your clothes, counting the minutes until you can get home and change into your comfy sweats. It all starts with getting a good fit.

Fitting is complicated, in part because it doesn't stand alone. Rather, it must be tackled within the larger framework of all that is required to make a garment, from design to pattern development. To achieve success, you must have the following:

1 A fitting method to follow

2 An understanding of good fitting practices

3 An understanding of good patternmaking practices

4 The ability to recognize specific fitting issues

5 The ability to put these specific issues within the context of the garment as a whole

This book is organized so that the information builds from one section to the next. In the first part of the book, I describe the conceptual foundation. In the second part, I explain the process of fitting garments and show how to develop fitting solutions for different body types. The last section shows you how to apply changes to auxiliary pattern components so all the pieces work well together, and I also suggest some creative variations.

Even though fitting is complicated, with patience and guidance, everyone can learn to fit.

LAYING THE FOUNDATION

Being a competent fitter requires both a conceptual and a practical understanding of the fitting process. Skipping the concepts and going straight to the fitting examples is like trying to build a house without first laying its foundation. Just as the house will develop cracks, your fitting will have weaknesses, which will cause confusion and less-than-perfect results.

Developing a Solid Approach to Fitting

Any skill requires training. Fitting requires training the eye to recognize what good fit is and what indicates a poor fit. For example, a novice often doesn't notice drag lines until they are pointed out. With practice, the eye becomes trained first to see the obvious fitting problems and eventually then to discern nuances. A good way to train your eye is to observe people's clothes wherever you go, from your work environment to stops at the grocery store.

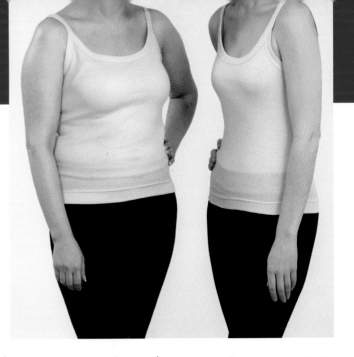

WHY FITTING IS COMPLICATED

Once the fitting problem is identified, it must be corrected. This requires knowing how to manipulate the cloth. However, the fitting problem cannot be dealt with out of context; it must be solved within the framework of the garment as a whole. In addition, the cloth must be manipulated in a manner that allows the change to be made in the pattern. As your fitting skills improve, your knowledge of pattern work will improve as well due to the interrelationship between fitting and pattern manipulation.

Obtaining a good fit is a process, rarely a one-shot experience. It takes time, patience, and usually multiple muslins to develop a perfect fit. Most sewers think the process is worthwhile, since the end result is that perfectly fitting pattern you've dreamed of.

Fitting yourself is possible but often time consuming. Accurately assessing a muslin on your own body is more difficult than making good observations on someone else. It's helpful to have a dress form that reflects your body; working with a fitting buddy can help even more. Two sets of eyes are useful when learning to identify fitting problems, and you can collaborate on figuring out the best solution. Plus, you can fit each other.

EACH INDIVIDUAL IS UNIQUE

Since no two bodies are exactly the same, fitting requires individualized problem solving. Fitting instructions will get you started, but they are generalized descriptions of a situation and a typical solution. You must then apply this information to the person being fitted. This requires experimenting with and interpreting the fitting instructions. Fitting is easier and more successful when you work with the cloth on the individual's body rather than insisting that a fitting "rule" be applied in a preordained manner.

Although picture-perfect bodies can depict standardized fitting solutions, very few of us have such bodies. This book is comprised of real fitting situations that are characteristic of typical fitting issues. The models are ordinary people with everyday lumps and bumps. Your own body might not be represented by these particular models, but you will find fitting examples throughout the book that are similar to your fitting problems.

In addition to finding solutions to fitting issues, a good fitter also needs a way to reflect on and approach the problems. This book provides a methodology that will help you interpret specific fitting examples and then apply the information to your own fitting issues, leading you to the best solution for your situation. The end result is beautifully fitting clothes.

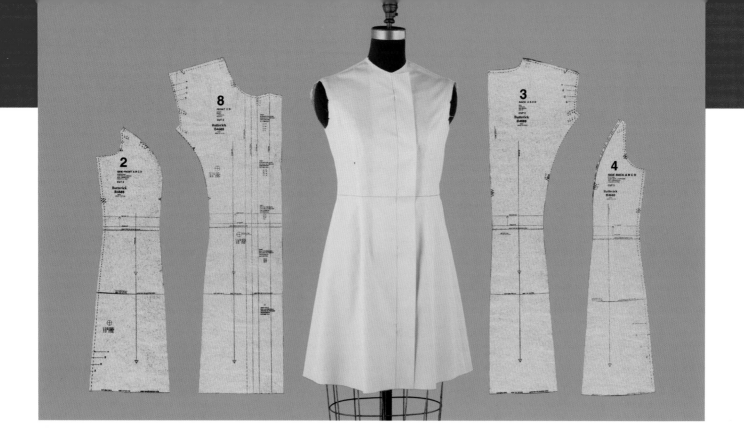

Pattern and Fitting Basics

Patterns are tools that help us make a garment. If that garment fits nicely, the pattern becomes more valuable, because it is the vehicle that lets us reproduce the garment. Most sewers are thrilled to have a pattern that fits well, because they can then concentrate on being creative with fabrics, embellishments, and small style changes.

HOW PATTERNS ARE DEVELOPED

Patterns are developed in two primary ways: drafting and draping.

A drafted pattern is based on body measurements. It can be computer generated utilizing patternmaking software programs. It also can be hand-drawn, with or without adherence to established drafting rules.

A draped pattern is derived from manipulating cloth directly on a dress form or person. Established draping rules can be followed as much or as little as desired. A paper pattern is often made from the draped garment sections. Draping is often used when the selected fabric or garment design does not lend itself to drafting a pattern.

Flat pattern development (or flat patternmaking) is a method of developing patterns from a basic set of patterns, sometimes referred to as working patterns, slopers, or blocks. Much of the ready-to-wear industry uses this method to create patterns for their styles. This book will use many flat pattern principles to manipulate the pattern in the process of getting a good fit.

FINDING YOUR WAY AROUND A PATTERN

Commercial patterns provide a lot of information to help the sewer make an educated selection when choosing a pattern and to assist the sewer when making the garment. Understanding the pattern envelope and its contents is the first step toward using patterns successfully.

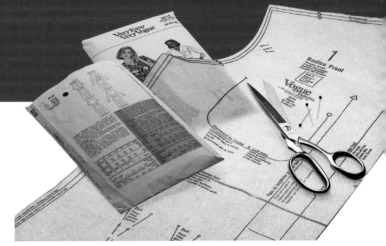

Almost all commercial patterns include a guide sheet that includes a list of pattern pieces, a description of pieces to use for specific views, fabric cutting layouts, seam allowance information, a key to reading the illustrations (how elements such as the right side and wrong side of the fabric are depicted), and step-by-step directions. Some patterns provide a short glossary of sewing terms, and some have helpful design tips.

In addition to these elements, some pattern envelopes also provide information such as a difficulty rating based on the sewing techniques required to make the garment, recommendations of figure types for the garment style, and stretch guides for knits-only patterns.

Remember, a pattern is a tool for you to use, not a dictum that you must follow precisely. It's important to view the information that the pattern supplies within the context of your knowledge about sewing, fabric, and pattern work.

The Pattern Envelope Front

Garment depiction is a fashion illustration or a photograph of the garment. Some patterns provide both.

Views show garment variations and options.

Size indicates size or sizes included. Multi-sized patterns usually print all cutting lines on the same tissue.

The Pattern Envelope Back

Line drawings often convey more information than the illustration or photo on the front of the pattern, because they provide style lines (seam placement) and fitting elements such as darts.

Descriptive caption describes how the garment is cut (loose or close to the body) and general stylistic elements of the garment.

Finished garment measurements also indicate how the garment is cut. For example, hemline circumferences

are usually given. Some pattern companies provide more information than others.

Size chart lists standardized measurements and correlating pattern sizes.

Notions list indicates items such as shoulder pads and buttons required for the pattern, including size specifications.

Fabric recommendations are suggested fabrics for the pattern's garment(s); use this information as a guide in conjunction with your own knowledge of fabrics.

Yardage chart indicates how much fabric to buy, usually with two different pattern layouts: with nap (all pattern pieces are oriented in the same direction) and without nap (the pattern pieces are oriented to use the least amount of fabric).

The Pattern Pieces

Dot, triangle, or square symbols are match points for adjoining pattern pieces. If you think of the pattern as a puzzle, these symbols help you put the puzzle together correctly.

Grainline arrow specifies the orientation of the pattern piece on the fabric. Grainline arrows usually indicate the length-of-grain and therefore should be placed parallel to the selvage of the fabric. Grainline is extremely important because it is what makes your garments hang correctly.

Placement lines indicate the position for elements such pockets, buttonholes, and trims.

(continued)

Double line provides an appropriate place to lengthen or shorten the pattern with minimal disruption of the pattern's style lines.

Finished garment measurements are sometimes provided for the bust, waist, and hip. This is useful information in determining how much ease is included in the pattern.

GARMENT SILHOUETTES AND EASE

Clothes create a silhouette on the body, falling into one of three general categories:

1 Clothes cut close or fairly close to the body create a fitted silhouette. Stylistically, tailored garments that have enough ease to move comfortably but without excess fabric fall into this category. Eveningwear and formal clothes can also be in this category. And depending on what is currently popular, trendy clothes might be cut quite close to the body.

2 Clothes cut with more ease but without being loose and baggy create a relaxed silhouette. Stylistically, these clothes often look more casual than tailored garments. They run the gamut, including office wear, everyday clothes, and weekend favorites.

3 Clothes that incorporate even more ease create a loose silhouette. Stylistically, the fullness can look proportionate on the body if the volume of fabric is well controlled. It can also look baggy and oversized, which periodically is popular.

It's important to be comfortable in your clothes, but comfort is not solely dependent on how much ease is in your garment. A very large garment can be uncomfortable and restrictive just as easily as a garment that's too small. Fabric selection impacts the way a garment feels on the body. But the biggest key to comfort is good fit.

1 Fitted silhouette

2 Relaxed silhouette

3 Controlled fullness silhouette

3 Loose silhouette

Two Kinds of Garment Ease

Garment ease refers to the difference between the finished measurements of the garment and the measurements of the wearer's body. With woven fabrics, the garment needs to be at least somewhat larger than the body; otherwise we cannot move in our clothes. This difference is referred to as wearing ease.

Some garments are intentionally bigger than the wearer's body in order to create a specific look. When a garment is purposely styled to be noticeably larger than the body, this is referred to as design ease.

A 1960s tent dress is a perfect example of design ease. There is a great deal more ease in the hip area than is needed to move comfortably in the garment. It is precisely this design ease that creates the style of the dress.

With knit fabrics, the garment's finished measurements often equal the wearer's body measurements, because the knit structure and its ability to give provide the wearing ease. Garments such as activewear and bathing suits that are made of stretch knits (knits with spandex) have negative ease. In this case, the garment's finished measurements are smaller than the wearer's body measurements, because the fit is partially obtained as the fabric stretches around the body.

1960s tent dress

CHOOSING A PATTERN SIZE

It's rare that a commercial pattern is ideal for your figure, because these patterns are developed for a standardized body. Some pattern companies base their patterns on a specific figure type; this is convenient if you find a pattern company that uses a figure similar to yours. For most women, however, commercial patterns are simply a tool—a good starting place for developing a pattern that fits.

Pattern envelopes provide a measurement/size chart to help you choose a pattern size. While using this chart is simple, there are a number of variables to consider in addition to your body measurements when selecting a pattern size.

Taking Your Measurements

Accurate body measurements are an essential starting point. Wear the undergarments that you normally would with the garment you intend to sew. Undergarments that fit well make the fitting process easier and the final garment more attractive. When taking measurements, assume a normal stance; do not pull the tape tight, but have it rest lightly on the body.

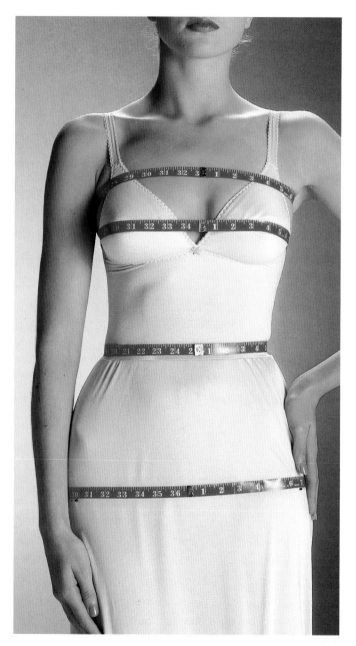

- **High bust/chest.** Measure directly under the arms, across the chest (above the full bust), and across the back, keeping the tape straight across the back.

- **Bust/full bust.** Measure over the fullest part of the bust and across the back, keeping the tape straight and parallel to the floor.

- **Waist.** Measure the natural waist, which is the smallest part of the torso, even if you usually wear your garments lower. A narrow elastic tied around the waist will seek the smallest part of the torso.

- **Hip.** Measure the fullest part of the hip/buttock, keeping the tape parallel to the floor. Use the abdominal measurement or a high, full thigh measurement if it is greater than the hip/buttock measurement.

Where's My Waist?

Although most people think of their waist as where they prefer the top of their skirts and pants to rest, the waist by definition is the smallest part of the torso. Many women wear skirts and pants not at the natural waist but sitting lower on the torso, often just resting on the top of the hip bone or at the navel. Style trends often have the "waist" even lower on the pelvis. Commercial patterns are developed with the waist at the smallest part of the torso, unless the pattern specifies otherwise (for instance, "1½" [3.8 cm] below waist" might be printed near the top of a skirt pattern). For fitting and pattern development purposes, think of a lowered waistline as a stylistic element.

Which Measurements to Use?

Having an accurate set of measurements allows you to go to the next step: deciding what size pattern to buy. Start with the size chart on the pattern envelope to determine which size the pattern company recommends.

For skirts and pants (bottoms), use your full hip measurement, or the abdomen or high thigh measurement if it is larger than the hip/buttock measurement.

For blouses and jackets (tops), choosing a pattern size is more complicated, because most commercial pattern companies develop their patterns for a B-cup size. Some specially marked patterns provide multiple cup sizes, and others are sized for a full figure.

Many women whose bust is larger than a B cup prefer to use the high bust/chest measurement to select the pattern size, because the full bust measurement puts them into a pattern size that is disproportionate to their frame. The smaller size pattern better fits their frame, and a full bust adjustment (see page 129) is made to the pattern to accommodate the larger cup size. If the full bust measurement is used to select the pattern size, then the shoulder width and armhole will likely need to be adjusted and made smaller. Both approaches are valid; use the one that makes the most sense to you.

For women with an A-cup size, the same situation exists but in reverse. If the full bust measurement is used to select the pattern size, the shoulder width and upper torso length will likely need to be adjusted and made larger. Alternatively, if the high bust/chest measurement is used, a small bust adjustment (see page 129) will need to be made.

Determining Your Cup Size

Subtract the chest measurement from the full bust measurement.

A cup = 1" (2.5 cm) or less

B cup = 1¼" to 2" (3.2 to 5.1 cm)

C cup = 2¼" to 3" (5.7 to 7.6 cm)

D cup = 3¼" to 4" (8.3 to 10.2 cm)

DD cup = 4¼" to 5" (10.8 to 12.7 cm)

Using a Standard Measurement/Size Chart

Pattern sizes are standardized among the major pattern companies, but these sizes bear no relation to ready-to-wear sizes. To select a pattern size based on your bust measurement, read across the "bust" line until you come to your measurement; then read up to find the pattern size. Use the same method if using a hip measurement. If your body measurement is between two sizes, considering the variables described in this chapter will help you make a logical pattern size selection. Remember, the pattern is just a tool to help you get started.

FIGURE SIZE CHART

Misses'/Miss Petite

Sizes	4	6	8	10	12	14	16	18	20	22	24	26
Sizes-European	30	32	34	36	38	40	42	44	46	48	50	52
Bust	29½"	30½"	31½"	32½"	34"	36"	38"	40"	42"	44"	46"	48"
Centimeters	75	78	80	83	87	92	97	102	107	112	117	122
Waist	22"	23"	24"	25"	26½"	28"	30"	32"	34"	37"	39"	41½"
Centimeters	56	58	61	64	67	71	76	81	87	94	99	105.5
Hip - 9" (23 cm) below waist	31½"	32½"	33½"	34½"	36"	38"	40"	42"	44"	46"	48"	50"
Centimeters	80	83	85	88	92	97	102	107	112	117	122	127
Back Waist Length	15¼"	15½"	15¾"	16"	16¼"	16½"	16¾"	17"	17¼"	17⅜"	17½"	17¾"
Centimeters	38.5	39.5	40	40.5	41.5	42	42.5	43	44	44	44.5	45
Petite-Back Waist Length	14¼"	14½"	14¾"	15"	15¼"	15½"	15¾"	16"	16¼"	16⅜"	16½"	16⅝"
Centimeters	36	37	37.5	38	39	39.5	40	40.5	41	41.5	42	42

Women's/Women's Petite

Sizes	18W	20W	22W	24W	26W	28W	30W	32W
Sizes-European	44	46	48	50	52	54	56	58
Bust	40"	42"	44"	46"	48"	50"	52"	54"
Centimeters	101.5	106.5	112	117	122	127	132	137
Waist	33"	35"	37"	39"	41½"	44"	46½"	49"
Centimeters	84	89	94	99	105.5	112	118	124
Hip - 9" (23 cm) below waist	42"	44"	46"	48"	50"	52"	54"	56"
Centimeters	106.5	112	117	122	127	132	137	142
Back Waist Length	17⅛"	17¼"	17⅜"	17½"	17⅝"	17¾"	17⅞"	18"
Centimeters	43.5	44	44	44.5	45	45	45.5	46
Petite-Back Waist Length	16⅛"	16¼"	16⅜"	16½"	16⅝"	16¾"	16⅞"	17"
Centimeters	41	41.5	41.5	42	42	42.5	43	43

EASE CHART

		Close Fitting	Fitted	Semi Fitted	Loose Fitting	Very Loose Fitting
Bust Area	Dresses	0 to 2⅞" (0 to 7.3 cm)	3" to 4" (7.6.2 to 10 cm)	4⅛" to 5" (10.5 to 12.7 cm)	5⅛" to 8" (13 to 20.3 cm)	Over 8" (20.3 cm)
	Jackets		3¾" to 4¼" (9.5 to 10.8 cm)	4⅜" to 5¾" (11.1 to 14.6 cm)	5⅞" to 10" (14.9 to 25.4 cm)	Over 10" (25.4 cm)
	Coats		5¼" to 6¾" (13.3 to 17.2 cm)	6⅞" to 8" (17.5 to 20.3 cm)	8⅛" to 12" (20.7 to 30.5 cm)	Over 12" (30.5 cm)
Hips	Pants/Skirts	0 to 1⅞" (0 to 4.8 cm)	2 to 3" (5.1 to 7.6 cm)	3⅛" to 4" (7.9 to 10.2 cm)	4⅛" to 6" (10.5 to 15.2 cm)	Over 6" (15.2 cm)

Information courtesy of The McCall Pattern Company ©2011.

Other Variables in Selecting a Pattern Size

The amount of ease built in to a pattern affects the way the garment fits. Some patterns include a garment description, which indicates how much ease there is. For instance, a garment might be described as semifitted or loose fitting. However, these terms are imprecise—they describe a range of ease, as seen from the ease chart.

The garment rendering or photograph on the pattern envelope also depicts how fitted or loose the garment is intended to be. Unfortunately, these illustrations and photographs do not always accurately reflect the amount of ease in the garment.

Finished garment measurements on either the pattern envelope or the pattern tissue are the most helpful, because they tell you precisely how much ease has been incorporated into the pattern. Simply subtract your body measurement from the finished garment measurement, and the result is how much ease the garment will have on your body. Deciding how much wearing ease and design ease you would like in your garment will guide you in choosing a pattern size.

Wearing Ease Recommendations

Wearing ease recommendations also vary. For instance, the Butterick chart lists 3" to 4" (7.6 to 10. 2 cm) of ease in the bust for garments in the fitted silhouette category, whereas I find less is necessary. How much wearing ease to include is a matter of personal preference. However, many women find that they need less wearing ease in a garment that fits well compared to a garment that does not fit well.

I recommend the following ease amounts for garments in the fitted silhouette category when the garment fits well. For the hip and the full bust, 1½" to 2" (3.8 to 5.1 cm) for a slender figure, and 2" to 3" (5.1 to 7.6 cm) for a full figure is adequate and comfortable. The waist depends on personal preference; some women like a bit of ease (perhaps ½" to 1" [1.3 to 2.5 cm]), while others actually like negative ease.

Pattern Selection

Altering the length of many patterns is very simple, and most patterns provide lengthen/shorten lines for your convenience. Adjusting a pattern's circumference is more difficult. Therefore, select a pattern size that will be close to your desired circumference (wearing ease + design ease), even if you know you will need to alter the length.

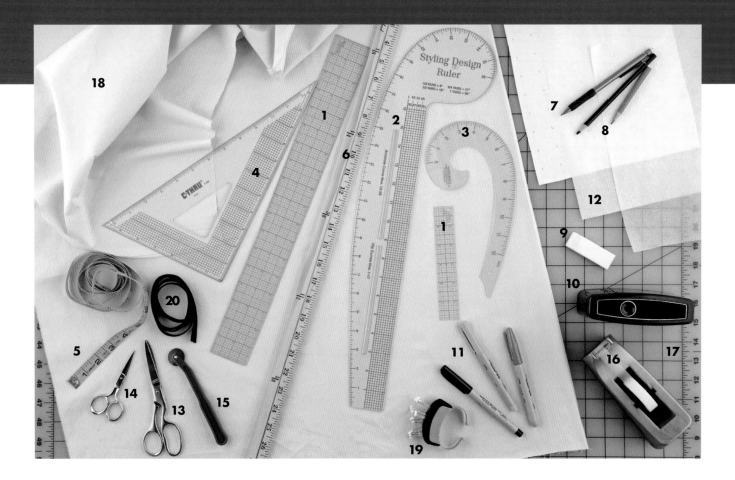

TOOLS FOR PATTERN WORK AND FITTING

A few specialized tools are handy when fitting muslins and adjusting patterns. Since people work more efficiently when tools are comfortable in their hands, try different pencils and paper scissors until you find those you like. There are a number of options for pattern work, such as Swedish Tracing Paper (an interfacing-like product), tissue paper, architect's trace, alpha-numeric grid paper used in the industry, and exam table paper. The advantage of using paper instead of an interfacing-type product or taking apart a muslin and using the fabric itself for a pattern is that paper is exact and cannot stretch out of shape.

Transparent straight edge rulers (**1**) allow you to view the pattern while drafting. See-through rulers marked in ⅛" (3 mm) increments are particularly handy and are available in several lengths.

Fashion ruler/styling design rulers (**2**) provide excellent curvature for pattern adjustments and pattern drafting.

French curves (**3**) provide additional curvatures; they are nice to have but not essential.

Right-angle rulers (**4**) are also convenient and can be triangles, L-squares, or T-squares.

Measuring tape (**5**) that does not stretch, either reinforced fiberglass or waterproof oilcloth.

Yardstick (**6**) for checking fitting axis during the fitting process.

Pencils (**7**) that make a precise, easy-to-read line and are comfortable in your hand. Mechanical pencils don't need sharpening.

Colored pencils (**8**) are particularly handy when making multiple pattern adjustments and you want to indicate which line to use; they're also helpful for drawing axis lines on a fitting muslin.

Fabric eraser (**9**) can be used to remove light pencil marks without abrading or marking the fabric.

Pencil sharpener **(10)** for wooden and colored pencils.

Fine-tip markers **(11)** for marking pinned adjustments on a muslin.

Pattern paper of your choice **(12)**, for example architect's trace, alpha-numeric pattern paper, exam table paper. Tissue paper designed for gifts tears easily and is not recommended.

Paper scissors **(13)** should be comfortable in your hand and allow you to cut accurately.

Small fabric scissors **(14)** are helpful when clipping fitting muslin during the fitting.

Tracing wheel **(15)** and carbon paper if you like to transfer pattern markings to the muslin this way.

Clear tape **(16)** for adding paper to patterns and making pattern adjustments. Some are more flexible than others, some are removable. I prefer ½" (1.3 cm) Magic tape in a desk dispenser.

Colored tape (not shown) for marking the yardstick; blue painter's masking tape is easy to remove and leaves no adhesive residue.

Table or work area **(17)** large enough to spread your pattern out. An elevated table prevents back strain. A clean kitchen counter works well. You can easily elevate a table with bed lifts or PVC pipe (that the table legs can slip into) cut to the appropriate length.

Muslin **(18)** or other stable fabric for test garments. Woven gingham is often off-grain, and so is not actually helpful. Some people like pattern tracing fabric or lightweight nonwoven interfacing, so the pattern itself can be used as a test-fitting garment; while convenient, this method is not as accurate as keeping a separate paper pattern.

Pins **(19)** for fitting the muslin should be sharp and easy to use. I prefer glass head pins. Some people find a wrist pincushion convenient.

Elastic **(20)**, ¼" to ⅜" (6 to 10 mm) wide, for anchoring skirts and pants during a fitting, and assisting in taking waist measurements.

Sewing machine and basic sewing notions for making test-fitting garments.

Iron and ironing board for pressing test fabric, constructing test garment, and pressing fitted muslin pieces flat.

Full-length mirror for fitting test garments. Having an additional mirror allows you to easily see your back and sides without turning the body and distorting the test garment.

Dress form made or padded to measurements is convenient but not necessary. Fitting test garments on the body is better for getting accurate proportions.

THE INTERRELATIONSHIP BETWEEN PATTERNS AND FITTING

To get a pattern to fit, use the pattern in conjunction with a test garment (or fitting muslin). The fitting muslin is your laboratory, where you can experiment with changes so the fit is good and the garment's proportions are flattering. The pattern is the record-keeping device where you make the fitting changes so that you can reproduce the garment.

Understanding the principles of flat pattern manipulation helps you become a more effective fitter. For example, you will know to make changes on the fitting muslin in such a way that they can later be made in the pattern. Understanding the principles of fitting advances your ability to alter and adjust patterns. For instance, you will be more aware of how a change to one pattern piece affects an adjacent pattern piece.

The two skills of fitting and patternmaking support one another in many ways. When you are fitting, you will know that you can fine-tune the subtlety of a curve with your ruler on the pattern. When you are adjusting a pattern, you will be guided by both the visual and tactile knowledge you have of the individual's body. Strengthening one skill leads to the enhancement of the other skill.

OVERVIEW OF THE FITTING PROCESS

Getting a pattern to fit is a process. Sometimes it's a simple and short process, and other times it's long and involved. Some garment styles are more straightforward to fit than others, and some individuals are easier to fit than others. But the general process is always the same. The following chapters describe the process in detail.

1 Make preliminary adjustments to the pattern, if desired.

2 Mark and sew a test garment.

3 Fit the test garment. This requires training the eye to recognize fitting issues, deciding which fitting changes to make first, and knowing when to stop a fitting.

4 Mark the changes pinned on the test garment and remove the pins.

5 Transfer the markings on the test garment to the pattern.

6 Alter and manipulate the pattern. This requires learning basic pattern manipulation techniques.

7 True the pattern (that is, check that adjacent seams on the pattern are the same length).

8 Mark and sew another test garment, repeating the process until the fit and the pattern are perfected.

Fresh Starts

Rather than trying to fit the entire test garment in one session, it can be helpful to stop a fitting after you pin a small number of changes. Making those changes on the pattern and sewing a new test garment often makes it easy to see which fitting changes to make next. Plus, you can double-check that what you've done so far is indeed improving the fit. If a large number of fitting changes are made in a single session and a new fitting issue is introduced, it can be quite difficult to assess what caused the new problem.

RECOGNIZING FITTING ISSUES

Training the eye to recognize fitting issues requires time. Masters at fitting have studied and practiced for years, and they have fit hundreds of garments on all types of bodies. Once you can recognize a few fitting issues, you'll be able to concentrate on others, gradually building a comprehensive understanding of fitting. Fitting is a skill that can be learned, but you may need to train your eye to see fabric in new ways.

Recognizing Drag Lines

Drag lines are diagonal or horizontal pulls in the fabric. They usually radiate from the point where the problem originates; however, since there is a beginning and endpoint to the drag line, determining which is the origination point can be confusing. Drag lines indicate that a garment is too tight or that there is not enough three-dimensional space for a mound of flesh. They can occur on any type of garment.

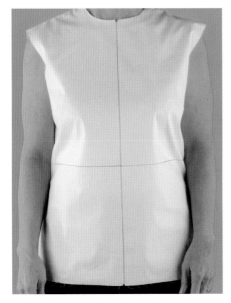

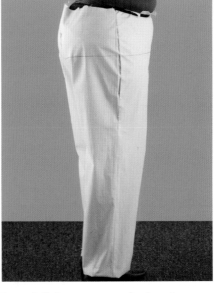

The diagonal pulls in the fabric starting at the bust and going to the side below the horizontal balance line (HBL) are typical drag lines. They originate at the bust, indicating that there is a fitting issue involving the bust.

In addition to several other fitting issues, there are quite a number of drag lines emanating from the full buttock. Together they indicate that the full buttock needs more three-dimensional space.

Although there a number of fitting issues in the shoulder area, the diagonal folds of fabric running from the bust to the side seam near the waist are drag lines that indicate the need for more bust shaping. The horizontal pulls in the fabric at bust level across the center front of the garment also indicate that the garment is too tight across the bust.

Recognizing Folds

Folds are symptomatic of fabric excess. Vertical folds indicate too much circumference; horizontal folds indicate too much length. Folds do not always form where the problem is stemming from. For instance, if a bodice has horizontal folds at the waist, there could be too much length in the upper torso between the underarm and the shoulder, or in the lower torso between the underarm and the waist.

The vertical folds of fabric at the sides from the mid-back through the waist indicate that there is too much circumference in this garment back.

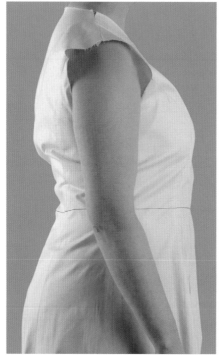

The horizontal fold of fabric across the mid-back indicates that there is too much length in the bodice above the waist.

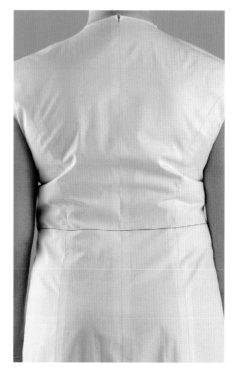

Here is the same garment viewed from the back.

Practice Seeing Fitting Issues

Any time you're around people, whether it's at the office or the grocery store, look at the fit of the clothes people are wearing. Does a blouse have a drag line radiating from the bust toward the hip? Does a jacket ride up on the buttock? Is a skirt hemline shorter in the back than the front? The power of observation—our ability to see and understand what we are seeing—grows with practice.

Recognizing Fabric Flaring Away from the Body

Except for designs where the fabric is intended to flare, fabric flaring away from the body signals a fitting problem. It usually indicates that the HBL is not level.

Small Drag Lines from Pins

Pins often create very small drag lines of their own. This is due to the path of the pin in the cloth, where the fabric is being pushed in one direction and then pulled back down in the opposite direction.

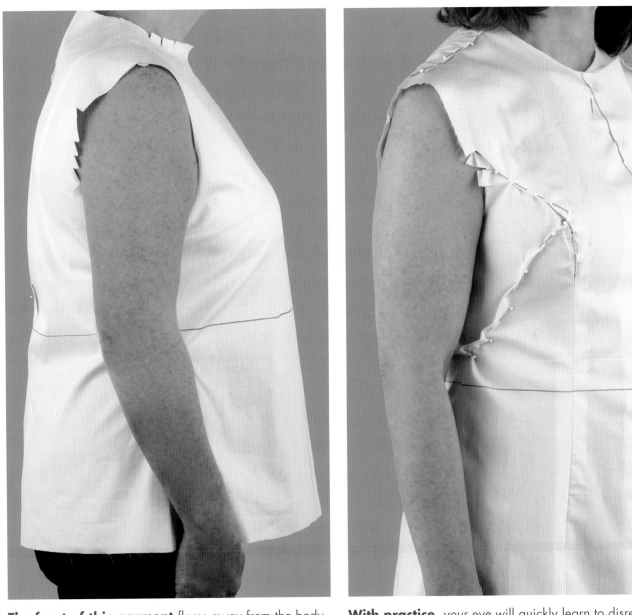

The front of this garment flares away from the body at the hemline. This suggests that the HBL is not level. In this example, the drag lines emanating from the bust indicate that more bust shaping is necessary.

With practice, your eye will quickly learn to disregard the small aberrations in the cloth created by pins.

A Framework for Fitting

Making fitting adjustments without a framework to work within relies on a lot of luck. Sometimes you'll make progress, and sometimes you won't. And when a fitting adjustment does work, you frequently won't understand why it did so—although you'll probably feel very grateful that it did. Using a fitting axis, described below, establishes a framework you can work in. This, in turn, allows you to conduct the fitting methodically. At each step, you'll know what you're trying to achieve, even if you have to figure out how to achieve it. The fitting axis is what puts you in control of the fitting process.

THE FITTING AXIS

A fitting axis establishes fixed lines around which the fabric is manipulated. Without such a fitting axis, correcting one fitting issue can cause a different fitting issue to develop. You're usually flying by the seat of your pants and hoping for the best. With a fitting axis, on the other hand, you approach fitting a muslin with purpose and direction.

To understand the fitting axis or framework, think of a straight skirt made with plaid fabric. Center front is a constant line that doesn't get altered, and it is the first component of the axis. It is a straight line that is perpendicular to the floor.

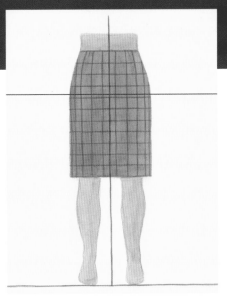

At the hem of the skirt, one color line of the plaid shows evenly all the way around the skirt. This line, the hemline, is parallel to the floor, and it is used to establish the second component of the fitting axis.

Move up the body to the hip, which is usually the fullest part of the buttock, to establish the second component of the fitting axis. Viewed from the front, the hip level is below where the body begins to taper toward the waist. The hip level, which is parallel to the hemline, is the second component of the fitting axis.

The fitting axis allows you to develop your most important fitting tool—the horizontal balance line.

THE HORIZONTAL BALANCE LINE

The line at the hip level of the skirt is referred to as the horizontal balance line, or HBL. Due to how the HBL is derived, the HBL is always parallel to the floor and perpendicular to the center front. On a skirt, most of the fitting takes place above the HBL, as the fabric is shaped to follow the contours of the lower torso. If the fitting axis is kept in correct position, the hemline will follow one color line of the plaid fabric, and the skirt will hang straight and plumb **(A)**.

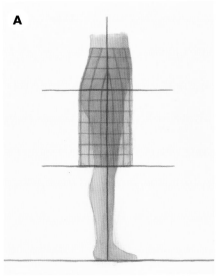

If the HBL is not employed when fitting the skirt, the fabric can be successfully shaped to follow the contours of the body. But depending on how the fitting was executed, the hemline might not follow one color line of the plaid fabric, in which case the skirt will most likely flare away from the body at either the front or the back **(B)**.

On garments that hang from the shoulder (tops, dresses, jackets, and coats), an HBL is placed between the bust and the waist. A dress is a good example of how the torso HBL is derived: it is an additional line that is parallel to the hem and to the hip-level HBL. If the garment length extends below the hip, another HBL drawn at hip level facilitates the fitting process. If the garment length ends

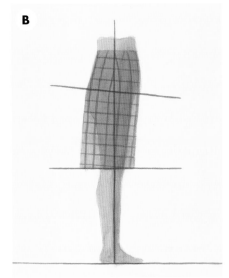

(continued)

Center Back Axis Line

Center back is not as useful as center front for the perpendicular component of the fitting axis, because back seams of garments often incorporate shaping. However, when fitting the back, it can be helpful to imagine a center back axis line, especially in relation to keeping the HBL level.

above the hip, use the one HBL on the torso between the bust and the waist **(C)**.

A garment with a shaped hem follows the same principles, because the shaped hem is actually a stylistic element. The fitting process is often streamlined if the fitting muslin has a straight hem. Complete the fitting, and then create the hem shaping **(D)**.

Establishing the HBL on the Pattern

On many commercial patterns, the lengthen/shorten line can be used for the HBL. But it's also easy to establish an HBL if there are no lengthen/shorten lines, and to check that the lengthen/shorten lines on the pattern are at the same level. The following process is the same for any type of garment.

In order to establish a horizontal balance line, you must be familiar with walking patterns (see page 59). Start with the front pattern piece. The HBL is perpendicular to the center front. Because the grainline arrow is parallel to the center front, the HBL is also perpendicular to the grainline arrow. In fact, horizontal balance lines are always perpendicular to the grainline arrow on garments cut on the straight-of-grain. On bias-cut garments, the HBL is at a 45-degree angle to the straight-of-grain.

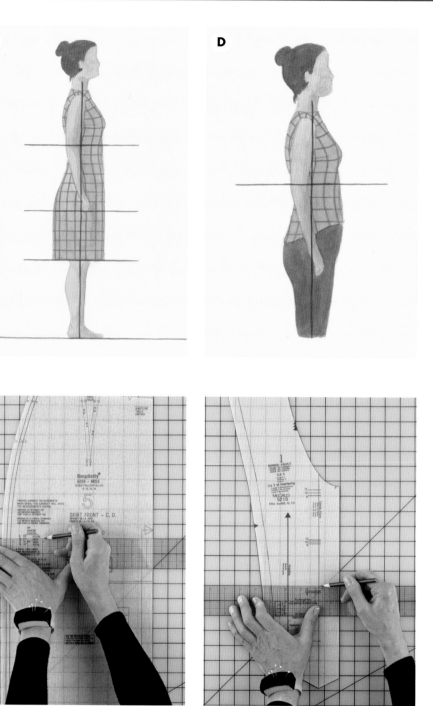

Place the HBL at or just below the fullest part of the hip on a skirt or pants.

Place the HBL between the bust and waist on a top, dress, jacket, or coat.

When the fitting muslin is prepared, the HBL will be drawn on the outside of the cloth so that it is easily seen. For instructions to do this, see page 35.

1 To establish the HBL on the adjacent pattern piece, walk the two pattern pieces from the hem to the HBL placement, and mark the HBL placement on the corresponding pattern piece at the seam line.

2 Place the adjacent pattern piece on a grid board, and move the grainline arrow along a vertical grid line until the match point at the seam line comes to a horizontal grid line.

3 Draw the HBL, using the horizontal grid line at the match point. Accurate work is important.

Fitting Tip

If it facilitates the fitting process, draw more than one HBL on the fitting muslin.

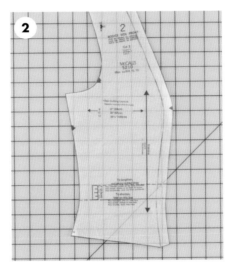

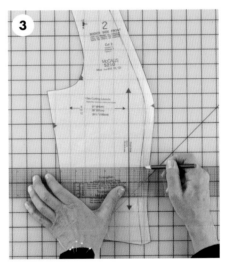

Using the HBL during a Fitting

During the fitting process, the HBL is a landmark to utilize, a concrete reference point. Learning to bring the fitting axis into position and to manipulate the fabric around the fitting axis takes practice. But luck is removed from the process and replaced with educated trial and error. With only a small amount of experience, you'll understand that fitting is simply a matter of manipulating the fabric around the fitting axis so that it creates the space required by a body's unique shape.

Fundamentals of Fitting Muslins

LEARNING TO LOOK

Fitting a muslin requires actively looking. Most of what we see during the day is processed passively, even though we are taking in a large amount of information. When learning to fit, it's essential to think actively about what you are seeing. At first, you must learn to notice that a fitting issue exists. With experience, you'll become a discerning observer, reading the fabric in a way that reveals the cause of the fitting issue.

Using a Mirror and Photographs

Because we need to pin and manipulate the fabric during a fitting, we work with the muslin at close range. However, an alteration that takes care of a particular fitting issue in one area might not be the best solution in terms of making the client look proportionate and balanced as a whole. So periodically it's helpful to look at the muslin within a larger context.

To do this, you can step away from the individual if you are fitting someone else, or you can sight in to a full-length mirror that's several feet away. When fitting yourself, using one or more mirrors lets you view the muslin while in a normal stance.

A mirror is helpful for several reasons: Using a mirror permits us to view the subject from further away, which reduces the size of the entire image and allows us to see the specific area of interest within a larger context. Also, when looking directly at a muslin, we are viewing a three-dimensional figure. The reflection in the mirror is two-dimensional, and this dimensional change often makes it easier to identify fitting issues.

A mirror also helps us view fitting issues creatively. When we fit, we tend to latch on to the first solution that comes to mind. Sighting in a mirror to shift the context encourages us to observe in a new way. This often leads us to other potential solutions.

Using photographs to study fitting problems provides the same benefits as sighting in a mirror. When fitting oneself, a photograph may seem less personal, and this step of removal makes it easier to look at our own body more objectively. Any tool that enables you to understand what you are seeing not only helps elucidate the problem at hand, but also increases your ability to observe in general.

THE BODY AS "VOLUME"

Fitting is a complicated process. Yet, in essence, the fitting process is simply a matter of making the space created by the fitting muslin match the space occupied by the body. There is no mystique—it is just a puzzle to solve. You manipulate the muslin so that its three-dimensional space reflects the volume of the body.

In addition to matching the total volume, the muslin must also reflect where the body mass is located. For instance, two women with exactly the same full bust measurement could have quite different body proportions. One could have a broad back and small breasts, and the other could have a narrow back and large breasts. The total full bust measurement is the same, but the two patterns and fitting muslins look very different. One will have a wide back pattern, and the other a narrow back pattern.

One will have less space for breast tissue, and the other more space for breast tissue.

However, the process of fitting is the same for both figures. Move the fabric of the muslin to bring the fitting axis into position, and then manipulate the fitting muslin's volume so that it reflects the body (volume) you are fitting.

FITTING OTHERS AND YOURSELF

Conducting a fitting on another person has many advantages. You can walk around the individual, viewing the muslin from all different vantage points. You can study the muslin itself as well as the reflected image in the mirror. Your hands can work independently or together. And you have easy access to all parts of the muslin.

Having a fitting buddy is a productive approach for many sewers. You have the advantages of fitting another person, plus another set of discerning eyes. Especially when you are learning to fit, one person might detect issues that the other doesn't happen to see. And you can problem solve the fitting issues together.

Weight Fluctuation

Some women have almost no variation in their weight, whereas other women experience a good deal of weight fluctuation. A few pounds of weight gain or loss can affect the way a garment fits. With some clients, I feel like I'm trying to fit a moving target from one fitting session to the next. For someone whose weight fluctuates, it's important not to overfit the test muslin and realize that, as the fitter, you might have a very difficult time getting an absolutely perfect fit.

Fitting Yourself

Fitting yourself is possible, but it requires patience. The limitations of not being able to see or touch every part of the muslin are the biggest obstacles. Setting up an extra mirror or two helps you see your sides and back.

Pinning changes to the muslin is especially difficult. On the front, try using your dominant hand to pin changes on the other side of the body. This also works for making most changes to the side of the garment. For the back, be prepared to take off and put on your garment a number of times.

Identifying fitting issues and imagining the pinned solution are valuable assets. Visualize the change that needs to be made, remove the garment, manipulate and pin the fabric, then put the garment back on. When assessing the results, differentiate whether you need to fine-tune the pinned correction, move the location of the adjustment, or start anew.

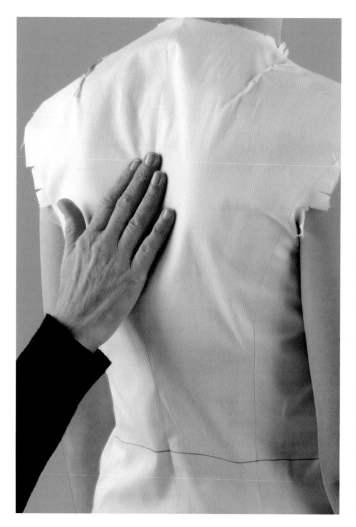

If your frustration level rises, set the project aside for a couple of hours or days and try again. Fitting yourself is largely a matter of perseverance and determination. A bit of assistance is very helpful. For example, you can teach a non-sewer how to pin. Then, using your ability to observe and assess the muslin, instruct your "helping hands" where to do the pinning.

Fitting Another Person

Fitting a muslin on someone else requires touching that person. An experienced fitter knows that the first task is to build trust between herself and the individual she's fitting. This will allow the client to relax, enabling the fitter to do her job.

To build trust, I have my client put on the fitting muslin, and I pin it closed. I then stand behind her while she faces the mirror. As I make my first visual assessment of the muslin, I lightly touch her upper back. I then walk around her and perhaps gently touch her shoulder. While she is becoming accustomed to my hand on her body, I'm becoming familiar with how the muslin fits.

If my client seems comfortable, I can start the fitting in earnest. If she doesn't, I talk about what I'm observing. For example, "This fold of fabric indicates that we need to increase the bust dart. I'll show you the difference." This provides a good transition to pinning one or two changes. At the next session, the client is likely to be more at ease because she already knows what a fitting session entails. Plus, when she sees that the new muslin fits better, her confidence in the process and trust in you grows.

Touching your client's body gives you additional information that your eyes alone cannot pick up. After a fitting has been completed, I'll have a sense of the client's body in my hands. This information "in my fingers" helps me tremendously as I use the fashion ruler to make the changes on the pattern.

To keep a client relaxed, I often engage her in conversation. I might ask her questions about her work,

Fitting Tip

Standing in one place for more than five or ten minutes is tiring, so be sure to have your client periodically move around and do a few knee bends.

how many children she has, how she fared in the latest snow storm, what her summer garden produced, what her plans for the upcoming weekend or holiday are—almost anything to get her talking. The time passes more pleasantly for her, because she's occupied. And I can concentrate on fitting her with just a little attention to keeping the conversation going.

Some clients are interested in the fitting process. In this case, you can talk about what you are doing to make the muslin fit. This often leads to exploration of what is flattering on her figure. Many clients find this exciting, because it puts the fitting stage of garment development into the context of clothes that will actually be worn. If you are fitting yourself, thinking about interesting fabrics and stylistic elements can help keep you motivated through this part of the process.

Comfort: One Indication of Good Fit

It's important to get feedback about how the muslin feels on the wearer's body. If you are fitting yourself, you'll need to play the role of both the fitter and the client.

Sometimes a client will voluntarily say that something feels much better after you correct a fitting issue. If the client does not spontaneously provide feedback, you'll need to ask (for example, "Does the armhole feel better now that I've clipped it?"). If you notice that a area of the garment is close fitting, ask the client how it feels (for example, "Does the bodice feel tight across the bust?"). Her comments are important clues as to how the fitting is proceeding, and they often reveal areas that need your attention as a fitter.

The ultimate goal is to have the client feel comfortable and relaxed in her garment. We all have quirks about what feels comfortable and what doesn't. Some people can't stand to have a tight sleeve; others don't like looseness across the bust. These are very real issues to the person being fit, even if you don't personally share these likes and dislikes.

Experimentation is part of the process. You might need to try several different things to achieve both comfort and good fit. In addition to asking yourself which change makes the garment look better, ask the client which feels better.

Take Your Time

Many people do not know what good fit is and have never owned a garment that fits properly. Taking small steps toward getting the garment to fit correctly is the best approach. Rather than trying to make all of the fitting changes in one session, make the most important changes first. Correct the pattern and make a new test garment. During the next fitting session, make a few more changes.

In this way, you make the fitting process easier on yourself as the fitter, and you will gradually lead the client to understand what good fit is. This strategy also works well if you are fitting yourself: as the fit slowly improves, you more readily will see what needs to be done next.

WHAT TO WEAR FOR A FITTING

Because foundation garments, layering garments, and shoes affect the way a garment fits, they must be taken into account during the development of a muslin.

Foundation Garments

Wear whatever undergarments you normally would wear under the garment being developed. Undergarments should fit properly; for example, a worn-out bra lowers the bustline, and too-tight panties create a bulge above and below the elastic band.

Layering Garments

When fitting a muslin such as a jacket, wear what you normally would wear under the finished jacket, perhaps a camisole, blouse, or sweater. I suggest to my clients that they wear the bulkiest potential layering garment during the fitting process. If a variety of garments will be worn under the finished jacket, the fit will likely be compromised at one end of the spectrum. For instance, if the finished jacket was fit to accommodate a sweater, it will probably look a bit loose with only a camisole. Deciding on the range of layering garments is simply a choice that the wearer must make.

Once you have a pattern that fits well, you can turn it into a bigger or smaller garment with a handful of pattern changes. For instance, if you have a shoulder princess blouse, you can scale it up to make a shoulder princess jacket or even a shoulder princess coat. You can also scale the garment down, turning a jacket into a blouse. For information on how to do this, see page 77.

Shoes

Wear the shoes that you intend to wear with the garment. Heel height impacts the length of garments, especially pants. But heel height also changes your stance, which in turn affects the fit. There might not be much difference at all between a 1" and a 1½" (2.5 and 3.8 cm) heel, but there will be a more noticeable difference between a 1" and a 2½" (2.5 and 6.4 cm) heel, and a sizeable difference between a 1" and a 4" (2.5 and 10.2 cm) heel. If you don't have shoes picked out for the garment, choose a shoe with a heel height that's close to what you envision wearing.

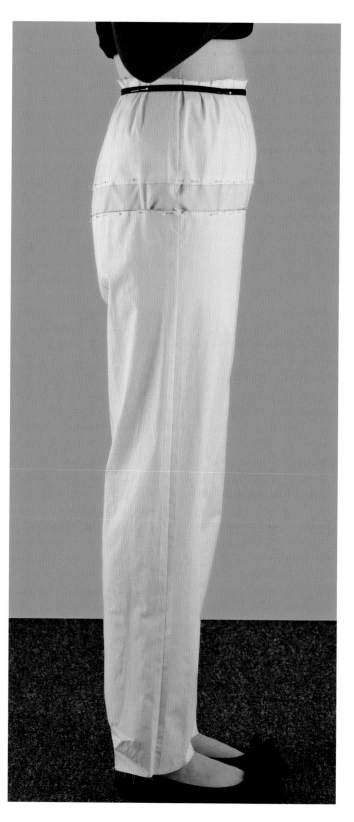

PREPARING THE TEST MUSLIN FOR A FITTING

Choosing Fabric for a Test Garment

For garments that will be made from a woven fabric, choose a stable woven fabric for the test garment. If the fashion fabric that will be used contains spandex, select a fabric for the test garment that has a similar amount of spandex. However, if the fashion fabric that will be used is drapey, I recommend using a stable (non-drapey) fabric for at least the first and perhaps the second test garment; this will ensure that you don't rely on the drape of the fabric to solve fitting issues. If the fashion fabric that will be used is thick, such as for a coat, it's helpful to use a similarly thick fabric for the test garment.

For garments that will be made from knit fabric, choose a knit for the test garment that has similar give and stretch qualities in the length-of-grain and the cross grain.

I prefer a light-colored fabric, which is easier to "read" (detect fitting issues) than a dark-colored fabric. With a light-colored fabric, it's also easier to see the markings transferred from the pattern and to make notations during the fitting.

Muslin fabric is often used—which is why a test garment is also referred to as "a muslin." Muslin fabric varies in weight and quality. With experimentation, you'll find test fabrics that you like to work with and that suit your budget. I like to keep a good supply of test garment fabric on hand, since I know I'll be making several different test muslins in the process of getting a pattern to fit well.

Muslin fabric and other inexpensive fabrics are frequently off-grain. Fortunately, most muslin and many other inexpensive woven cottons are stable enough that the fabric being slightly off-grain isn't a big issue. While straightening the grain of fashion fabric before cutting out a pattern is very important because of the impact grain line has on how a garment hangs, do the best you can with test garment fabrics without driving yourself crazy.

I do not preshrink my test garment fabric because I like the extra stability provided by the small amount of sizing in muslin and other inexpensive cottons.

Cutting Out and Marking the Test Muslin

I cut out most test muslins by placing the pattern on fabric that has been folded in half, so that I cut a right and a left side of the garment at the same time. Making test garments as efficiently as possible without sacrificing accuracy helps speed up the entire process.

Marking the test muslin with pertinent information from the pattern facilitates the fitting process. With experience, you'll learn what information is helpful to you and what is extraneous. And with experimentation, you'll also figure out the method you like to use to transfer this information.

Information to Transfer

The landmarks listed below and on the next page should be transferred from the pattern to the right side of the muslin. Some fitters also like to mark the bust apex, grainlines, seam lines, hemlines, notches, and match points.

Center front. This is one of the axis lines and therefore it should be noted on the fitting muslin. For a garment with an asymmetric front, having center front marked provides a visual reference.

Garment opening. Mark the seam lines of the garment opening so that you accurately pin the fitting muslin closed. On garments with a center front opening, the center fronts are the match lines; having them marked is important since the amount of fabric between the center front and the cut edge will vary depending on the size of button or other type of closure. For asymmetric garments, mark the match lines, which might also be center front.

(continued)

Horizontal balance line. Make sure that the HBL is easy to see, since it is a very important fitting tool. Mark more than one HBL on the fitting muslin if it would be helpful. For example, on a sheath dress, I would mark one HBL between the bust and the waist, and another HBL at or just below the full hip. See next page for how to mark a HBL on the pattern.

Darts. Mark all darts on the muslin, whether or not you sew them before conducting a fitting. On first muslins, I don't sew waist darts on skirts and pants because I prefer to drape them in as I assess the client's body. However, having them drawn on the muslin provides a convenient frame of reference in fitting the right and left side symmetrically. Even though I sew bust darts

and shoulder darts prior to fitting, having the dart legs drawn on the muslin is helpful if I need to reposition them during the fitting.

How to Transfer the Markings

I use both dressmaker's carbon and colored pencil. I rarely thread trace the pattern markings because of the risk of the threads coming out of the fabric during the fitting process, and because I can't see the thread tracing as easily. Mark the test muslin after it's been cut out, but before removing all the pins holding the pattern to the fabric.

To use dressmaker's carbon or transfer paper:

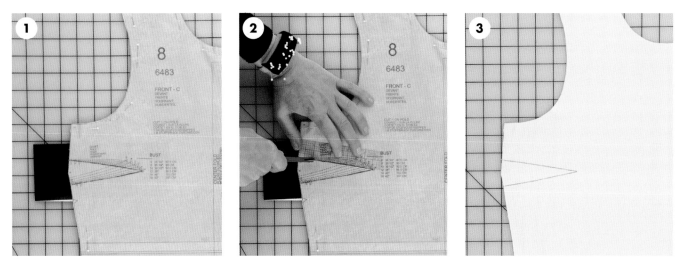

1 Insert two layers of carbon paper between the layers of fabric, with the carbon facing each layer of fabric.

2 Using a tracing wheel, go over the lines or symbols on the pattern to be transferred.

3 An accurately marked dart.

Test Garment Openings

Decide where you want the garment access (opening) to be on the fitting muslin. It is often helpful to have the opening in a different location than where it will be on the finished garment. For instance, I prefer a center back opening when fitting pants, which eliminates the bulk of a front fly and allows me to see the fit of the front crotch curve more easily.

To get very accurate, straight lines, I mark horizontal balance lines and center fronts with the method described below:

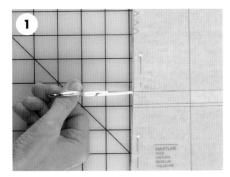

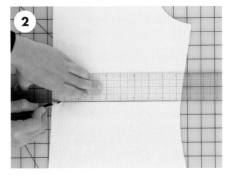

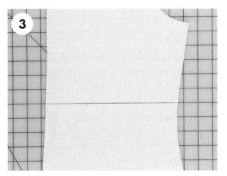

1 Make a small clip at the HBL. In this example, the bodice back pattern piece has a seam at center back, so the HBL is clipped along both the center back seam and the side seam.

2 Open the fabric, align a ruler with the clips, and draw the HBL. Repeat for the other back piece.

3 The accurately marked HBL.

Sewing the Test Muslin

Use a long stitch length when constructing the test garment so that it is easy to release a seam or dart during the fitting process. Check that the lengthened stitch does not, however, produce a puckered seam.

Press the seam allowances and darts as you would for a real garment. I prefer to have the seam allowances against the body. Some people like to fit with the seam allowances on the outside of the garment because it's easier to adjust and pin the seams. While this is true, I find the seam allowances very distracting when reading the fabric for fitting issues and when assessing how the finished lines of the garment look on the body. If the muslin is simply turned inside out in order to put the seam allowances on the outside of the test garment, it can also lead to confusion if the client's body is uneven (for example, has one high shoulder), because the left side of the test muslin would be on the right side of the body.

Stay stitching seam lines is not necessary except in areas where the fabric would stretch out of shape very easily. If my test garment fabric is quite stable, I stay stitch seam lines such as the waist or neck only when I am working on a final muslin. When stay stitching, use a regular stitch

length (ten to twelve stitches per inch [2.5 cm]), and check that the stitching is not causing the fabric to pucker.

Do not put zippers in initial fitting muslins, because they make it very difficult to pin some fitting adjustments, such as shortening a garment. It's fine to put a zipper in a final muslin. If you are fitting yourself and have a garment with a back closure, feel free to change the placement of the opening for the purpose of fitting the muslin so it's easy to get in and out of the garment by yourself.

Sew together the basic garment sections but omit stylistic elements and details. For instance, do not conduct initial fittings with collars, because a neckline that reflects the client's body must first be established. Do not conduct initial fittings with sleeves sewn into the garment, because a sleeve can distort the fit of the rest of the garment. Distill the garment down to its most basic pattern elements, and this is where you want to start the fitting process.

After constructing the test garment, give it a final press so that the fabric is not wrinkled. Do not starch the fabric, however, as this might prevent the fabric from relaxing on the client's body.

CLIPPING AND MARKING DURING A FITTING

Tightness in a test garment distorts the fit. The first step in the fitting process is to release seams and clip garment areas that are tight. This allows the garment to relax on the body, which is essential before proceeding with the fitting. Periodically during the fitting process, check the test garment again for signs of tightness.

Alleviating Tightness at the Perimeter

Horizontal or diagonal pull lines in the fabric can—but don't always—indicate tightness. As is often the case when fitting, it's important to "read" the fabric. If you suspect tightness at the perimeter of a garment, for instance at the neckline or armhole, it's easy to check. Make several ⅜" (1 cm) clips in the seam allowance. If the fabric spreads apart between the clips, the fabric is telling you there is tightness. If the fabric does not spread apart, tightness is not the cause of the pull lines.

Gradually making the clips deeper and increasing the number of clips is a safe way to proceed. When the clips no longer spread apart or when the original pull lines in the test garment disappear, you have clipped enough.

This neckline is too tight, indicated by the slight strain lines between the bust and the neck. If you slipped a finger under the front neckline, you would also feel the tension against your skin. Sometimes a client will give you feedback. A neckline or waistline that is too tight will often cause the test garment to creep upward as the too-tight area seeks a smaller circumference on the body.

The test garment can relax on the body once the perimeter is clipped. Sometimes the clips will be within the seam allowance, but often you will need to clip beyond the seam allowance further into the garment fabric.

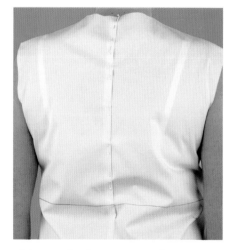

This armhole is too tight, causing slight distortion at the underarm, indicated by the small fold of fabric at the back armhole and the crumpling of fabric below the armhole. Sometimes the distortion of fabric is very noticeable, as seen on page 87.

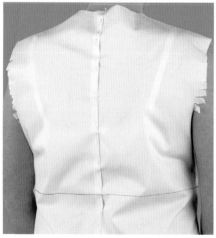

Clipping the armhole allows the fabric to relax. In this example, the armhole seam was clipped well beyond the original seam line. The back armhole and sometimes the front armhole are typical places where this situation occurs.

Alleviating Tightness on the Interior

Tightness can also occur in the middle of the garment. In these instances, you must release seams in order to alleviate the tightness, since the tightness does not occur at the perimeter of the garment. Occasionally, an area of the garment that seems to be tight in the first assessment of the test muslin will no longer be tight once the proper fitting change is made. For example, if the bustline is too tight, the back of the garment might also look tight; but when adequate room for the bust is provided, the back no longer shows sign of strain.

Another example is when the back hemline of a bodice is tight across the buttocks when the HBL is lower in the back than in the front. Bringing the HBL to a level position often alleviates the tightness across the back hip. However, if you don't initially notice that the uneven HBL is the cause of the tightness at the back hip, no harm is done. Your fitting order will follow a different path. For instance, you would probably release the side seams to alleviate the tightness across the buttocks. Through the course of the fitting, you would eventually notice that the HBL was low in the back. Correcting that would likely let the side seams close up again. In this example, you would have gone through some extra steps, but the end results would be the same.

Although it is not as obvious as in the previous example, this bustline is also too tight, indicated by the slight strain on the fabric at the center front where it is pinned at bust level.

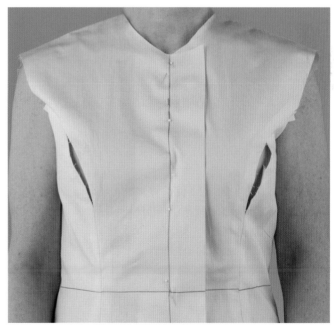

Releasing the princess seams over the bust allows the test garment to relax on the body. Be sure to work on both sides of the body, in this case releasing the princess seam on the right front as well as the left front.

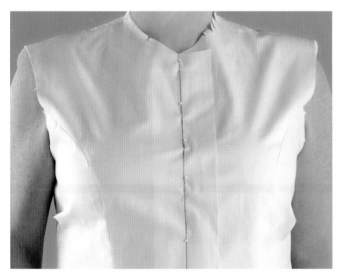

This bustline is too tight, indicated by the drag lines forming from the bust toward the center front at bust level.

Marking a Muslin during the Fitting

I frequently draw on my test garments while I'm conducting a fitting. To indicate the placement of a seam, draw the seam line, not the cut line. Fitting and pattern work hold this in common: always think and mark seam line.

Occasionally I'll draw a seam line on a test garment that's not quite where I want it. If this happens, two hatch marks mean "no," as is the case with pattern work.

Making notes directly on the muslin means the notes can't get lost, and they'll be right there when you're transferring the fitting changes to the pattern. As your fitting skills become more adept, you can also use notes to speed up the fitting process, although this isn't as precise as actually making the adjustment on the muslin.

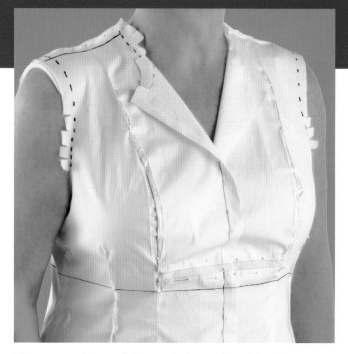

The seam lines of the armholes and neckline have been marked as well as a new placement for the shoulder seam.

To determine the placement of the seam line, several tools can be used. A narrow piece of cording or soutache braid gives you something to sight on, and it's easy to move. You can also use a row of pins to mark a tentative seam line, but they aren't as fast to reposition. In some instances, such as with a shoulder line, sighting along a pencil works.

Two short lines or hatch marks indicate that the line should be disregarded.

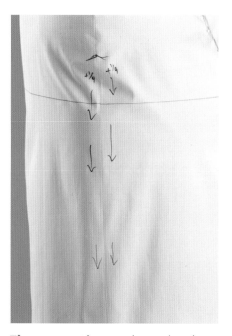

These notations indicate that the skirt is to be let out from the mark above the HBL to the bottom of the skirt. In the pattern work, I would know to add the amount indicated down the side seam and then blend the new side seam to the upper portion of the hip curve.

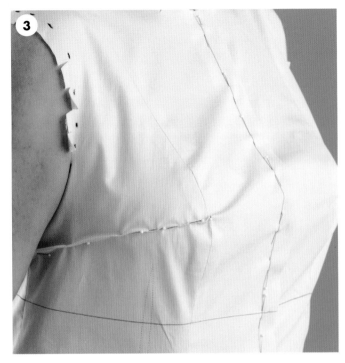

This adjustment is pinned correctly.

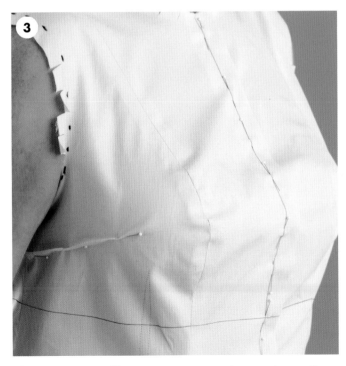

This pinning adjustment is incomplete and actually indicates the need to create a dart rather than make a close-wedge adjustment.

PINNING

Pinning changes on a test garment so that you don't accidentally poke the wearer takes some practice. Sometimes you can place your free hand up under the garment, but most of the time you cannot without distorting the fabric. Developing a pinning technique facilitates the fitting process.

Developing a Pinning Technique

I often reposition one of the seam allowances so that both are pointing in one direction in the area of the adjustment, and then proceed as follows. First, gently push the point of the pin through the top layer of fabric only. Next, rather than pushing the pin completely through the bottom layer of fabric, which is when you might poke the client, pin into just the uppermost fibers of the bottom layer. As you do this, use the pin to gently pull the fabric of the bottom layer slightly away from the client's body. Then guide the pin a bit further into the bottom layer of fabric. Finish by arcing the pin and coming back through the top layer of fabric.

General Pinning Practices

1 Pin the alteration where the fitting issue occurs. This often means you will be pinning into the middle of the garment, rather than at or along a seam.

2 Pin the fitting change so that it flatters the figure. Sometimes there's a trade-off between obtaining the most effective fit and the most flattering fit.

3 Pin the fitting change on the muslin in a way that the adjustment can be made on the pattern. For example, when increasing the bust shaping on a princess seam, pin the close-wedge to the opposing seam and not partway across the side princess panel.

(continued)

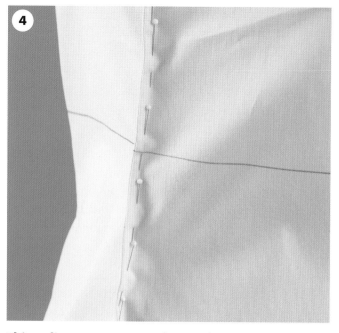

This adjustment is pinned correctly.

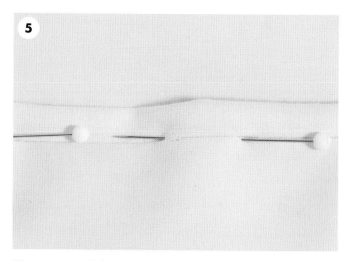

This pinning adjustment is incomplete.

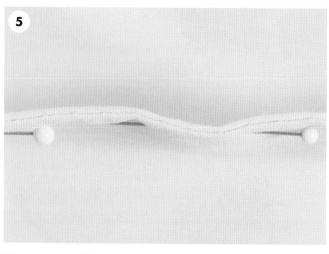

The excess fabric on this seam has been pinned out equally on both seams.

The excess fabric on this seam has been pinned out on only one side of the seam.

4 When pinning, resolve the endpoint. For example, when pinning out ¼" (6 mm) excess on a side seam, don't leave the uppermost or lowest pin with the ¼" (6 mm) intake. Rather, pin so the adjustment is blended back to the seam line.

5 Pin seam adjustments so it's clear whether just one or both sides of the seam are affected.

6 Be a considerate fitter when placing pins. Even if the pin won't poke the client, it feels threatening when the point of the pin is at the edge of the fabric and close to the skin. Place the pin so the head of its pin is nearest the garment edge.

KEEPING THE MUSLIN BALANCED

There is no such thing as a perfectly symmetrical body. Everyone has differences on one side of the body in comparison to the other. For example, the dominant arm might be larger, one shoulder might be lower, one hip might be higher, or one leg might be shorter.

Fitting the muslin very precisely on each side of the body will result in a finished garment that actually accentuates the unevenness of the figure. Rather than emphasizing the differences between the two sides of a person's body, it's preferable to fit the garment in a way that makes the body look balanced and symmetrical. Many beginners have a tendency to fit too closely, which is referred to as "overfitting." However, for most women, a balanced garment is what shows her figure to its best advantage.

When the test muslin is balanced, the pattern can also be balanced. This means there is need for only a half pattern, as is the norm for commercial patterns unless the garment is an asymmetric style.

Some women have figure variations that necessitate fitting each side of the body separately. For instance, scoliosis can cause so much curvature in the spine that the two sides of the body are quite different. In this case, each side of the body must be fit individually and a complete pattern developed. For example, a complete skirt pattern would consist of a right back and a left back, and a full front pattern that was not on the fold. When fitting

Even Fitting

- For a high/low shoulder, I place a shoulder pad on the low side to even out the body; the thickness of the shoulder pad should equal the amount the shoulder is low.

- To avoid overfitting, fit the high or larger side: fit the high shoulder or hip, and fit the larger arm or hip.

unbalanced figures, the challenge is to obtain an effective fit that makes the body look as symmetrical as possible.

FITTING ORDER

Fitting is rarely a linear process that proceeds in a specified and unvarying order. There is usually a lot of going back and forth between different areas of the body. In part this happens because the test garment is not a stationary item, but it settles on the body as the fitting issues are addressed. And at the beginning of the fitting process, each time the test garment settles and relaxes on the body, it fits somewhat differently.

The fitting order also varies because you might not notice every fitting issue at the beginning of the fitting session. In addition, you must familiarize yourself with the client's figure as well as how the fabric is lying on the body. And because of the variations in patterns, you may need to work with the fitting muslin a bit to understand the peculiarities of the pattern used for the test garment.

All of these variables contribute to the complexity of the fitting process. However, the following steps provide a general, easy-to-follow fitting order.

1 Release any area of the test garment that is tight.

2 Make the HBL level. If you aren't sure how to accomplish this, make a temporary adjustment until you can figure out the best solution. Having the fitting axis in place will help you identify and assess the fitting issues in the garment.

3 Correct any length issues, elongating or shortening the fitting muslin as needed.

4 Fit the mounds or fleshy areas of the body.

5 Revisit the HBL and fitting axis.

6 Stop anytime you feel that a new muslin reflecting the changes you've made will be helpful.

- The fitting axis is one of the most important tools you have. Manipulate the fabric of the test garment to bring the fitting axis into correct placement. Then, within each quadrant formed by the fitting axis, manipulate the fabric to eliminate drag lines, fold lines, tightness, and excess fabric.

- Periodically during the fitting session, check the placement of landmarks such as center front, the HBL, and side seams.

- If a test muslin keeps shifting from front to back or from side to side, this usually indicates that one or more fitting issues have not been addressed and are preventing the garment from settling on the body.

- If a test muslin creeps upward on the body, this might indicate that the garment is tight. It also might be due to the garment(s) that the client is wearing under the test garment. For instance, if the client is wearing a cotton knit top that is tucked in at the waist, a skirt muslin tends to creep upward.

- Darts create three-dimensional space. Therefore, they should point to a mound or fleshy area, not to a flat or hollow area of the body.

- How large a dart is (the dart intake) affects how much three-dimensional space is created. A larger dart intake creates more three-dimensional space than a smaller dart intake.

- There is frequently more than one way to solve a particular fitting issue. Trying several options and assessing the results of each one is the best way to determine the most effective solution.

- Don't spend a lot of time fine-tuning the exact shape of every seam during a fitting. Much of this will be taken care of when the fitting changes are transferred to the pattern and the pattern work is done.

- Don't make too many changes at once. Make the most obvious changes—those you are sure about—and then make the pattern changes and a new test garment. The extra step of making a new test muslin is often a time-saver in the long run. If lots of changes are made at one time and a fitting problem is introduced or worsened, it's very difficult to determine which change caused the problem.

- Fit bodices without collars, sleeves, or other details. These additional elements can mask basic fitting problems.

- Finalize the fit of a bodice before fitting a set-in sleeve. Part of the comfort of the sleeve depends on the fit of the bodice. First get the sleeve to fit the arm; then deal with the relationship between the armhole and the sleeve cap.

- Fit tops and dresses that have waist seams (natural, empire, or dropped waist) by first fitting the bodice portion of the garment. Add the skirt after the bodice fits well.

Seams

The center front seam is fixed; only in rare instances is it curved.

Side seams should hang straight and plumb.

Center back seams can be straight or curved.

ASSESSING THE FIT

Looking at a garment with a discerning eye is essential for a fitter. There are obvious things to check at the end of a fitting session: the HBL should be level, the side seams should be straight and plumb, there should be no signs of strain or tightness, and there should be no drag lines. But it's often difficult to assess a test garment after a number of adjustments have been made and it's full of pins, especially since the pins themselves can cause very small drag lines and dips in the fabric. This is when it's helpful to transfer the fitting changes made on the fitting muslin to the paper pattern, adjust the pattern, and make a clean test garment.

Making a second or third muslin lets you see how the adjustments have translated to the pattern and gives you the opportunity to fine-tune these changes. With a few of the most obvious fitting issues solved, a new muslin also makes it easier to identify the remaining problems.

Looking at a photograph of the fitting muslin on the body often makes it easier to identify fitting issues, as discussed on page 28. Or ask a sewing buddy for help in assessing the fit. Someone who has not been involved in the initial fitting process can frequently see fitting issues that you are missing. And talking about what you are both seeing often leads to a better understanding of what is going on and how to solve it.

In addition to a visual assessment of the fit, it's also important to assess how comfortable the garment is. Areas that are uncomfortable frequently mean that there is an underlying fitting problem.

The Benefits of Multiple Muslins

For most garments, I expect to make at least two or three fitting muslins, perhaps even more for difficult-to-fit figures. Some garments, like pants, are also more difficult to fit, so more muslins will be in order.

I don't think of making multiple muslins as "extra work." The time I put into getting a good fit is what allows me to feel relaxed when I'm ready to cut into the fashion fabric. Not only am I confident that the garment will fit nicely, but I've also become familiar with how the main portions of the garment are constructed. This results in very few, if any, unexpected problems when constructing the garment in fashion fabric.

Wearable Mock-ups

When I feel that the fit of a garment is in good shape, I often make a wearable mock-up. This is a garment made of less expensive fashion fabric that is similar in hand and weight to the "real" fashion fabric.

A wearable mock-up provides another level of checking the fit. It gives you the chance to wear the garment and go about normal activities. This often brings to light issues that were not noticed when you were just standing in front of the mirror. And if fitting issues are discovered, you've not ruined costly or irreplaceable fabric. If the fit is good, then you have another garment to wear.

Special-occasion garments do not lend themselves to making a wearable mock-up as readily as day-to-day clothing. However, sometimes you can make a slight modification; for instance, a floor-length column gown could be made as a street-length sheath dress using a less glamorous fabric.

Is It Good Enough?

Deciding when to stop making muslins is an important part of the fitting process. As your eye becomes better trained, you'll tend to see very small fitting issues, and it's easy to get mired in making muslins and never sew an actual garment. Sometimes "good enough" means that you're ready to make a garment, whereas with other garments, you'll decide to strive for perfection.

Fundamentals of Altering Patterns

Each time you have adjusted the muslin, you need to make corresponding changes to the original pattern pieces. Altering the pattern is a crucial step that requires patience and thought.

GLOSSARY OF PATTERNMAKING TERMS

The language of fitting and pattern alteration includes the following terms and phrases.

Apex: The furthest protruding point of the bust.

Blending a seam: Redrawing a seam to eliminate jogs or angles by making a smooth and continuous line.

Bust point: See "apex."

Close-wedge: A manipulation used to shorten a fitting muslin or a pattern by an uneven amount.

Cut line: The line indicating where to cut the pattern.

Dart intake: The distance between dart legs, measured at the seam line.

Dart legs: The lines on each side of a dart; the stitching lines for a dart.

Dart point: The point or dot indicating the end or termination of a dart.

Dart equivalent: The amount equal to a dart intake.

Dart extension: The area to the side of a dart that is frequently triangular in shape and protrudes further out than the rest of the pattern or garment until the dart is closed and folded in the proper direction.

Dart transfer: Moving a dart to another location.

Fine-tune: To make a small adjustment that results in further improvement.

Fold line: A line indicating that the pattern piece is to be positioned on fabric that is folded in half when cutting the garment out.

Grainline arrow: A straight line on the pattern indicating how to position the pattern piece on the fabric; the grainline arrow on the pattern is placed parallel to the selvage of the fabric.

Grid board: A flat board marked with a series of regularly spaced parallel and perpendicular lines.

Intersecting seam line: A seam that crosses or intersects another seam.

Notch: A registration mark on the pattern, often shaped as a small triangle.

Open-wedge: A manipulation used to lengthen a fitting muslin or a pattern by an uneven amount.

Seam allowance: The distance between the seam line and the cut line.

Seam line: The line on the pattern indicating where the garment is to be stitched.

Spread: A manipulation used to lengthen a fitting muslin or a pattern by an even amount.

Stacking pattern pieces: Placing adjoining pattern pieces one on top of the other, matching the seam lines

and any notches. Often the top pattern piece has been folded along the seam line.

Tick mark: A short line. A series of tick marks are used to indicate an approximate seam placement, which can then be finalized and drafted permanently.

Tuck: A manipulation used to shorten a fitting muslin or a pattern by an even amount.

Truing a seam: Checking that seams on a pattern are blended nicely and that two adjoining seams are the same length or incorporate the desired amount of ease, then making any necessary corrections.

Waist-fitting dart: A vertical dart starting below the bust.

Walking a seam: The process of comparing the same seam on two adjoining pattern pieces.

Wedge: A manipulation used to shorten or lengthen a fitting muslin or pattern by an uneven amount. See "close-wedge" and "open-wedge."

MAKING FLAT
PATTERN ADJUSTMENTS

Altering patterns can seem daunting. It's easy to feel confused or overwhelmed when you have a lot of changes to make, especially if you don't see how those changes are possible with the pattern alteration method you know.

There are a number of pattern alteration methods that you may have heard of or that you currently use, including the seam method, the pivot method, the slash method, and the box method. Depending on how your mind works, some are easier to understand and execute than others. Most simplify pattern alterations so that the method is easy to use. However, simplification almost always sacrifices precision. Most methods are also based on the assumption that a commercial pattern is intrinsically correct. Having this attitude toward patterns encourages you to search for a pattern that has been designed for your body type, so that you fit into the mold of the pattern.

My approach to pattern alteration is somewhat different in that it places the wearer's body as the focal point. There is a direct correlation between the changes made to a test muslin while it's on the body and the changes one makes to the pattern. Occasionally, only a few adjustments are necessary, but usually there are quite a number of alterations. At times there are such substantial changes to the pattern that the final product is yours more than the pattern company's.

While it may seem scary to alter patterns so freely, remember that the pattern is nothing more than a tool, a convenient starting place. This freedom is what allows for the level of precision necessary to create a garment that truly fits. And what is more, with this method it doesn't really matter which pattern you start with—the end result will be a pattern that fits.

Thus, with this method of fitting and pattern making, the key to making successful pattern alterations lies in making appropriate and precise fitting adjustments to the test garment. After fitting the test garment, you directly transfer the fitting changes to the paper pattern. Then you adjust the paper pattern in much the same way as you manipulated the muslin. Undertaking pattern work in this way puts you in control of the process. Although other pattern alteration methods may seem safer because they keep the pattern more intact, they do not allow for this level of effectiveness and exactness.

With basic patternmaking skills, you can make almost any pattern change. This chapter describes basic patternmaking techniques. More specialized techniques are discussed as they arise in conjunction with the fitting examples.

Patternmaking, like many skills, has its own specialized language. For a glossary of patternmaking terms, see page 44.

Tips for Adjusting Patterns

- Work methodically, carefully, and neatly.

- Make the pattern alteration where you made the adjustment on the fitting muslin. This is where the fitting issue occurs, so change it there.

- Think seam line. In your pattern work, concentrate on the placement of the seam lines, just as you do when fitting a test garment. It's easy to adjust the seam allowances after new seam lines are established.

- Draw new seam lines using an appropriately shaped ruler, rather than freehand.

- Patterns must be flat after adjustments have been made. If there are bubbles or wrinkles when the pattern is lying on the table, this indicates that the pattern manipulation has been done incorrectly.

- Make a new copy of the pattern if prior changes make it difficult to see important landmarks. This may happen along seam lines due to redrawing or fine-tuning, or in areas where there is so much tape and added paper to be bothersome.

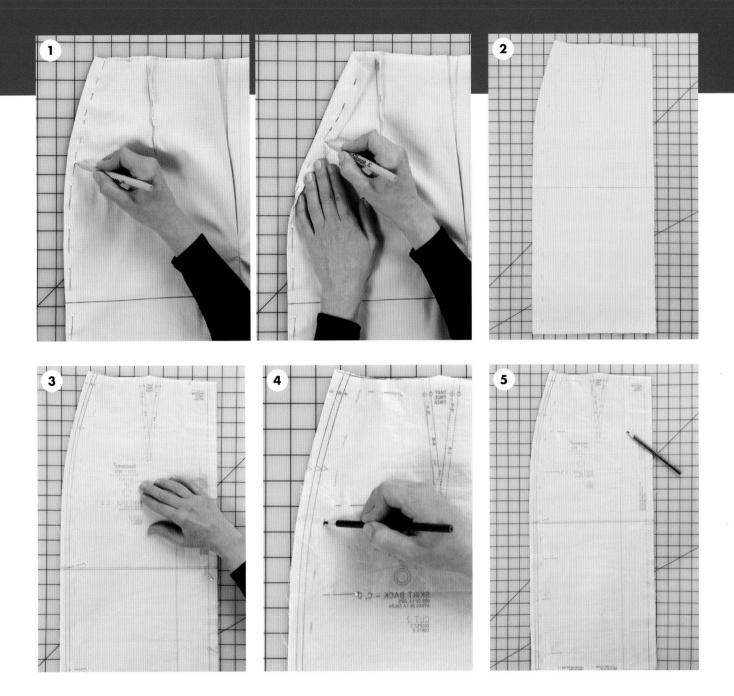

TRANSFERRING MUSLIN MARKINGS TO THE PATTERN

First, mark the fitting changes on the muslin. Use a marker or pencil in a contrasting color so that the fitting changes are easy to see and are different from muslin markings such as dart legs and grainlines. A bright color works best. Then transfer the markings to the pattern.

1 Mark both sides of each pin used in the fitting process.

2 Take all pins out and press the muslin flat.

3 Lay the pattern over the muslin, aligning the edges and markings such as the HBL. Taking the muslin apart often makes it easier.

4 Transfer the markings to the pattern with a series of tick marks.

5 The pattern piece with all of the fitting changes indicated by tick marks is now ready to be altered and manipulated. For beginners, transfer all of the fitting changes from the muslin to the pattern pieces before making any pattern changes.

(continued)

The tick marks represent alterations that need to be made to the pattern. Some seams might have little or no change, while others have substantial changes.

For many people, making significant changes like completely redrawing a seam line feels unorthodox and risky. However, if the fitting changes you made to the muslin while it was on the body improved the fit, and if you accurately transferred the muslin changes to the pattern, then it's logical that you can trust those alterations. When approaching fit and pattern work in this way, it's not important to keep the pattern intact; rather, your goal is to make the pattern changes based on discerning fitting changes.

BLENDING SEAMS, USING THE RULERS, AND ADDING SEAM ALLOWANCES

Blending Seam Lines

Because pinning during a fitting can be challenging and awkward, it's difficult to pin a seam smoothly and in a perfect blend. Blending seams is an important part of patternmaking, since abrupt transitions are noticeable in the garment. For most pattern alterations, long and gentle blends translate to a garment that's more flattering. Short and choppy blends produce less flattering seams.

Therefore, when you blend a seam on the pattern using the tick marks as your guide, there will be times that one or two tick marks do not fall on a well-blended line. It's more important to capture the intention of the line than it is

Sides of the Pattern

It doesn't matter which side of the pattern you work on. Sometimes during pattern work you'll work on the side with the writing, and other times you'll work on the opposite side.

Intersecting Seams

Seams that intersect center front and center back require special attention at the point of intersection. Waistlines and necklines are good examples. Draft waist and neck seams so they are straight and perpendicular to center front or center back for approximately ⅜" (1 cm) before they begin to curve. Otherwise, there will be an unsightly dip or point in the waist or neck seam at the intersection.

to connect every single tick mark. As your patternmaking skills improve, you'll feel more confident interpreting the tick marks. And you'll always have the chance to fine-tune how a seam lies on the body if you make another test garment.

When part of a seam line changes, the new seam is blended to the existing seam. Many commercial patterns, especially multi-sized patterns, do not have seam lines drawn on the pattern paper. When connecting a newly drawn or altered seam to the original seam line, it's important to first draw the existing seam line on the pattern paper so you have something to blend the new line to. If you are new to pattern work, I recommend drawing all the existing seam lines on the pattern before starting to alter the pattern.

Using the Rulers

Pattern work requires precision in order for the garment to fit as intended, which is why it's important to use rulers. For example, if you inadvertently added just ¹⁄₁₆" (1.6 mm) to each seam on an eight-gore skirt, the skirt would be 1" (2.5 cm) larger than desired. Another example is the curvature of the seams over the bust: an inexact line could change not only the overall size of the garment, but it also the placement of the fullness over the bust, leading to an unflattering fit. Using rulers makes your pattern work exact.

A straight edge ruler and a fashion ruler (Styling Design Ruler) are the most frequently used rulers, although a hip curve and one or more French curves are also handy. With practice and experience, your rulers will become extensions of your hands. If I were shown a seam line to blend, I might not be able to verbally describe what part of the fashion ruler to use. But when I picked up the ruler, my hands would automatically know how to orient it for an effective blend. Your eyes and hands will also learn to use the rulers adeptly—all it takes is practice.

With the fashion ruler, you are able to produce a wide variety of curved and arced lines. The subtle shaping in seam lines can greatly influence how the garment looks on the body. For example, if a woman carries weight on the outside of her upper thigh, you can accentuate or minimize her build by the way you blend the side seam from the fullest part of the thigh to the knee on a skirt or pants. As a patternmaker, you therefore have the ability to control not only the fit, but also how a viewer's eyes perceive the body.

If the blend requires slight reshaping, you usually have several options, so it's important to think about what you want to accomplish and to experiment with different ruler positions. For instance, if the intent of the alteration is to increase the room in the bust, you wouldn't want to place the ruler so that it removed ⅛" (3 mm) or more from the bust area. Keeping the fullness at the bust might require slightly reshaping the blend under the bust in order to get a smooth transition. In these instances, choose the scenario that makes the most sense for the body you are fitting.

Finesse the Curve

While learning to use the fashion ruler to draw seam lines, it is sometimes difficult to visualize the shape of the seam while also trying to find the corresponding part of the ruler that will produce the shape. When this happens, lightly draw the line freehand, and then use the ruler to finalize and finesse the line.

Visualizing Blends

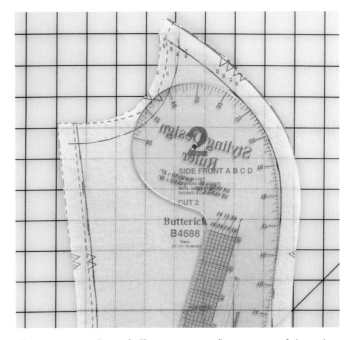

If you want less fullness, use a flatter part of the ruler.

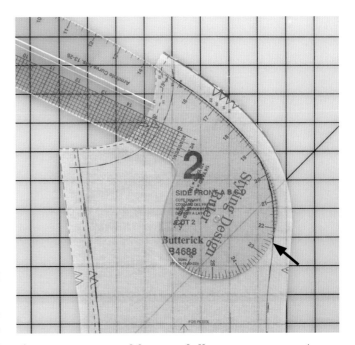

If you want to add more fullness, use a rounder part of the ruler. Note that with this ruler position you'll need to blend a second time lower down in order to smoothly transition to the seam line below in the area indicated by the arrow.

Working with the Fashion Ruler

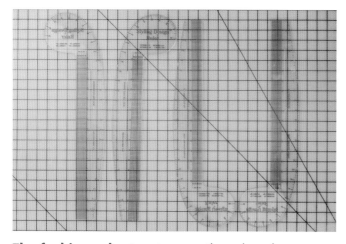

The fashion ruler is quite versatile and produces a wide variety of shaped lines, especially because it can be used in four different orientations. Sometimes the solution to blending a seam is to flip the ruler over.

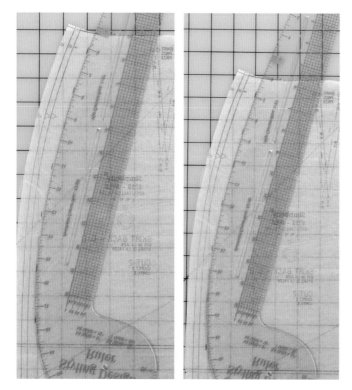

To find the best area of the ruler to use when blending seam lines, slide the ruler back and forth a few inches (cm), rather than picking up the ruler. Seeing a potential blend that is not very good along with a choice of blends often helps you to find the area of the ruler that is effective.

Working with a Straight Edge Ruler

With experimentation, you'll find a straight edge ruler that you like to work with. The thickness and the flexibility of the ruler will influence how comfortable it is in your hand. The fashion ruler has a straight edge on one side, but the ruler is rigid and thick. I like to use 2" × 18" (5.1 × 45.7 cm) and 1" × 6" (2.5 × 15.2 cm) flexible rulers marked in ⅛" (3 mm) increments. The markings form a grid, which is useful to check lines that need to be perpendicular to each other.

Use a straight edge ruler to draw lines such as the horizontal balance line, the grainline, and center front, as well as any other seam line that needs to be straight. I also use these flexible rulers with grids to accurately measure and mark seam allowances.

Blending a Seam Line Using the Rulers

To get long and gentle blends, position the fashion ruler so that as much of the ruler as possible touches the lines to be blended. In achieving a long blend, you often will need to reshape a part of the seam slightly. Experiment with ruler positions to do this. The following photos show this process.

Blending Seams

Make thoughtful and logical decisions when blending seams, but work efficiently and don't agonize over what to do. You can always make another test garment, which gives you the opportunity to fine-tune. And it's usually easy to see what needs to be done once the test garment is on the body.

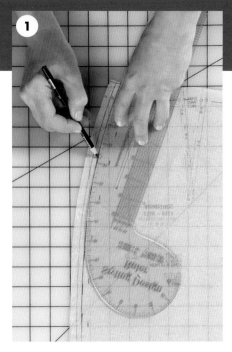

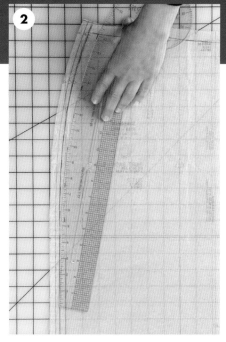

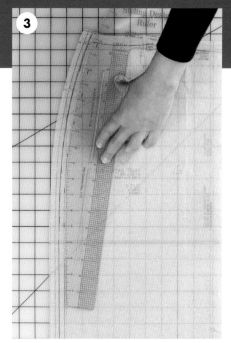

1 Since many patterns do not include seam lines, draw in all original seam lines.

2 This ruler position smoothly blends the tick marks of the new seam near the waist, but the transition to the lower straight portion of the new seam (marked in red) is not good.

3 In comparison, this ruler position nicely blends the straight lower portion of the side seam with the first few tick marks of the new seam line. Once the initial transition has been made, the rest of the seam can be blended, as follows.

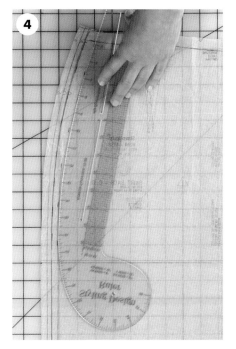

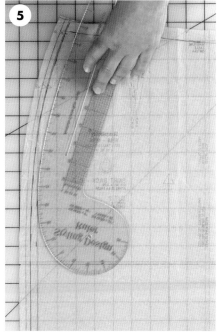

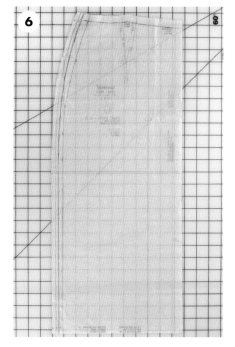

4 This ruler position is okay, but does not pick up the fullness in the hip curve.

5 In comparison, this ruler position shows the fullness of the hip and nicely blends into rest of the new seam line.

6 The new blended seam (in red).

Adding Seam Allowances

After fine-tuning a seam line, add the seam allowance. The amount of seam allowance is your choice as the patternmaker. If you use varying seam allowances for different types of garments or within one garment, clearly mark your pattern.

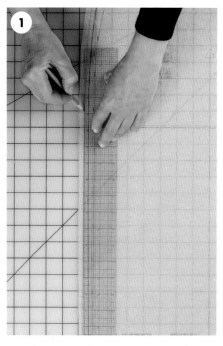

1 For a straight seam, measure the desired seam allowance using a ruler for accuracy and draw the cut line (in blue).

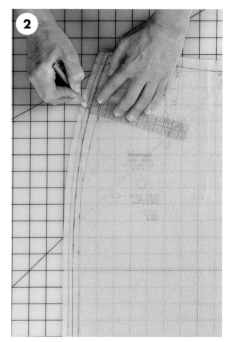

2 On curved lines, it's often best to mark the seam allowance with a series of tick marks.

Working Over a Grid

A cutting surface marked with a grid is an excellent place to do pattern work. Aligning the pattern pieces on the grid helps you make accurate pattern adjustments, and it encourages the eye to visualize the fitting axis on the pattern pieces.

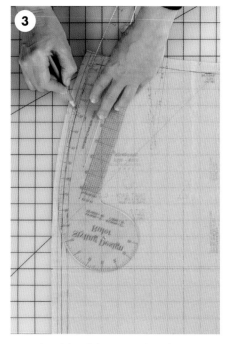

3 Then blend the curved cut line with a fashion ruler.

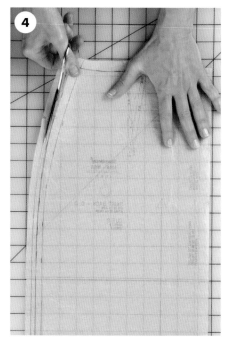

4 Once the cut line is drawn in, trim away the excess paper.

Lengthening and Shortening Patterns

It is best to lengthen and shorten patterns at or near the location where you made the alteration on the fitting muslin. This is typically done above or below the HBL in order to preserve the reference point that the HBL provides.

There are two types of length adjustments: even adjustments alter the pattern the same amount across the pattern piece; uneven adjustments alter the pattern a different amount on one side of the pattern piece compared to the other side. Both adjustments are made across the entire pattern piece in accordance with good patternmaking practices; this keeps the pattern flat.

Accurate Tucks

To keep your pattern flat and precise, cut and tape the pattern when making a tuck adjustment rather than making a fold in the pattern paper.

Even Adjustments: Tucks and Spreads

Make even adjustments using a tuck to shorten the pattern and a spread to lengthen the pattern. It's easiest to make even adjustments parallel to the horizontal balance line.

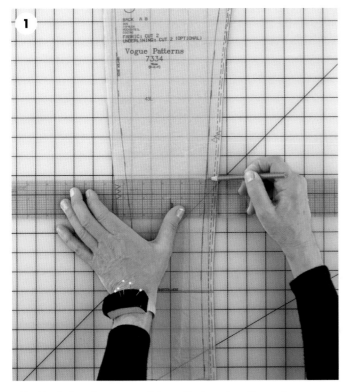

1 Mark the placement of the adjustment on the pattern. Position the pattern so that the grainline is along a grid and so that the placement mark is at a cross grid. Use this cross grid to draw the adjustment line.

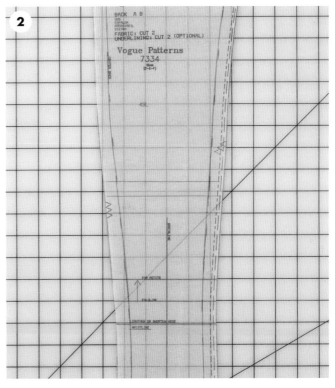

2 For a tuck, which shortens the pattern, measure and mark the amount of the adjustment, and draw a line here that is parallel to the adjustment line. The part of the pattern between these lines indicates the amount to be removed.

(continued)

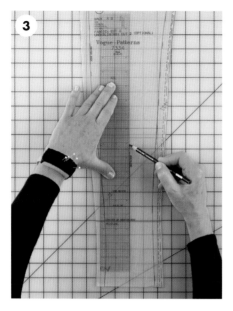

3 Extend the grainline so it is marked on both sides of the adjustment.

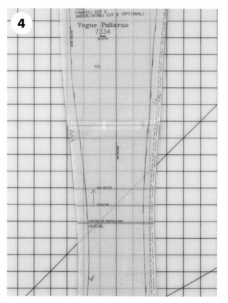

4 Cut the pattern apart along either line. Lay one cut line on top of the other, matching them precisely and keeping the grainline of each pattern segment aligned on the same grid line. Tape the pattern pieces together.

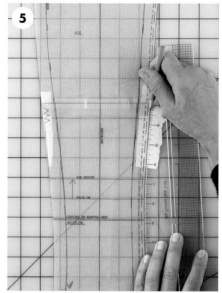

5 If necessary, blend the seam lines and the cut lines. In this example, both the center back seam and the back princess seam need slight blending.

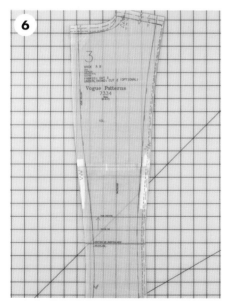

6 The finished pattern.

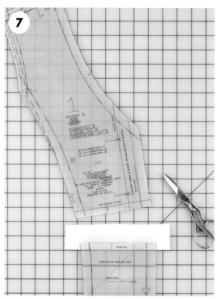

7 For a spread, which lengthens the pattern, cut the pattern apart along the adjustment line. Add paper to one side of the separated pattern; it doesn't matter which side.

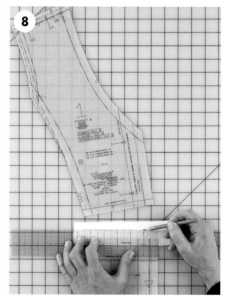

8 Measure and mark the amount of the adjustment, drawing a line parallel to the adjustment line.

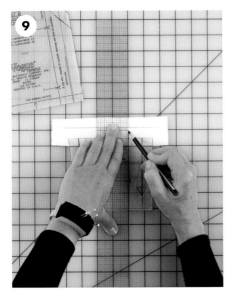

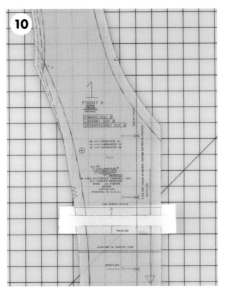

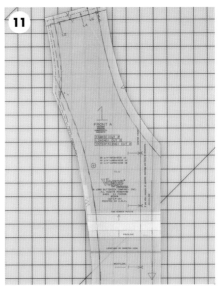

9 Extend the grainline on the added paper. Here I use the center front line as the grainline because the grainline arrow marked on the pattern is too close to the edge of the pattern and the seam line to be easily recognizable.

10 Align the other segment of the pattern with the new adjustment line that indicates the amount of the spread, matching the grainline arrow, and tape in place.

11 The blended and finished pattern.

Uneven Adjustments: Open-Wedges and Close-Wedges

Make uneven adjustments using a wedge, which can either lengthen or shorten a pattern. Only make wedge adjustments on pattern pieces that have seams on both sides. It is *not possible* to make a wedge adjustment when one side of the pattern is the center front or is on the fold. This is because a wedge adjustment causes both sides of the pattern to bend, and these two situations require a straight line.

To make wedge adjustments, transfer the placement of the wedge from the muslin to the pattern. Wedge adjustments do not need to be parallel to the HBL or perpendicular to the grainline.

(continued)

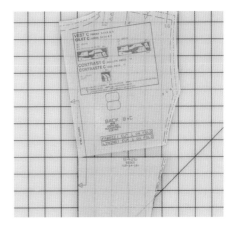

Here you can see the fold line "breaking" in the attempt to make an impossible wedge.

Unusual Curved Center Front Seams

Occasionally an unusual garment design has a curved center front seam. This is the only exception where a wedge adjustment can involve the center front seam.

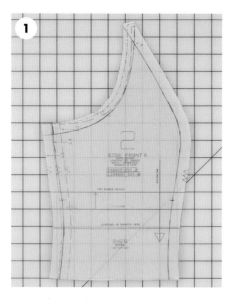

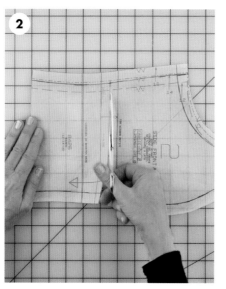

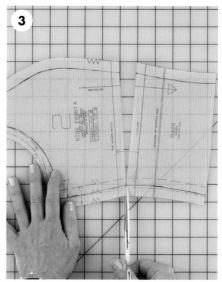

1 When making either an open-wedge or close-wedge, start by marking the placement of the wedge adjustment at each side of the pattern along the seam lines. Draw a line between the marks using a straight edge ruler. Note that it's important to mark wedge adjustments **on the seam line,** not on the cut line of the pattern.

2 To lengthen the pattern with an **open-wedge** adjustment, cut along the adjustment line, starting at the side of the pattern that will be lengthened or shortened. Cut to, but not through, the opposite seam line.

3 On the side of the pattern where the wedge adjustment ends, cut through the seam allowance up to the seam line, leaving a hinge of paper at the seam line.

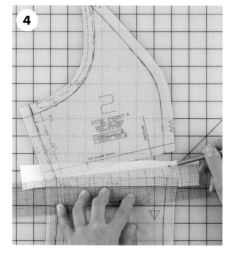

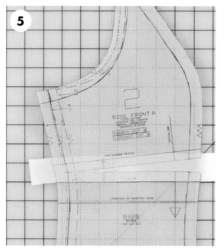

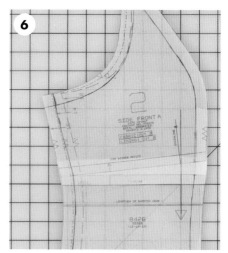

4 Spread the cut portion of the pattern and tape in additional paper on one portion of the pattern. On the added paper, measure and mark the amount of the spread, which in this example is ⅝" (1.6 cm).

5 Bring the free side of the pattern to the mark on the added paper made in the previous step, and secure the pattern with tape. The pattern paper should be absolutely flat.

6 Blend the vertical seams on each side of the pattern and, lastly, adjust the seam allowances.

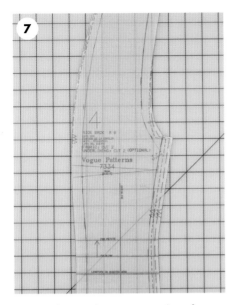

7 To shorten the pattern with a **close-wedge** adjustment, measure and mark the amount of the closure along the seam line where the pattern has been cut. Draw a line from the mark indicating the amount of the closure to the hinge mark on the opposite side of the pattern.

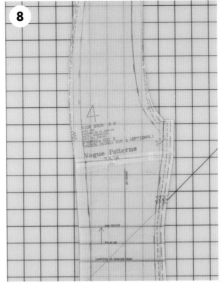

8 Cut a hinge, as described above, along one of the adjustment lines. Move one side of the pattern to make it overlap the other pattern piece by rotating the paper at the hinge point, bringing the wedge lines together. It doesn't matter which portion of the pattern is moved on top of the other. The pattern paper should be absolutely flat. Tape the pattern in place.

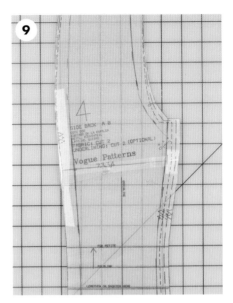

9 Blend the vertical seams on each side of the pattern and then adjust the seam allowances.

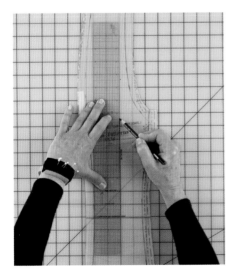

After making a wedge adjustment, redraw the grainline arrow by extending the grainline from the lower portion of the garment.

Grainline Arrows

After making open-wedge and close-wedge adjustments, redraw the grainline arrow. This is almost always done by extending the grainline from the lower portion of the pattern through the upper portion of the pattern. The logic of this is evident if you think back to a plaid skirt. Since the hem of the garment must remain parallel to the floor and perpendicular to the grainline, it's the upper portion of the garment above the HBL that is allowed to go off grain.

On bodices, allowing the upper portion of the garment to be a bit off-grain often improves how the garment fits. This is because fabric on a slight bias grain tends to mold to the body more readily than fabric on the straight of grain.

However, when making adjustments to sleeves, the grainline arrow is extended downward from the sleeve cap. This preserves the grainline in the upper portion of the sleeve. On a long sleeve, the lower portion will be a bit off-grain, which often helps the sleeve follow the natural curvature of the arm.

Adjustments to Adjoining Pattern Pieces

If you perform any length adjustments to one pattern piece, the adjoining pattern piece must also be adjusted to keep the seam lines the same length. It is important to keep this rule in mind during the fitting process. A common length adjustment is a tuck and wedge combination, as shown in the examples below. In the photographs of fitting garments, you will see that this occurs in many different areas of the garment and in different combinations of manipulations, such as tucks, wedges, and increased dart intakes.

One way to shorten the center back of a princess seam garment in relation to the front is to make an even tuck in the center back pattern, and then make a wedge on the side back panel that goes to nothing at the side seam, where the length adjustment ends.

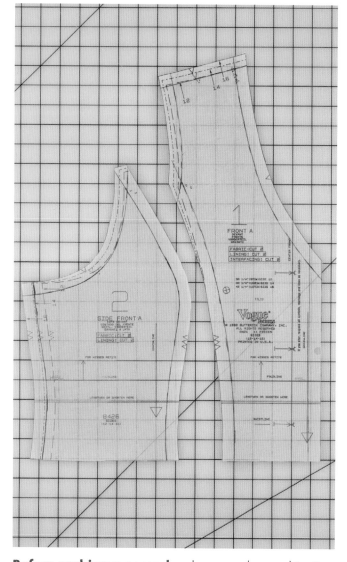

Before making a spread and open-wedge combination.

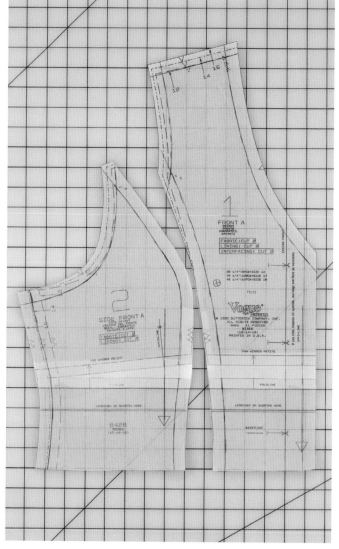

After making a spread and open-wedge combination.

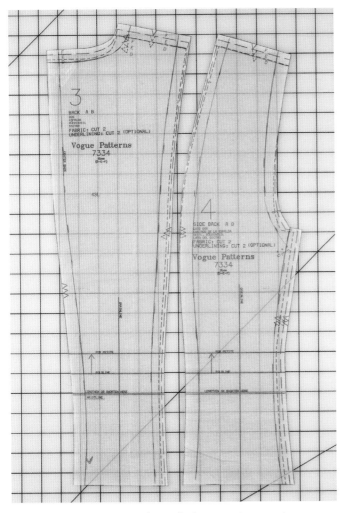

Before making a tuck and close-wedge combination.

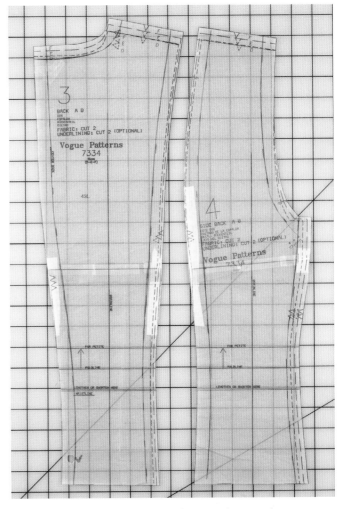

After making a tuck and close-wedge combination.

WALKING AND TRUING A PATTERN

Seams that will be sewn together need to be the same length, unless there is a specific reason to vary their lengths, in which case the fabric is either eased or stretched in the sewing process. It's relatively simple to compare two straight seams, but if one or both seams are curved, it's more difficult. To compare two seam lines with complete accuracy, they should be "walked." The process of comparing seam lengths and making adjustments so that the adjoining seams are exactly the same length is called "truing."

When walking two adjoining pattern pieces, the seam lines are compared. It's important to focus on the seam line and ignore any seam allowance or cut lines. If you are working with a pattern that intentionally does not have seam allowances, as in most couture sewing, be sure to note that the seam line is most likely the edge of the paper.

Where to Begin the Pattern Walking Process

If the pattern pieces have an HBL that intersects the seams being checked, start the process at the HBL, since it is a fixed point. Side seams of a bodice are a good example. Walk the seams from the HBL to the underarm, and then repeat the process from the HBL to the hem.

For other pattern pieces that do not have an intersecting HBL, start at a notch if there is one. A shoulder seam is a good example: start at the notch and walk the seams to the neck, and then repeat the process from the notch to the shoulder.

If there is no fixed point at which to start, you will need to make an educated decision about where to begin. I often start at the hem of the garment and walk the seam up, or I start at the outer edge of the garment and walk the seam toward the inner edge of the garment.

Walking Patterns

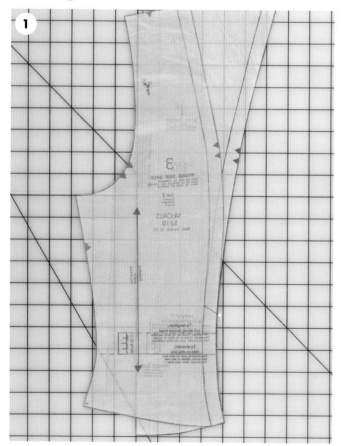

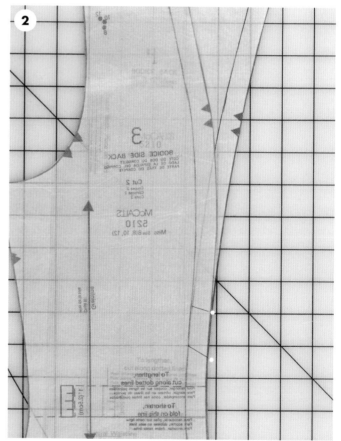

1 Lay one pattern on top of the other, matching the seam lines. Anchor the patterns with a pin through the seam line at the starting point, which in this case is the HBL. You can see that the bottom of this pattern already walks correctly since the top and bottom pattern pieces match from the HBL down to the hem of the garment.

2 Where the two seam lines diverge, place another pin directly on the seam. Note that the two cut edges also diverge.

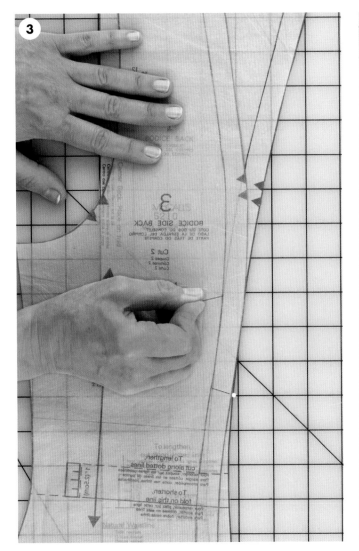

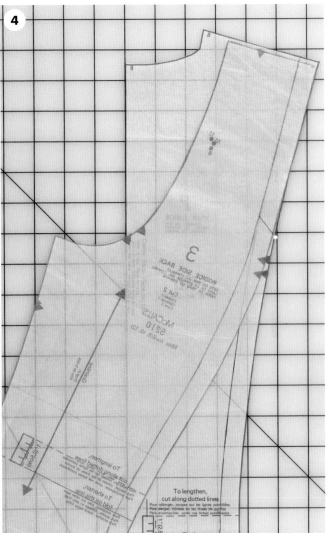

3 Remove the first pin, and pivot the top pattern so that the seams are brought into alignment starting at the pin. Where the two seams diverge, place another pin; repeat the process to the end of the seam.

4 In this example, the notches line up nicely on the two pattern pieces. After walking the entire seam, note any discrepancy in the seam lengths: here the bottom pattern is approximately ⅛" (3 mm) longer than the top pattern.

How to Adjust Seams with Discrepancies

If the two seam lines are not the same length and they should be (that is, there is no ease built into the pattern), then you have to make an educated decision about which seam to adjust. Knowing the intent of what was being done in the fitting is a good guide. For instance, if I'm widening a neckline on a garment and the shoulder seams are not true, then I would cut off the excess of the longer piece at the neck. If I were making the neckline fit closer to the neck, then I would add to the shorter piece at the neck.

(continued)

If the discrepancy is ½" (1.3 cm) or more, then splitting the difference is always safe. Cut off ¼" (6 mm) from the long piece, and add ¼" (6 mm) to the short piece.

Since I frequently will sew another test garment after such pattern alterations, I'll have the opportunity to check that what I have done in the pattern work makes sense on the body.

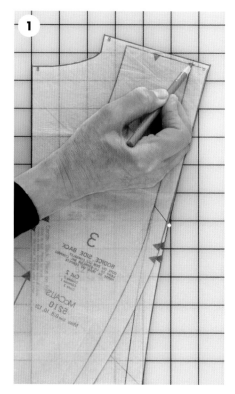

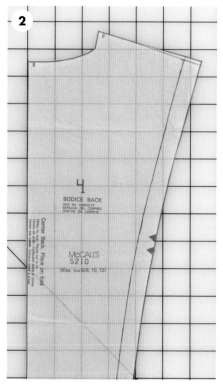

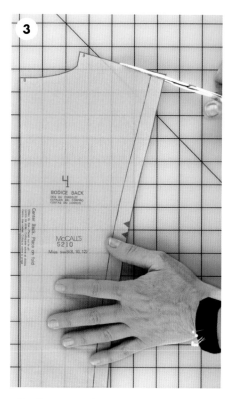

1 Continuing the example above, I will cut off the excess length from the bottom pattern, which is ⅛" (3 mm) longer when walked. First, mark the bottom pattern. Normally this would be done at the seam line, but in this case, there is such a small and obvious adjustment, it is okay to make the adjustment at the cut line.

2 Blend the new cut line, going to nothing along the shoulder toward the neck. In this example, it is only the princess seam that needs to be changed.

3 Cut away the excess paper.

Keeping Patterns Accurate

I like to execute pattern work as accurately as possible and rarely have more than ¹⁄₁₆" to ⅛" (1.6 to 3.0 mm) of discrepancy. You will need to decide what degree of accuracy is important to you. Many sewers say that working from a trued pattern makes sewing a garment quite a bit faster.

Walking Patterns with Darts

When truing a pattern with darts, skip the area between the dart legs, since the dart will be sewn before the two pattern pieces are joined. If you prefer, fold the dart out in the paper before walking the pattern; note that this can make walking the seams a bit awkward, as the pattern piece will not lie flat on the table.

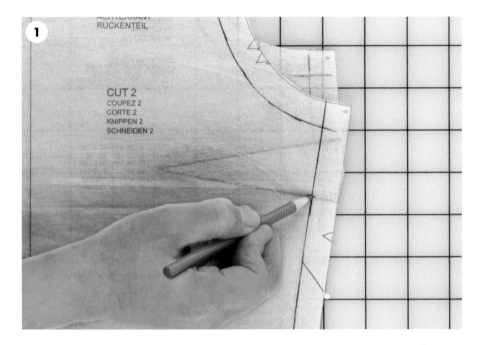

1 Have the pattern piece without the dart on top of the pattern piece with the dart. Walk the pattern pieces up to the lower dart leg. Mark the lower dart leg placement along the seam line.

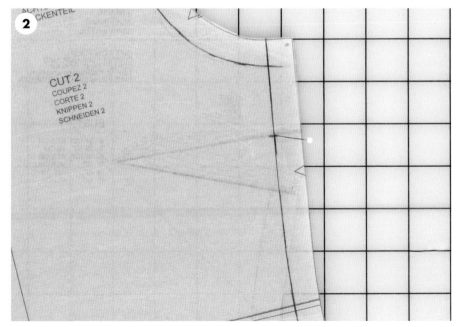

2 Shift the top pattern piece so that the mark indicating the lower dart leg matches the upper dart leg at the seam line. Then finish walking the seam.

PLACING AND CREATING NOTCHES

Notches are tools to help you sew the garment pieces together accurately. Sewing is like a puzzle. You have a number of pieces that go together, and notches help you put the puzzle together correctly. In the same way, notches are useful tools when doing pattern work.

There are some traditional notch usages. For instance, one notch on a sleeve indicates the sleeve front, and two notches indicate the sleeve back. These will correspond to the one notch on the garment front armhole and the two notches on the garment back armhole. With some commercial patterns, there is a recognizable system of how notches are used. As you take control of your pattern work, you might find you need fewer notches on some garments and

many more in other garments. Remember that notches are tools—utilize them according to your needs.

Notches are used in two primary ways. First, they are used to indicate which pattern or garment sections are adjoining. Notches are extremely helpful when two or more pattern pieces look similar and when there are lots of pattern pieces for a garment. For example, on a skirt pattern with princess lines, the placement and number of notches used in one location make it impossible to mistakenly sew garment sections together that are not adjoining. Second, notches are used to control where ease is put in a garment, which I discuss in detail in the following section.

Adding a Notch to a Pattern

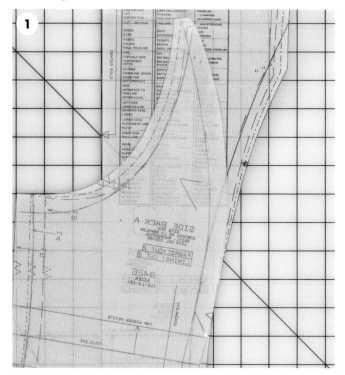
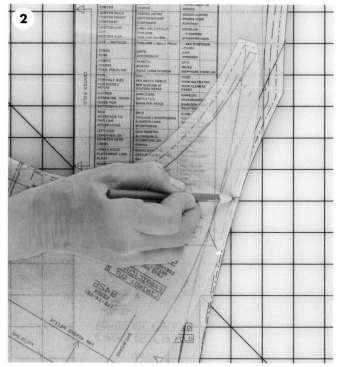

1 To add a notch to a pattern, draw the placement of the new notch on one of the two adjoining pattern pieces. Place the other pattern piece on top, matching up two pre-existing notches.

2 Accurately walk the top pattern piece, stopping when you come to the new notch and drawing it in on the upper pattern piece.

CONTROLLING PATTERNS WITH BUILT-IN EASE

Occasionally a garment fits better when two adjoining seams are not exactly the same length, but rather one seam is slightly longer than the other. The excess in the longer seam is referred to as "ease," since it is eased into the shorter seam during the sewing process. For example, on a princess line bodice, the side front princess seam often has a small amount of ease in relation to the front princess seam. This bit of ease helps fit a rounded bust shape. When there is built-in ease such as this, notches indicate to the sewer the specific portion of the seam where the ease should occur.

Another example is the back inseam of pants, which is frequently a bit shorter than the front inseam. In the sewing, the stretched back inseam improves the fit under the buttock. Good notch placement indicates exactly where to stretch the back inseam.

Repositioning Built-in Ease

To adjust the placement of built-in ease in a pattern, use notches to control where the ease is distributed on the adjoining pattern piece. In the following example, the front princess seam is true from the HBL up to the lower notches, and from the armhole down to the upper notches. When the patterns are walked between the notches, the side front is ⅜" (1 cm) longer than the front, which means there is ⅜" (1 cm) of ease.

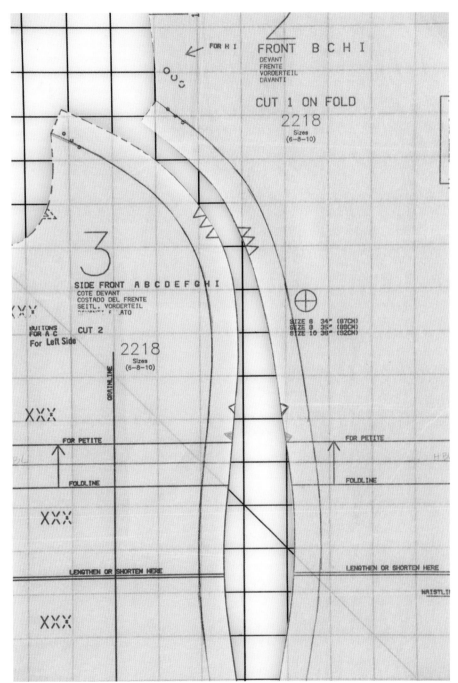

If distributing the ease across a greater distance enhances the fit, move the corresponding notches on the adjoining pattern pieces. For instance, the lower notches of this pattern could be moved downward ½" (1.3 cm). This allows the total amount of ease to remain the same, but it is distributed over a greater distance.

Removing Built-in Ease

Sometimes patterns have more built-in ease than is desirable. On a princess bodice, for example, smaller and more pointed bust shapes require less ease than fuller and rounder busts. And if a princess line garment fits very well, there is often no need for any ease at all. Also, some fabrics, such as taffeta weaves and polished cottons, are extremely difficult to ease. In these cases, take control of your pattern and reduce or eliminate the amount of ease to get a nice looking finished garment.

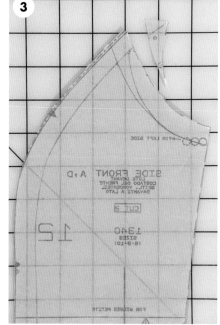

1 With the pattern containing the ease on top, walk along the seam line from the notches to the end of the seam containing the ease, which in this case is at the armhole. At the end of the seam, mark the position of the seam line from the bottom pattern onto the top pattern (in red).

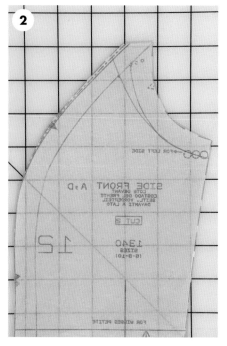

2 On the top pattern, blend the new seam line to the existing seam line.

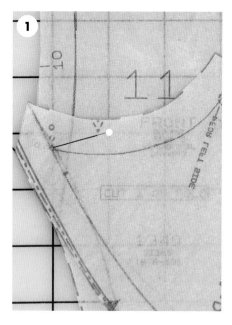

3 Correct the seam allowance and trim along the new cut line.

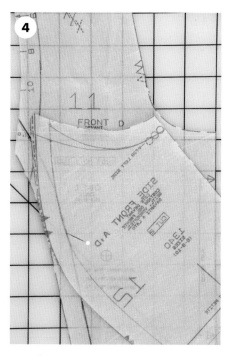

4 Then, reposition the notch that indicated the location of the ease. In this case, reposition the notch that is closest to the armhole on the side front pattern. To do this, walk the side front pattern to the front pattern starting at the armhole. When you come to the notch on the front pattern, mark the side front pattern.

TRUING DIFFICULT SEAMS

When walking two adjoining pattern pieces, you occasionally will encounter situations as you approach the end of the seam where it is unclear what the pattern pieces should look like. This is most common when the seam on each adjoining pattern piece is shaped differently, as is the case with an armscye princess seam or when the intersecting seam is steeply angled. In these types of situations, many commercial patterns square off one of the seam allowances or provide a match point at the termination of the seam itself. However, truing your pattern precisely makes sewing the garment much easier.

Anytime that I cannot visualize what the ends of two adjoining seams should look like, I "stack" my pattern pieces so that they mimic how the seams would look as if they were sewn, as shown below.

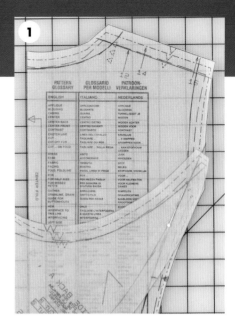

1 After walking this back princess seam from the notches (in red) up to the armhole, it is difficult to see what will line up with what when sewing the seams together.

Stacking Patterns

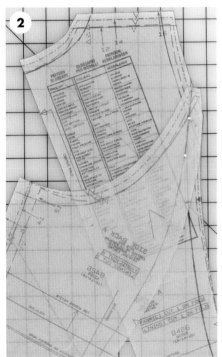

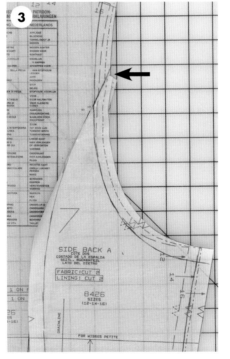

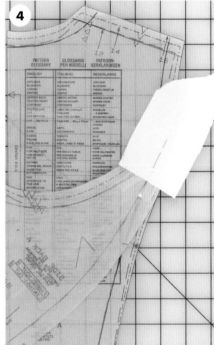

2 To clarify this, pin the pattern pieces together as though sewing the seam. Note that sometimes you can only pin the top inch (cm) or so if the seam is very curved.

3 Fold back the top pattern piece to see what the seam intersection would look like if it were sewn. In this example, you can see that the side back pattern is the wrong shape and doesn't extend enough, leaving a small gap, as indicated by the arrow.

4 To correct this, tape on additional paper to the side back pattern.

(continued)

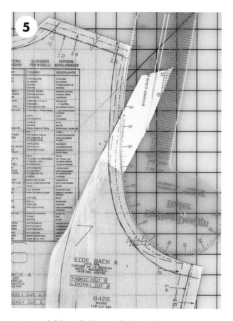

5 Fold back the side back pattern again. If it's helpful, pin it in place to prevent the patterns from shifting. Blend the seam, drawing across the patterns where they join.

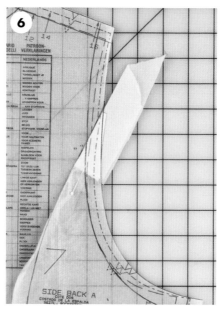

6 Add the seam allowance (in blue).

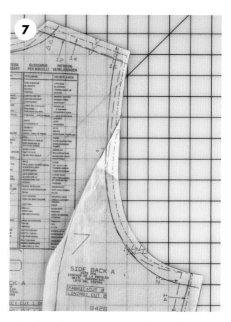

7 Cut along the new cut line. This is the trued armhole.

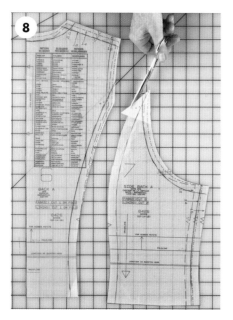

8 Unpin and trim off excess paper along the princess seam.

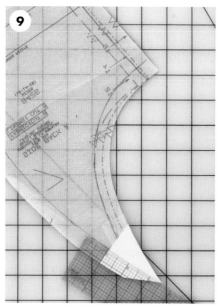

9 The tops of the adjoining princess patterns might look odd because commercial patterns do not usually true their seams like this. However, placing a ruler on top of the pattern clarifies the seam line.

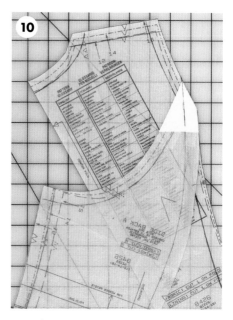

10 The seam will now match perfectly when sewing the princess seams.

MOVING THE PLACEMENT OF A SEAM

When a seam requires repositioning during a fitting, this can be reflected on the fitting muslin in two ways: you can release the seam and re-pin it in the new location, or you can indicate the new placement of the seam by drawing a line. Establishing a notch placement in both cases makes the pattern work more accurate, as you will see below.

Pattern Work for Repositioning a Seam by Pinning in the Fitting

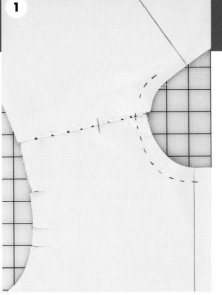

1 Before unpinning the muslin, mark the pin placement (black) and create a new notch on the muslin (green). To create the notch, simply draw a short line perpendicular to the seam. It should clearly show on each of the adjoining garment sections.

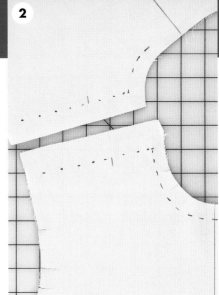

2 Unpin and press the muslin flat.

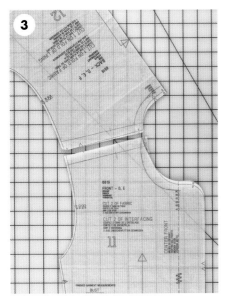

3 Transfer the new seam placement (red) and the notch (red) to the pattern. Adjust the seam allowances along the shoulder seam and cut along the new cut line.

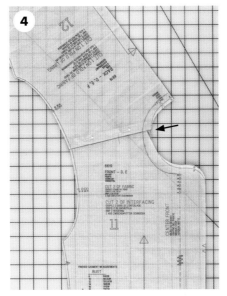

4 Stack the patterns to true the neckline intersection as follows: Fold one of the pattern pieces along the shoulder seam line; it doesn't matter which one. Align this seam with the adjoining shoulder seam, matching the new notch. Pin the pattern pieces together. In this example, the neckline seams match but the cut lines do not.

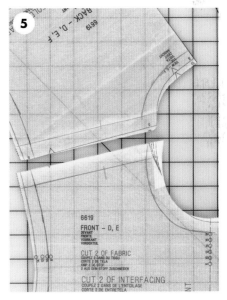

5 To true the cut lines, add seam allowance on the front pattern piece at the shoulder, as follows: Draw the intersecting neckline and armhole seam lines, and add the seam allowances. This is what the pattern pieces look like when finished.

Pattern Work for Repositioning a Seam by Drawing in the Fitting

Note that in this example the center front is on the fold.

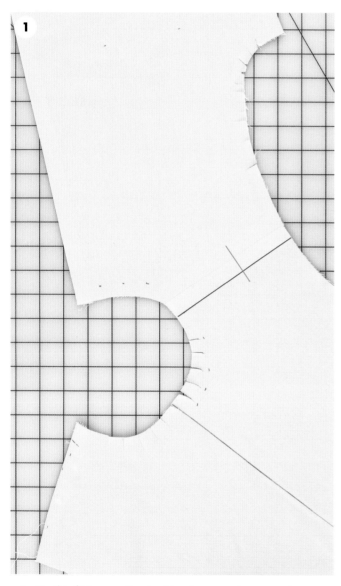

1 On this fitting muslin, the blue line was drawn on the muslin during the fitting, indicating the new position of the shoulder seam. Measure the distance between the existing seam and the new seam placement. In this example, the shoulder seam is being moved forward ⅝" (1.6 cm) at the armhole and ¾" (1.9 cm) at the neckline. Draw a notch (green) on the muslin through the new and existing seam lines somewhere along the shoulder seam.

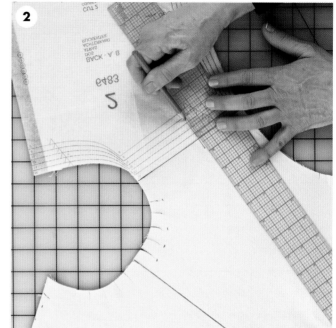

2 Before moving the seam position on the pattern, pick up the new notch from the previous step at the original seams on each pattern piece.

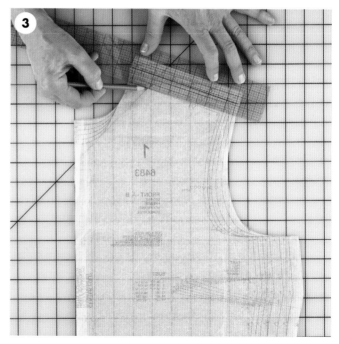

3 To reposition the front seam, measure and mark the position of the new seam line on the patterns. Draw the new front seam using a straight edge ruler.

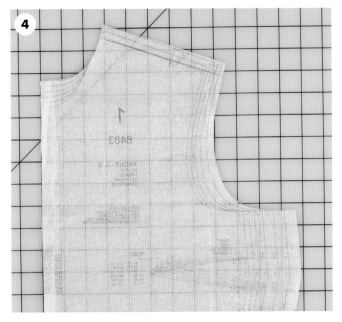

4 Add the seam allowance to the front shoulder seam. Extend the notch, if necessary, so it intersects with the cut line. Cut along the cut line.

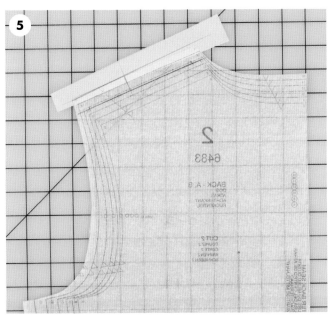

5 The back seam line is being moved forward, so you will need to tape in extra paper on the pattern. Measure, mark, and draw the position of the new seam line (in red) as was done for the front. Add the seam allowance for the back shoulder seam. Extend the notch, if necessary. Cut along the cut line of the shoulder seam.

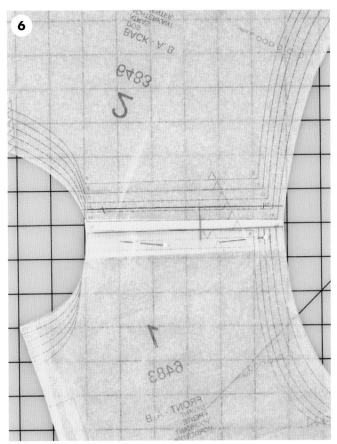

6 Proceed with truing the intersecting seam lines by stacking the patterns as follows: Fold one pattern piece along the shoulder seam line. Match the notch marked in the first step. Note that the original notches along the shoulder seam are no longer valid due to the change in shoulder seam placement, which is why it's so important to establish the new notch. Reblend the seams and cut lines, if necessary, and cut along new cut lines.

Patternmaking Tip

If there is a fitting adjustment on a seam that also needs to be repositioned, do the pattern work in separate steps. For instance, if a shoulder seam needs to be taken in as well as repositioned, first make the pattern changes to take the seam in. Then make the pattern changes to reposition the seam. Working methodically is the best way to prevent confusion.

MOVING A DART TO A NEW LOCATION

The theory of dart manipulation in flat pattern development allows you to move a dart from its original location to a new location. Moving a dart position can be useful in order to get a better or more attractive fit. The ability to move the dart location on the pattern is also helpful when fitting, because then it's possible to pin out excess fabric where the excess occurs, which facilitates getting the optimum fit. Then, if you don't want a dart in that location on the body, it can be moved to a more flattering position.

When a dart is relocated, the fit is not substantively changed in the relocation process, although it's best to check and fine-tune the fit in a test garment.

In the fitting examples, I often move a dart to a location I prefer by manipulating the fabric, which is called "draping." See page 10. Draping a dart during a fitting and transferring the dart in pattern work both produce good results. Some people prefer one method over the other, but many people use both methods depending on what is expedient in a given situation.

Some dart transfers are done at the apex, meaning that the apex becomes the rotation point where a hinge is created and around which the dart is moved. The dart point can also be used as the rotation point in simple situations, such as the example to the right.

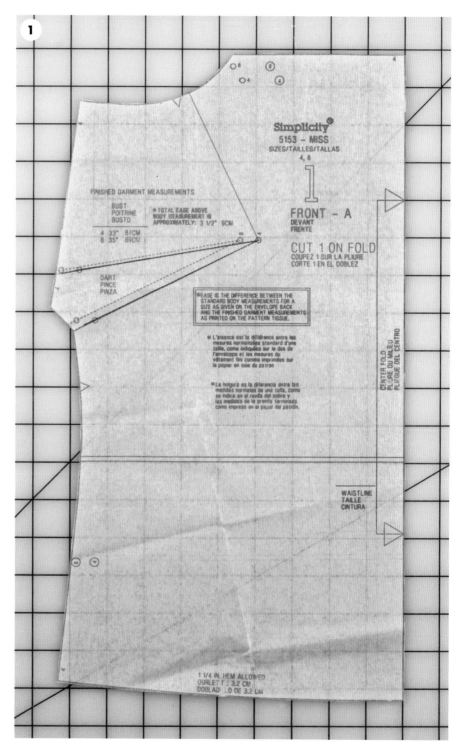

1 Draw the new dart position (in red). Here the dart is being moved from the bust to the armhole on a tank top.

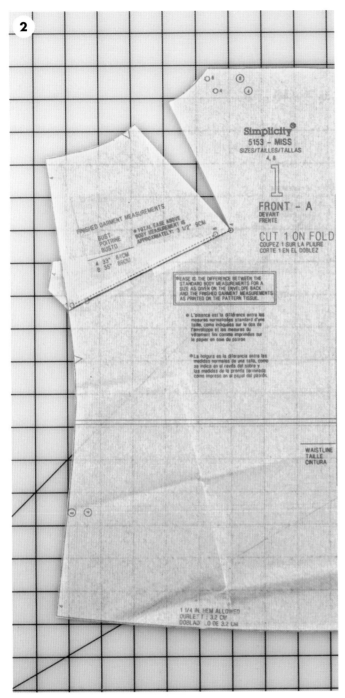

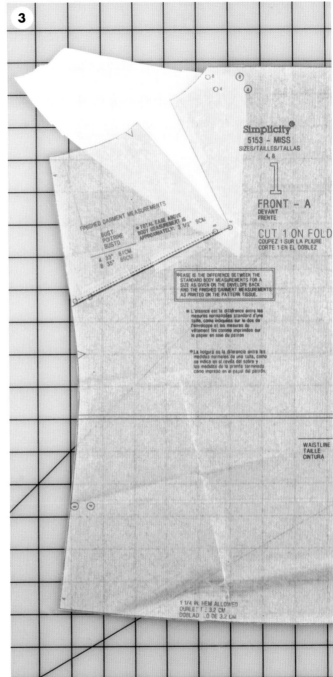

2 Cut through the original dart (it's okay to cut along either one of the dart legs or through the middle of the dart) up to, but not through, the transfer point. Also cut along the line for the new dart up to, but not through, the transfer point; this creates a hinge. Rotate the dart intake to the new position by bringing the two original dart legs together, and tape in place.

3 Trim off the old dart extension. Tape in additional paper at the new dart legs, making sure that it extends well beyond the dart. The dart legs must be trued in order to create a new dart extension, which is discussed in the following section.

TRUING DART LEGS

Truing a dart ensures that both dart legs are the same length. The process of truing a dart will form a perfect dart extension, which is the area of the pattern between the dart legs at the intersecting seam. Working with trued darts makes the task of sewing darts easier and promotes accuracy.

When truing a dart in the pattern, fold the dart in the direction that it will be pressed in the fabric. Vertical darts, such as waist darts and neck darts, are traditionally pressed toward the center front or center back of the garment. Horizontal darts, such as side bust darts and elbow darts, are traditionally pressed down toward the hem of the garment.

Determine the direction the dart will be pressed. If the dart will be pressed down, begin the process of truing the dart legs with the lower dart leg. If the dart will be pressed toward the center of the garment, begin the process of truing the dart legs with the dart leg that is closest to the center.

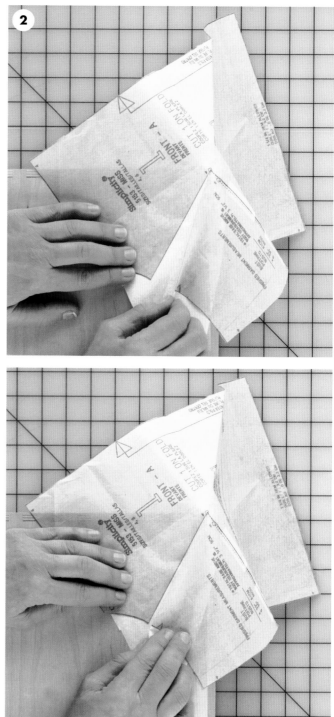

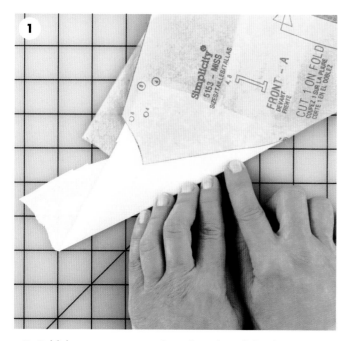

1 Fold the pattern paper along the selected dart leg.

2 Bring the folded dart leg to the other dart leg, pivoting the paper at the dart point. It's helpful to work on the corner of a table, having the dart on the table surface and letting the rest of the pattern hang off the table. Pin or temporarily tape the dart closed.

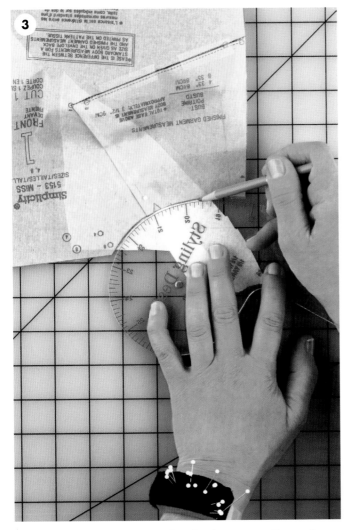

3 Reposition the pattern so that the dart area is flat on the table, and reblend the intersecting seam and cut line, if necessary. Here it is only necessary to correct the cut line.

4 Cut the pattern along the cut line. Unpin the dart. When the dart is opened up, the dart legs will be perfectly trued.

Shaped Darts

Shaped darts, which have curved dart legs, often improve the fit of a garment. However, it's very difficult to match curved dart legs when truing a pattern. Therefore, with all darts that intersect a seam, draft the dart legs with a straight edge ruler to facilitate truing the dart legs. Then draw the curved dart legs or make a note on the pattern to sew curved darts.

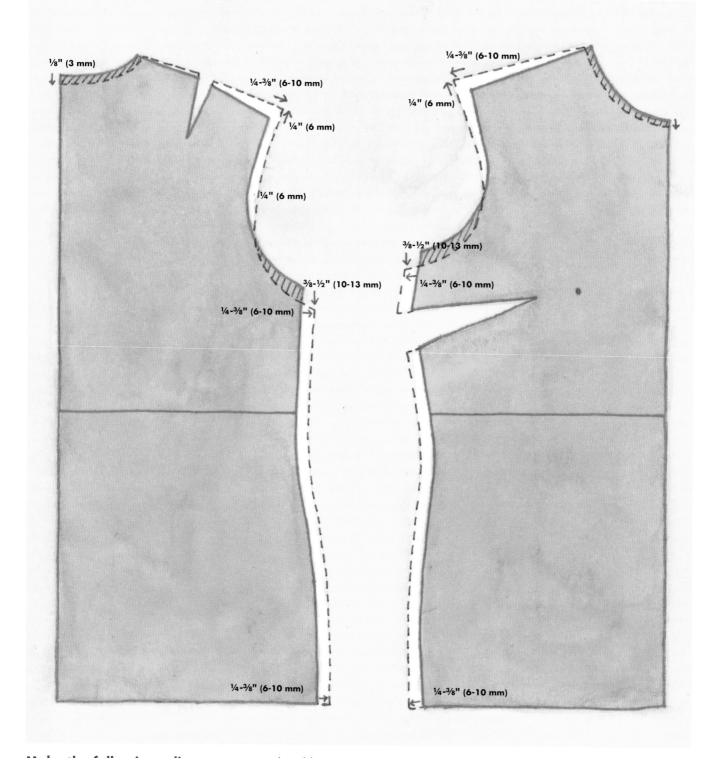

1/8" (3 mm)

1/4-3/8" (6-10 mm)

1/4-3/8" (6-10 mm)

1/4" (6 mm)

1/4" (6 mm)

1/4" (6 mm)

3/8-1/2" (10-13 mm)

1/4-3/8" (6-10 mm)

3/8-1/2" (10-13 mm)

1/4-3/8" (6-10 mm)

1/4-3/8" (6-10 mm)

1/4-3/8" (6-10 mm)

Make the following adjustments to scale a blouse pattern up to a jacket or a jacket pattern up to a coat. To scale a blouse pattern to a coat, double the measurements. The measurements can also be used to scale a pattern down by making these adjustments in reverse.

SCALING PATTERNS UP AND DOWN

In many of the fitting examples, I fit the garments fairly close to the body, which is what I think of as a clean but not a tight fit. This allows me to actually address all of the fitting issues, since with a stylistically loose garment, it can be difficult to distinguish between a fitting issue and the largeness of the garment.

If the client intends to wear a layer under the garment that is being fit, have her wear this layering garment during all of the fitting sessions. See page 31 for more information.

Once you have a pattern that fits well, it's easy to scale the pattern up and down. For instance, you can scale a blouse up to a jacket or scale a jacket down to a blouse. The theory of how to do this is shown in the opposite illustration.

For princess seam garments, first start with these changes made to the perimeter of the garment. To make the garment roomier still, add a small amount (perhaps ⅛" [3 mm]) to the princess seams themselves.

WORKING IN AN EFFICIENT ORDER

Deciding what order to use when making pattern changes might seem overwhelming at first. To simplify the process, try to limit the number of changes you make on each test garment. Making three or four pattern changes at one time is much easier than making ten or twelve.

Limiting the number of changes does mean that you will make more test garments, which may seem like a lot of work. However, fitting multiple clean muslins allows you to check that the changes you've just made are working. And fitting a clean muslin also makes it easier to see the remaining fitting issues.

It is most efficient to first make pattern adjustments that affect the interior of the pattern, and then make changes to the perimeter of the pattern. If you make pattern changes in a different order, no harm is done. The end result will be the same, but you'll find yourself blending and truing some seams more than once, and you'll probably have more bits and pieces of paper taped to the pattern.

As you gain experience and confidence in altering patterns, you'll develop your own work habits that put you in control of the pattern. It's more important to work cleanly and methodically than it is to follow a specific order.

General Order for Pattern Work

1 Make length adjustments, such as horizontal tucks and wedges.

2 Make width adjustments, including reshaping vertical seams, adjusting the bust area, and reworking waist darts.

3 Fine-tune the placement of the shoulder seam and side seam.

4 True dart legs.

5 Fine-tune the placement and shape of the neck, armhole, and waist seam.

6 Blend seam lines if not done above.

7 Walk and true seams.

8 Measure seam allowances and draw cut lines.

9 Cut along cut lines.

DEVELOPING
YOUR ABILITY

There are two aspects to fitting that are addressed in this section: the process of fitting a garment from beginning to end and fitting the variations that occur due to differences in individual bodies. To gain an understanding of the entire process and develop your fitting ability, read through all the steps and study the photographs, even if you think certain details may not apply to you.

The Process of Fitting Garments

This chapter shows the process of fitting six different garments from start to finish, which is important in order to understand the flow of a fitting. It is organized by the type of garment being fit. The style lines in these garments are those most commonly used, such as a bodice with side bust darts and a bodice with princess lines. The models have average, but by no means "perfect," figures.

The next chapter describes how to fit different figure variations with these same patterns. It is organized according to different areas of the body, with descriptions provided for a range of typical fitting problems. Fitting pants, which carries many specialized and unique fitting problems, is described in a separate chapter.

Although these three chapters are written in the form of step-by-step directions, not all steps are appropriate for every body type. In fitting, it's of utmost importance to read the fabric on the body you are fitting and to solve each individual's unique fitting problems. The following fitting sequences are examples of thousands of potential fitting problems that can occur in endless combinations. To fit an individual's body, you will need to pick and choose the examples that apply to your situation; not every step in the sequence will apply to your situation. However, reading through the sequences will help you develop your ability to recognize and solve fitting problems.

For these examples, I intentionally chose patterns that were new to me, so that the fitting process you see is real, not merely staged problems with generalized solutions. You will see me deal with quirks of particular patterns, which is a realistic aspect of fitting. And even though I can get all of the bodices to fit the models, some are simpler to fit than others and some are more flattering than others. This is all par for the course when it comes to fitting.

SKIRT

A straight skirt is the easiest garment to fit, because it's the simplest garment to understand conceptually. Visualizing a plaid skirt helps establish the fitting axis in your mind, which is useful when fitting other garments as well.

Style/Fitting Considerations

It's best to fit a straight skirt with the skirt anchored at the natural or true waist (the smallest part of the torso). If you prefer to wear your skirt lower, as many women do, this is a stylistic change and is done after the skirt has been fit at the waist. Fitting at the natural waist allows the skirt to settle on the body, resulting in an excellent fit. If the skirt is lower on the torso, it often shifts on the body during the fitting process.

Front darts are typically used to narrow the skirt circumference from the hip to the waist, as well as to fit the body. As shown in the process below, front darts are not always flattering and can be eliminated.

Whether to use a waistband or a waist facing is a stylistic consideration; the fit of the skirt is the same. The comfort of the wearer is another factor, in conjunction with what works the best for her body type.

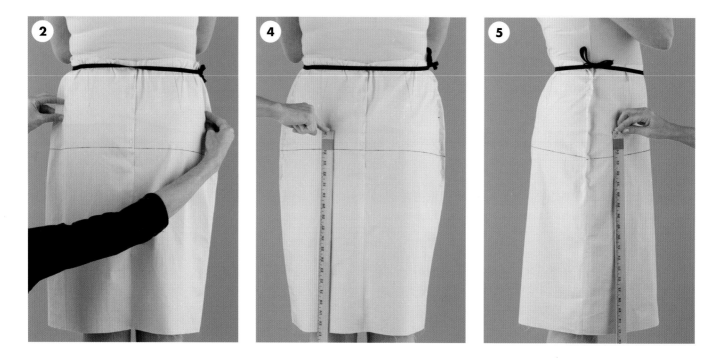

Process of Fitting the Skirt

1 Tie a piece of elastic around the body at the waist of the skirt. The elastic will naturally find the smallest part of the torso. The elastic does not need to be exactly at the waist seam of the muslin.

2 Assess the circumference of the garment at the hip.

3 If there is too much ease, pin out the excess, leaving enough wearing ease. If there is not enough ease, release the seam; remember, it is not good fitting practice to fit a muslin that is too tight.

4 Begin the process of getting the HBL level. Place a yardstick (meterstick) against the buttocks and note where the HBL falls. Marking the yardstick (meterstick) with a piece of tape provides an easy-to-see reference point.

5 Check the HBL at the side of the skirt.

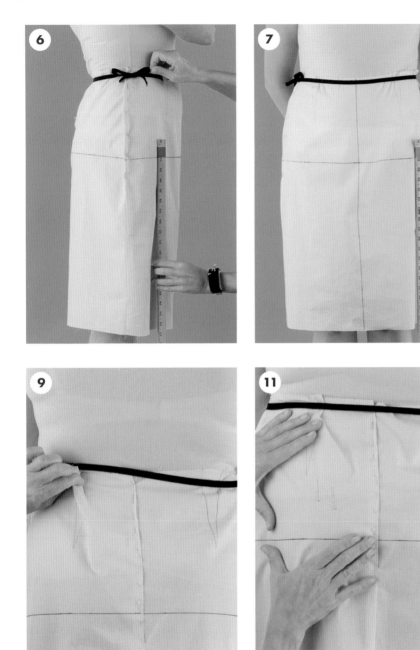

Fitting Tip

If the HBL continues to move as you measure and remeasure, the skirt may be too tight (usually across the buttock or high hip), or the skirt fabric may be "crawling" against the fabric of the bodice. Releasing tight areas and having some slack or blousing in the bodice solves these problems.

6 If the HBL is low, gently pull at the waist of the skirt, bringing the HBL to its proper level. If the HBL is high, gently pull at the hem of the skirt.

7 Check the front of the skirt, bringing the HBL level.

8 Continue this process until you are certain that the HBL is level all the way around the skirt. You are establishing your fitting axis, so accuracy is important.

9 Assess the total dart intake on one half of the skirt back. Pinching out the dart amount on both sides at the same time will prevent pulling the center back seam to one side.

10 Determine how many darts to use. Because the total dart intake here is large, use two smaller darts.

11 The dart placement should be visually attractive and provide a good fit. Finding the roundest part of the buttocks and marking the dart points facilitates draping in the darts. The two pins mark the dart points just above the fleshiest part of the buttocks.

Fitting Tip

Darts with large intakes look ungainly on the body. If a single dart intake is greater than 1¼" (3.2 cm), you get better results splitting the dart intake between two darts.

12 Drape in the darts, following the contours of the body. This takes practice. Let your fingers "read" the body. Pinching the fabric at the top and bottom of the dart can be helpful. Note that this dart placement does not follow the dart specified by the pattern. However, having the pattern's dart placement drawn on the muslin provides a good point of reference when draping in the other side.

13 After draping and pinning the darts, check the HBL and bring it back to position.

14 Commercial skirt patterns typically use front darts to reduce the circumference of the skirt at the waist relative to the hip. Front darts are flattering on some figures, but not on others. Experimenting with darts and their placement is the best way to get a flattering fit. When the darts are pinned using this pattern's placement, the roundness of this client's stomach is visually accentuated.

15 If the darts are moved toward the side seam, the waist looks quite wide in proportion to the hip.

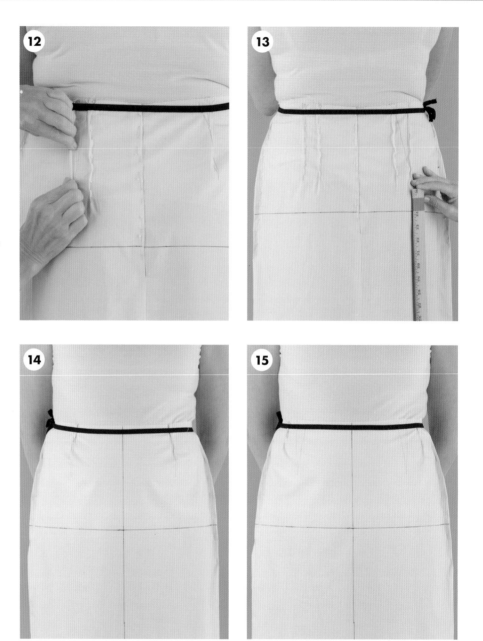

The Function of a Dart

The function of a dart is to create three-dimensional space in the garment. The dart should point toward the fullest part of the fleshy mound that this space will accommodate. Place the dart points just before the fleshiest part of the mound. If dart points extend beyond the mound (where the body begins to taper off), the dart creates space that will not be filled by the body; the result is unattractive.

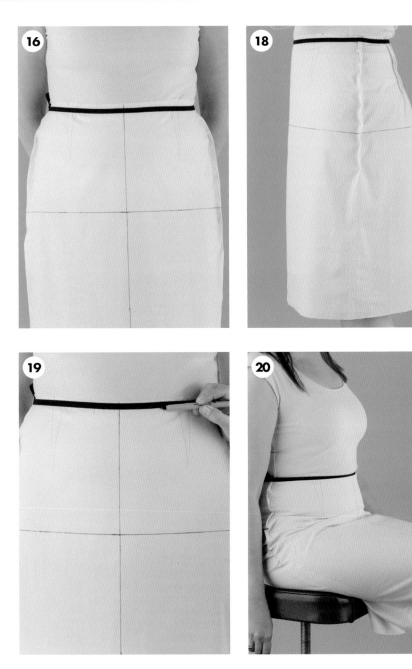

16 The client and the fitter agreed that having no darts in the front was the most flattering. The equivalent of the front dart intake can be removed from the pattern at the side seam.

17 Recheck the HBL.

18 Check that the side seam hangs straight. The side seam should be positioned approximately at the person's side and placed to make the body look proportionate. In this example, if the side seam were moved forward, it would make the stomach look smaller, but then it would fall to the front of the leg. One is not "right" and the other "wrong"; it's a judgment call the fitter makes.

19 Move the elastic so that it follows the client's natural curvature at the waist and creates a smooth line. Draw under the elastic to mark the client's waist.

20 Have the client sit to check tightness and comfort. If the skirt is too tight, there will be pull lines in the cloth radiating from the side seam toward the middle of the skirt. As in this example, no wrinkles means there's adequate ease.

(continued)

Placement of the Side Seam

Get help determining where the side seam should be. Ask the person you're fitting to close her eyes and put her thumbs on her sides at waist level. This tells you what she considers to be the middle of her body, and it's almost always accurate. You can make a visual assessment from there.

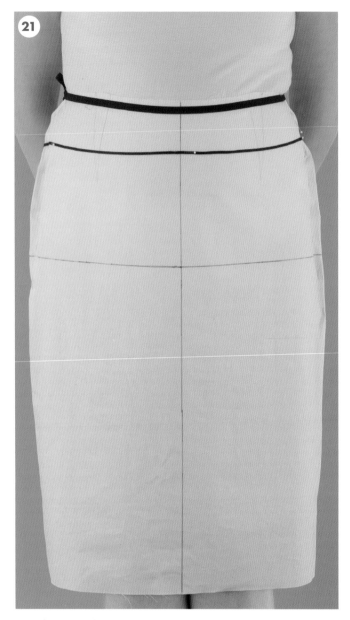

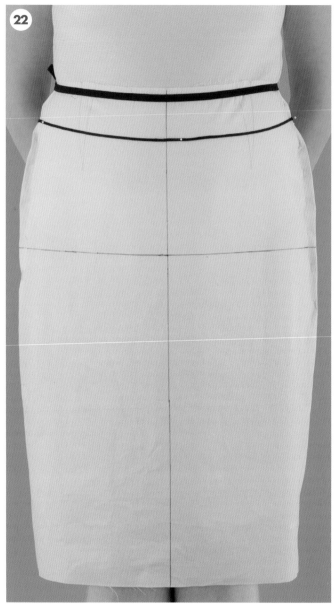

21 If the skirt fits well and doesn't require a second muslin, establish the actual waist of the skirt. This is a combination of what the client wants and what is visually pleasing. Some women prefer a lower waistline, often near the navel. Use a piece of cording or ribbon to help you establish the new waist placement. If the waistline is too straight, it makes the skirt look unflattering and like it's falling off the hips.

22 A slightly curved waistline is usually more flattering and natural looking.

Pattern Work Examples

See Fundamentals of Altering Patterns (page 44) for basic patternmaking techniques.

Waist Adjustments

The front waist seam drawn, with the front dart eliminated.

The back waist with the dart legs trued.

Hip Curve Differences

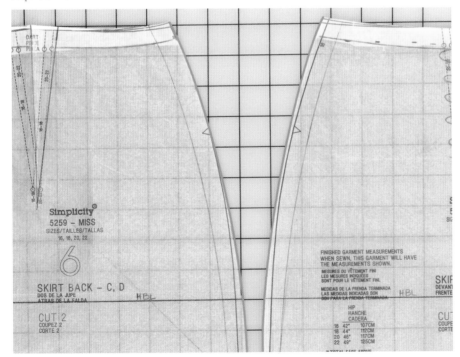

For many figures, the front and back hip curves are slightly different, because the back waist is often smaller than the front waist.

BODICE WITH DARTS

Side bust darts are an excellent fitting tool. Like all darts, they add dimensionality to a garment. To understand this concept of dimensionality, take a sheet of paper and fold a dart in it so that the dart point is somewhere in the middle of the page. Then put the paper on a table. The paper no longer lies flat but looks like a pup-tent, arcing above the table with space underneath. In a bodice, the three-dimensional space created by the dart provides room for the bust to sit within. And this is what allows the front of the garment to hang straight rather than flaring away from the body at the hem.

Style/Fitting Considerations

Bustlines vary in shape as well as in size. Some women's breasts are pointed, others are rounded. Some women have a lot of breast tissue on the side of the bust; others have a deep bust, top to bottom. Some women are "hollow" above the bust; others have a prominent chest structure. All of these variations must be taken into account during the fitting process.

Some figures are harder to fit nicely than others with a darted pattern. Using two parallel darts (see page 133) might help, especially on fuller bustlines. If you're having a lot of trouble, consider switching to a pattern that has princess lines. A shoulder princess line is an excellent fitting tool and works very well for all figure types and bust shapes.

Bust darts can be "straight" and level, or they can emanate from the side seam at any angle you wish. Their position impacts the way the garment looks on the body. In all cases, the dart should point toward the apex or the fullest part of the bust.

Without a dart, the fabric flares away from the body at the hemline.

With a dart, the fabric no longer flares away from the body.

The length of the dart will vary according to the bust shape and size. As a rule of thumb, the smaller the bust, the closer the dart point will be to the apex. The larger the bust, the farther away the dart point will be to the apex.

Process of Fitting the Bodice with Side Bust Dart

1 The bodice front. Note the drag lines emanating from the bust. They are especially noticeable above the bust ending in the gaping armhole and below the bust ending at the side seam just below the HBL.

2 The bodice back. Note that the back of the arm is crushing or pushing down on the fabric at the back armhole. This indicates that the back of the garment is too wide and that the back armhole needs to be clipped. Another way to conceptualize this is that the back armhole seam is not in the correct place, but needs to be farther in on the garment. This is equivalent to a tightness issue and must be addressed at the very beginning of the fitting process.

3 The bodice back after the armhole is clipped, which allows the fabric across the mid-back to relax. Note that there are still folds of fabric at the underarm, which suggest that there might be excess girth at the underarm. There is also excess fabric above the HBL. Address the fit at the bust and get the HBL level before moving on to the girth issue. At this time, you could temporarily pin the back to bring the HBL to level.

4 Increase the side bust dart intake by removing the stitching of the existing dart and draping a new dart, and pin an armscye dart to eliminate the drag lines identified in step 1. For instructions on how to drape a dart, see page 104. The armscye dart is usually rotated into the side bust dart in the pattern work. Note that the model's body has tilted due to the position of her arm.

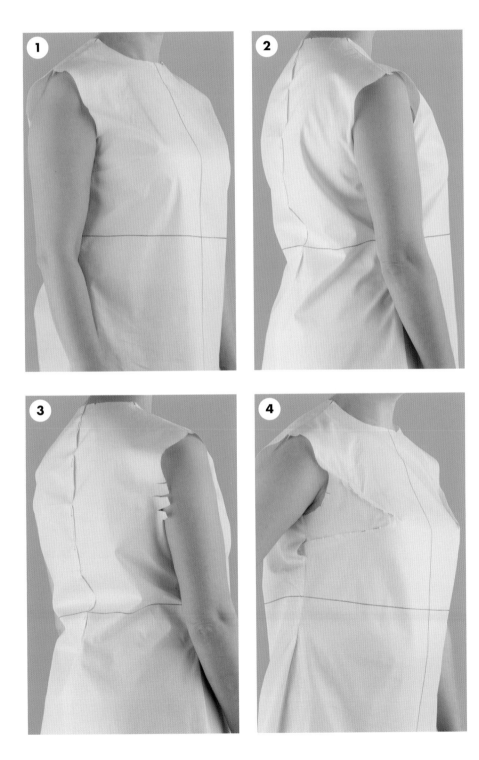

(continued)

5 Pin a tuck above the HBL across the entire back, making the HBL level. The tuck intake equaled the amount that the side bust dart was increased, which is very often the case.

6 Now check the amount of fabric at the underarm identified in step 3. Although I am pinching ⅝" to ¾" (1.6 to 1.9 cm) from each seam allowance, how much I pin out will depend on how fitted the client wants the garment to be.

7 When pinning out the excess girth, do so in a way that keeps the side seam straight. In this case, the back seam line remained the same, and all of the excess was taken out on the front. It's important to "let the fabric tell you what to do." I released the side seam at the underarm and then experimented to see where the excess girth actually was, using the position and straightness of the side seam as a guide.

8 If the side seam is taken in, as was done in step 7, check the back and front armholes again for tightness, clipping more deeply if necessary. This back armhole required more clipping; slowly we are discovering where the back armhole seam really needs to be. See pattern work on page 94.

9 Pin out the excess in the side seam from the HBL to the hem. Also note the slight looseness just below the underarm on the back. Even though the front side seam was taken in at bust level to reduce the total girth, this looseness shows that the garment is still not tight. This is partly because more space was provided for the bust when the side bust dart intake was increased. Take in the side seam more if you want a tight fit.

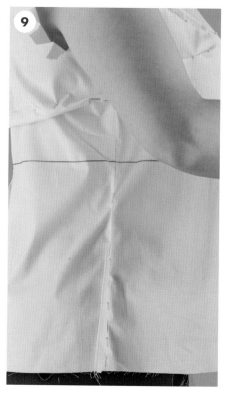

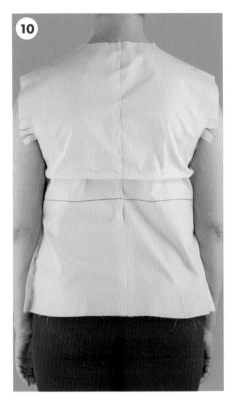

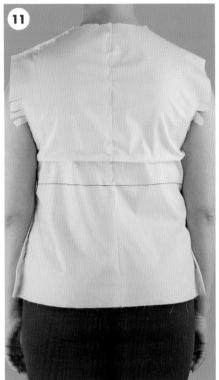

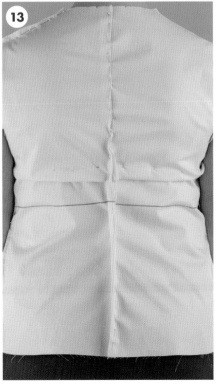

10 The muslin is starting to fit much better. For beginners, this would be a good time to transfer the fitting changes to the pattern and make a new test garment. Continuing with the fitting process, now that there are not so many distracting fitting issues, note that the HBL on the left back is slightly lower than on the right. Also note that the left armhole is slightly crumpled. Both are indications that the left shoulder is lower than the right.

11 To make the shoulders even for the fitting process, pin out the excess along the left shoulder seam; follow the contour of the shoulder line, making the HBL level while taking care not to overfit. Alternatively, use a shoulder pad on the low side only. Moving to other fitting issues, note that there is excess fabric at the small of the back.

12 Assess how much excess fabric there is in the small of the back— quite a lot.

13 One option for eliminating the excess fabric is to pin it out along the center back seam, as shown here. Below the HBL, the diagonal drag lines that point to the center back seam are due to the large amount that was taken out right at the small of the back.

(continued)

14 Another option is to take a small amount out along the center back seam and add waist darts. Taper the waist darts to nothing a few inches (cm) below prominent shoulder blades for a flattering fit. The amount you pin out depends on how closely fitted you want the garment to be. See pattern work on page 95.

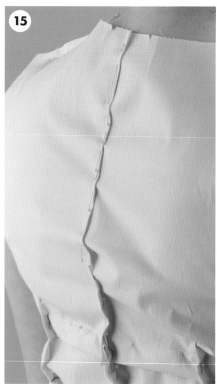

15 Note that the back neck stands slightly away from the model's body. This indicates the need for neck darts, which frequently make the garment more comfortable and prevent the garment from shifting around on the body.

16 Drape in and pin the neck darts, following the contours of the body. Note that the right and left upper backs are different, which is accentuated by the way each dart has been draped. To help the model look balanced and even, I would make both darts the same, using the left back neck dart in the pattern work. Also note the slight drag lines between the center back seam and the prominent right shoulder blade.

17 Let out the center back seam, starting about 2" (5.1 cm) below the neck and tapering to nothing a few inches (cm) above the HBL. This allows the fabric to relax and reduces the drag lines noted in step 16. See pattern work on page 94.

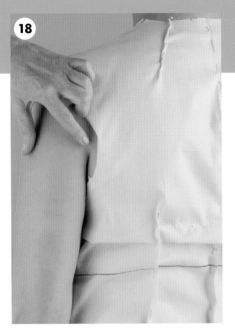

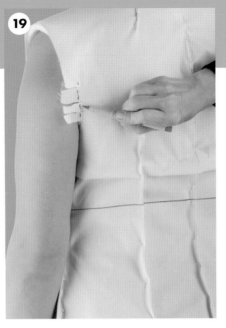

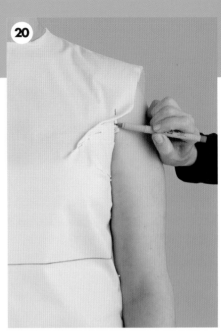

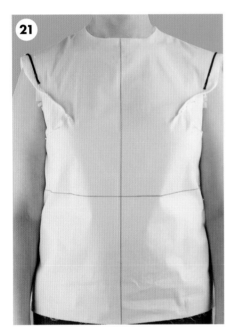

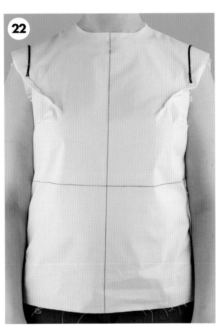

18 To establish the armhole placement, find the back and front "crease." This is where the arm attaches to the body. I have folded back the test garment fabric to reveal the back crease.

19 Mark the back crease.

20 Mark the front crease.

21 Establish the placement of the armhole at the shoulder so that it makes the body look proportionate. This is a judgment call. The most flattering placement is often farther up along the shoulder line than the "hinge" of the shoulder, which is the traditional landmark. These shoulder seams, indicated by the black tape, are too far out in my opinion, and the placement makes the model's shoulders look disproportionately broad.

22 To my eye, this armhole placement is too far in, making the model's hips and waist look large.

23 This placement, in my opinion, is the most flattering. Draw the armhole placement from the shoulder seam to the front and back crease.

(continued)

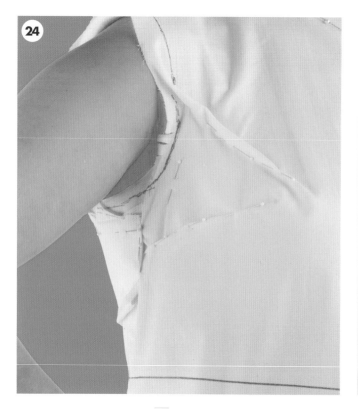

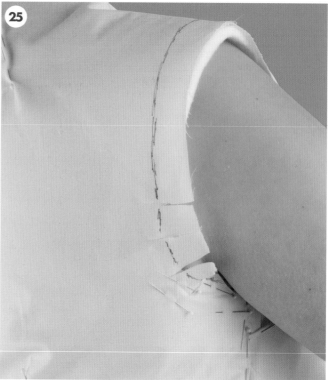

24 Establish the underarm. A high underarm provides more rotational movement and "reach" than a low underarm when using a set-in sleeve. The underarm should not be so high, however, that it is uncomfortable. (If you like a very high underarm, it's helpful to trim out the underarm seam allowances in the finished garment between the front and back crease.) The underarm of this test garment was too low, so I added fabric and then drew in the underarm placement that I wanted, connecting the underarm to the front and back crease. See pattern work on page 94.

25 The back armhole.

26 Establish the shoulder line placement, making the body look proportionate and balanced. As with the armhole placement, this is largely a judgment call. The black tape here follows the original shoulder seam. In my opinion, it's too far back.

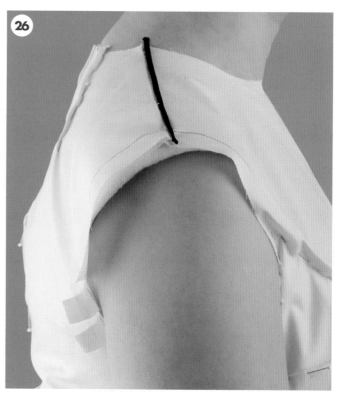

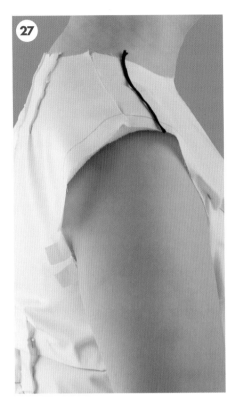

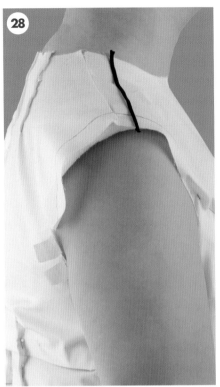

27 This placement, to my eye, is too far forward.

28 I prefer this placement, with the shoulder seam in the middle of the arm and in a pleasing position at the neck.

29 Establish a neckline. For a basic pattern that will be used as a block or sloper, the base of the neck is a useful reference point. Here, the front neck is drawn.

30 For the back, extra fabric was needed in order to draw in the neckline.

31 Transfer the fitting changes to the pattern, adjust the pattern, make a new mock-up, and fine-tune the fit. Once a test garment is fitting well, you can fit the sleeve. Sleeve fitting is shown in upcoming examples.

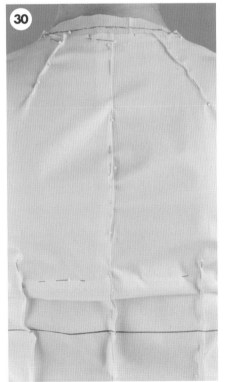

Pattern Work Examples

See Fundamentals of Altering Patterns for basic pattern-making techniques, page 44.

Back Armhole Adjustments

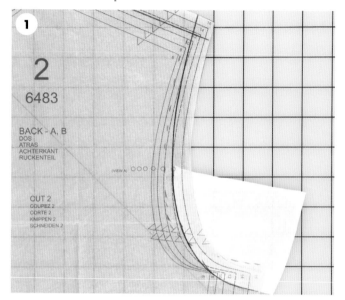

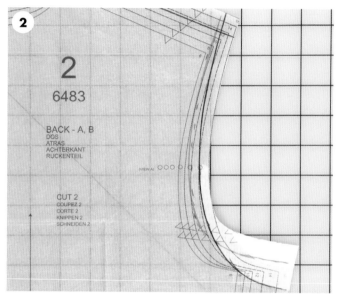

1 The red tick marks taken from the muslin indicate the new back armhole seam line. Note that paper was added in order to raise the underarm.

2 The completed pattern with the new back armhole.

Center Back Curvature

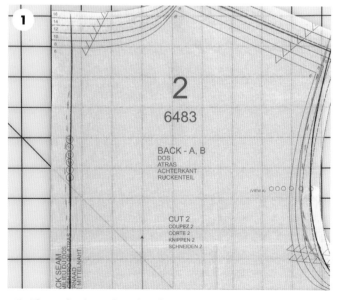

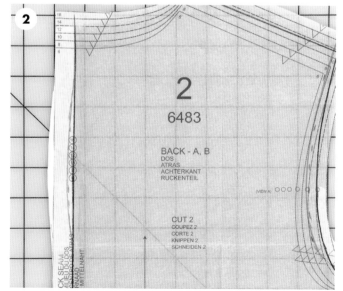

1 The red tick marks taken from the muslin indicate the new center back seam line.

2 The center back seam blended. To provide more ease through the mid-back, blend the original seam to the new seam line just a few inches (cm) above the waist.

Adding Waist-Fitting Darts

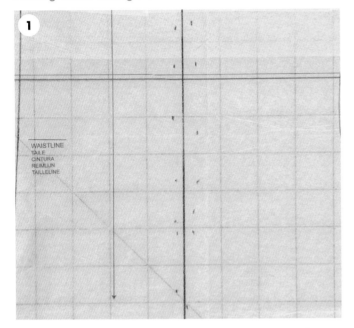

1

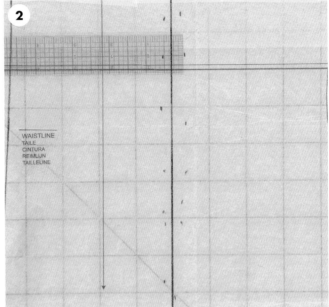

2

1 The black tick marks taken from the muslin indicate the waist-fitting dart. It's best to have an equal amount of intake on each side of the dart. To do this, draw a straight line between the mark that indicates the top of the dart and the mark that indicates the bottom of the dart.

2 Measure the total dart intake at one set of the tick marks.

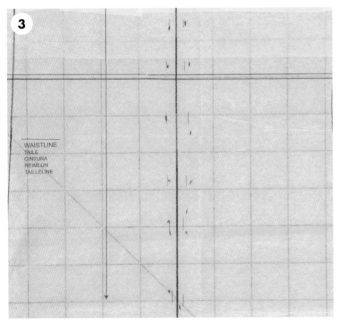

3

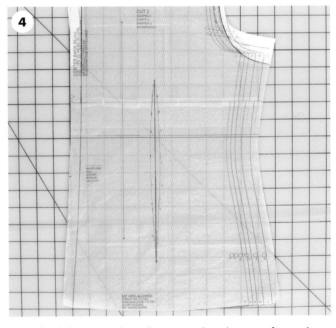

4

3 Divide the total intake in half, and mark one-half of the intake on each side of the center line of the dart. Repeat for all sets of tick marks.

4 Blend the new tick marks to complete the waist-fitting dart.

BODICE WITH SHOULDER PRINCESS LINE

Shoulder princess lines nicely accommodate all bust sizes and shapes, and are useful to fit a wide variety of back issues as well. They are often less complicated to fit than armscye princess lines, and the resulting pattern work is usually simpler too.

Style/Fitting Considerations of Princess Lines

Princess lines in general are extremely effective fitting tools, because the seam line goes over or near the apex of the bust. In addition to their effectiveness in obtaining a good fit, they are easy to modify to achieve a garment that is flattering visually. Princess lines start at the hem, go over the bust, and can end in a number of places on the upper body.

Shoulder princess lines **(A)** intersect the shoulder seam, usually at the midpoint, and the vertical line is visually slimming

Neckline princess seams are not frequently found in commercial patterns, but they also produce a pleasing vertical line. Changing where the princess line intersects the neck can make the bust appear smaller **(B)** or fuller **(C)**.

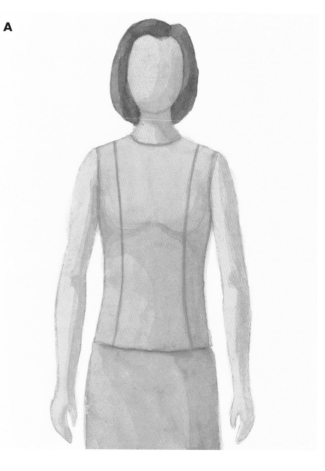

A

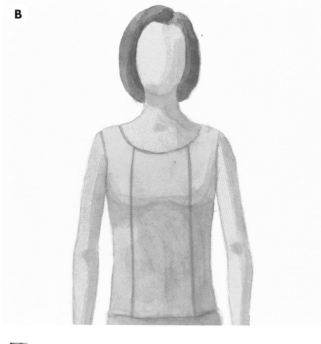

B

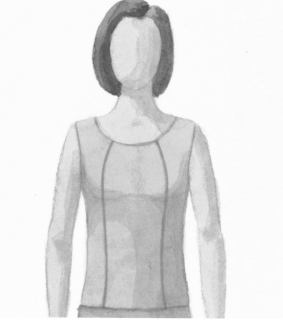

C

D

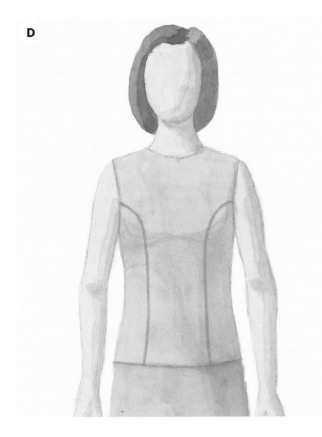

E

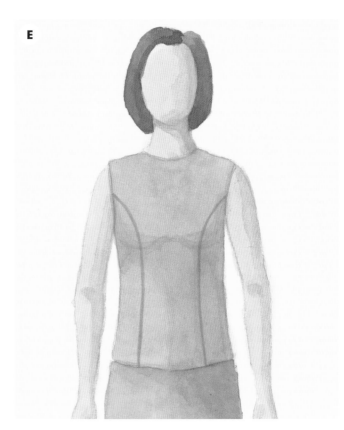

F

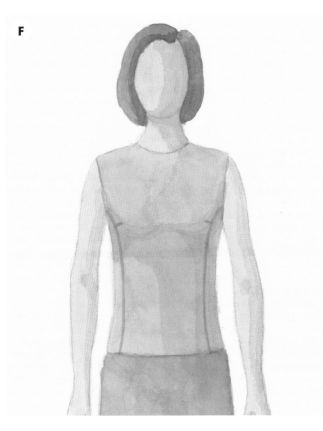

The position of armscye princess lines also carries a visual impact, making the bust appear rounder **(D)** or making the upper torso appear longer **(E)**. The need to join a concave and a convex curve in armscye princess lines can make them difficult to sew; raising the intersection point on the armhole makes sewing easier.

If a princess line does not go over or very near the apex of the bust **(F)**, the bust area cannot be fit effectively. With princess lines that fall to the side of the bust, a short dart completes the fit and produces an interesting style variation.

Process of Fitting the Bodice with Shoulder Princess Line

1 The bodice front. Although the garment does not close over the bust, the shoulders fit well. Rather than assuming that the client needs a larger size, first assess how the rest of the garment fits.

2 When viewing the garment from the side, note the excess fabric in the back above the HBL. Also note the drag lines emanating from the bust and pointing toward the waist and hip. The combination of these issues suggests that a full bust is the reason the bodice did not close at center front.

3 Viewed from the back, the bodice looks snug across the upper back but otherwise not tight. Note the low left shoulder.

4 Release the front princess seams over the bust. The princess seams spread, allowing the center fronts to match. Clip the neckline and front armholes to eliminate tightness.

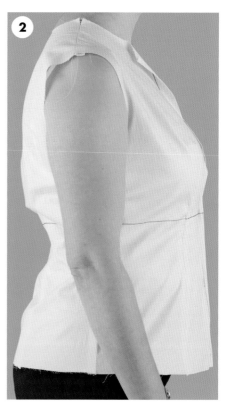

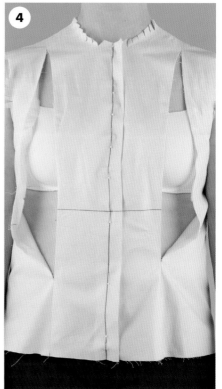

5 Releasing the front princess seams allows the bodice back to relax.

6 Note the excess fabric below the shoulder.

7 Pin out this excess fabric in a wedge. Begin to pin the princess seam working from the top downward. Note the bagginess on the side front panels.

8 Release the remainder of the front princess seams. The difference in length between the front panel and the side front panel is typical when making a full bust adjustment. For more information on full bust adjustments, see page 129.

(continued)

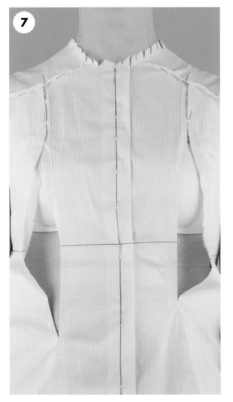

9 Slash the front panel above the HBL, and add a piece of fabric to lengthen the upper portion of the bodice, bringing the HBL into position so that it matches the HBL on the side front.

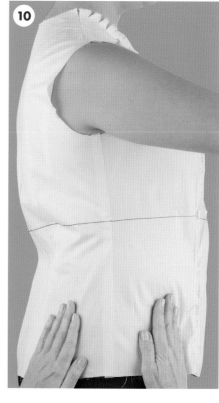

10 In order to pin the front princess seam over the bust, assess where the extra front girth needs to be added. The side seam is straight and there is no strain. This indicates that all of the extra fabric needs to be added at the bust.

11 Add extra fabric and pin the princess seams to it, smoothing the mock-up fabric so that it is neither tight nor loose over the bust. Slip in a small shoulder pad on the low shoulder. This could have been done during an earlier step, but I chose to wait until the garment had really begun to settle on the client.

12 Once the extra girth for the bust is added, establish the new front princess seam placement. Using a narrow piece of soutache or other trim lets you experiment with the seam placement. In order to get a flattering princess seam placement on the figure, both the front and the side front will need to be adjusted. In your pattern work, use the new princess seam placement to guide you in determining how much to add to each pattern piece.

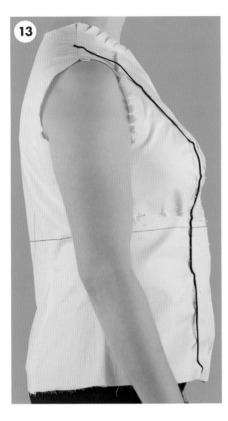

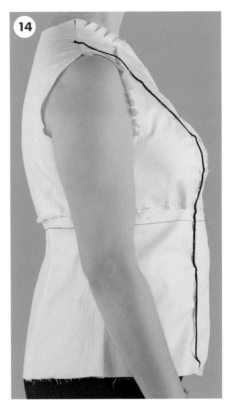

13 Viewed from the side, the back HBL is low in comparison to the front. When the extra fabric was added to lengthen the bodice front (step 9), more length could have been added. However, because the garment is a bit snug over the buttocks, I chose to raise the back HBL a small amount.

14 The back HBL raised. Note the drag line emanating from under the bust going to the side seam at elbow level.

15 The drag line identified in the previous step can be eliminated by either increasing the dart intake (pinned on the client's right) or by adding a waist-fitting dart (pinned on the client's left).

16 If the client prefers a snug fit through the back, take in the back princess seams.

JACKET WITH SIDE PANEL WITH SET-IN SLEEVE

Jacket patterns are often designed with side panels, a style element that eliminates the need for a side seam. The seams connecting the side panel to the jacket front and jacket back are about 2" to 3" (5.1 to 7.6 cm) to either side of the underarm where a side seam is usually located. Because these seams are not true princess seams due to their location on the body, the approach to obtaining a good fit is different from fitting a garment with a princess seam.

In this garment, I will fit a sleeve. For detailed information about fitting a sleeve, see pages 172.

Style/Fitting Considerations

Since the front side panel seam is not near the bust apex, it's difficult to get a clean fit on this type of garment without the addition of a bust dart unless you make the jacket oversized or you are truly small busted. As you will see, however, it's easy to add a bust dart, and the resulting garment is quite stylish.

Developing Reasonable Fitting Expectations

As your eye becomes better trained to recognize fitting issues, try not to let yourself become hypercritical. You don't need to figure out how to get rid of each and every little fold or bump of cloth on a test muslin. In fact, once you make up a garment in fashion fabric, some of those small imperfections disappear due to using "real" fabric, and many others are far less obvious. While having a high standard is good, feeling compelled to get clothing to look absolutely flawless is unreasonable. Unfortunately, an unrealistic view of picture-perfect clothing is presented to us every day by the advertising industry and the technological advancements in photography. Also, remember that during waking hours, we're moving in our clothes most of the time and are rarely motionless for more than a few seconds. Being able to move comfortably in our clothes is an important factor to consider when conducting a fitting.

Process of Fitting the Jacket with Side Panel

1 The garment front. Note the excess fabric in the front armhole. Also note the drag lines emanating from the bust to just below the waist at the side, as well as the tightness over the bust.

2 Viewed from the side, the front side panel seam is quite a distance from the bust apex. Note the drag lines identified above and the excess length in the back.

3 The garment back. Note the tightness across the upper back and at the hemline across the buttock and hip area. Also note the excess fabric in the back armhole and the excess length.

4 To eliminate the excess in the front and back armhole, pinch and raise the shoulder seam and pin along the shoulder line. It now becomes more apparent that the left shoulder is low.

5 As an alternative to pinning out the excess along the shoulder line, you can insert shoulder pads, which produces a stronger shoulder line on the garment. Women like this model often use shoulder pads to make their sloping shoulders look squarer. Because this model also has a low left shoulder, a second pad was inserted on the left; you could also use different sized pads on each side.

6 If you prefer, remove the second shoulder pad on the left. To my eye, the model looks more natural with just one pad on each side.

(continued)

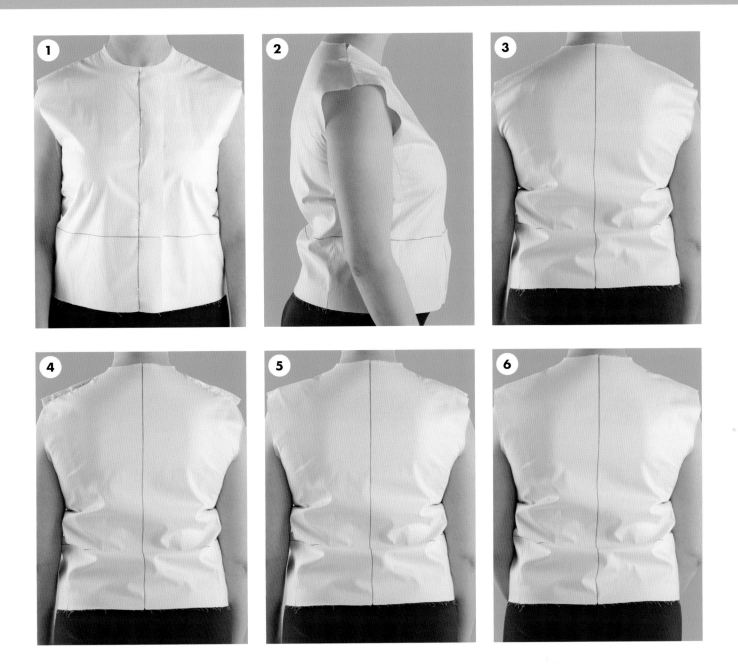

Body Asymmetries

Since very few people have perfectly symmetrical bodies, our eyes are accustomed to seeing body variations. As a result, using padding in a fitting in order to make a body look absolutely symmetrical can actually make a body look unnatural. Conversely, fitting each side of the body too exactly and out of context to the other side of the body can accentuate the body's asymmetry and make it appear more uneven than it is.

7 Clip the neckline and front armholes to alleviate the tightness. The drag lines identified in step 1 are the result of insufficient bust shaping. Releasing the front side panel seam helps you read the fabric: a side bust dart is practically forming on its own. Note that the HBL is dipping at the side.

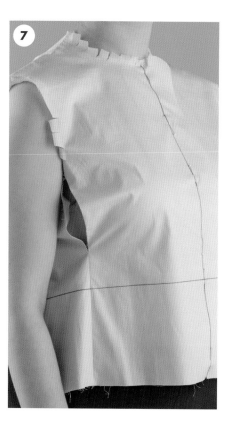

8 To create or drape a bust dart, first identify the apex and mark it, indicated on the fitting muslin with an "X." Next, mark the dart point, indicated by the pin. Smooth the fabric over the side of the bust, gently pushing the excess fabric together.

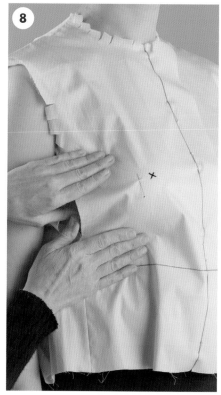

9 Pinch the excess fabric, which will become the dart intake. If you pinch too much, the HBL will rise on the side. If you pinch too little, the HBL will dip at the side. The correct amount of dart intake brings the HBL to level.

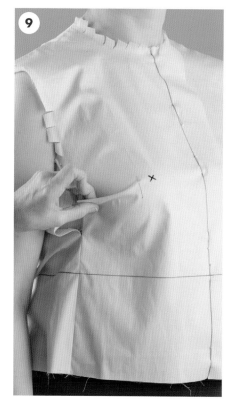

10 Fold the pinched fabric upward on the body, not letting the dart extend beyond the dart point. The angle of the dart should be flattering on the client's body. If you don't like the angle or placement of the dart, drape the dart again using a different angle or change the position of the dart. See pattern work on page 111.

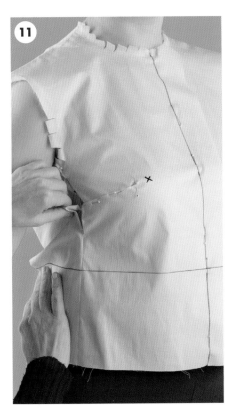

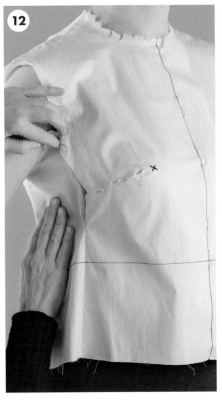

11 To keep the seam lengths the same, the side panel must also be altered. A wedge could be formed, starting at the front side panel and going to the back side panel seam. If this is done, the amount of the wedge pinned out should bring the HBL to level.

12 You can also resolve the discrepancy of seam lengths by releasing the upper portion of the front side panel seam and smoothing the side panel fabric. Draping the fabric in this way is often very effective. Note that the HBL on the side panel dips toward the back.

13 To bring the HBL to level across the back and the side panel, pin a tuck across the back and a wedge from the back side panel seam to the front side panel seam. Note both that the back side panel seam was released and allowed to spread open to accommodate the hip but that the front side panel seam hangs straight above the hemline.

14 Pin the back side panel seam below the HBL. Note that even with the side back panel seam let out, there is slight tension at the lower edge of the garment at center back, indicated by the vertical folds of fabric just below the HBL that do not continue through the hemline.

(continued)

15 If you are unsure whether there is tension or tightness in an area, cutting the fabric or releasing a seam will answer your question: if the fabric spreads, as is the case here, there was tightness.

16 Pin in a piece of fabric. To make this alteration in the pattern, you'll need to create a center back seam. This decision is the fitter's choice. I often use a center back seam because it allows me to provide a little more room across the upper back, to fit the small of the back better, and to provide plenty of room at the buttock. See pattern work on page 111. Also note the excess fabric in the armhole and the prominent shoulder blades.

17 Creating back shoulder darts helps to accommodate the shoulder blades and eliminates the excess fabric at the back armhole (see page 90 for step-by-step instructions). Draw in the back armholes (see page 91).

18 Draw in the front armholes (see page 91). Drape in front waist-fitting darts if you want a more tailored fit.

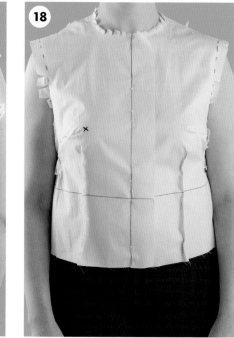

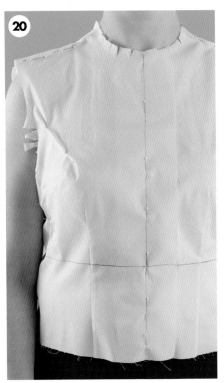

19 It's routine to make a second mock-up, which allows you to assess how the fit is progressing and to fine-tune areas that were adjusted in the first mock-up. Here, the shoulder seam and front panel seam were adjusted. Note the small amount of excess fabric between the bust apex and the armhole.

20 This excess fabric could be pinned out in a small dart and the dart amount transferred into the existing side bust dart in pattern work. However, fitting too closely above the bust often produces an unattractive fit. For many women, the fabric between the bust and the shoulder needs to "float" over the body rather than follow the exact contours of the body.

21 Now that the bodice is fitting well, it is time to drape in the sleeve, which is the process of fitting and pinning the sleeve cap to the bodice armhole. Here, I will show you the draping process with a sleeve that is proportionate to the client's arm. There are other examples of typical sleeve problems you will encounter, shown on pages 172. First, slip the sleeve onto the client's arm and pin the top of the sleeve cap to the bodice, matching the center of the sleeve to the shoulder seam.

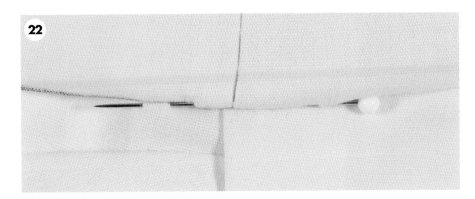

22 Pin the underarm of the sleeve to the bodice underarm. Have the client *slightly* raise her arm, match the underarm seam of the sleeve to the underarm seam of the bodice, and weave the pin through the fabrics. You can also have the client take off the bodice, pin the sleeve to the bodice in a few places, and put the bodice back on.

(continued)

23 About 1" (2.5 cm) away from the center of the sleeve cap, fold under the seam allowance of the sleeve. Sometimes you will need to fold under more or less than the pattern's designated seam allowance to get a nice looking sleeve cap. The order in which you drape in the sleeve front and the sleeve back doesn't matter.

24 Place the fold of the sleeve against the armhole seam that you've drawn on the bodice.

25 To create the ease in the sleeve cap, keep the hand closest to the center of the sleeve stationary, and with the other hand, slightly push the fabric back up toward the center of the sleeve.

26 Pin the sleeve to the bodice just to the side of where the fabric ease was created.

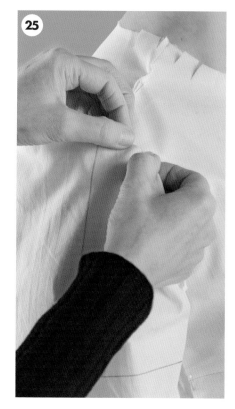

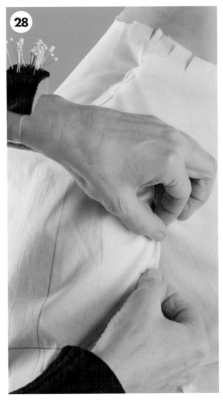

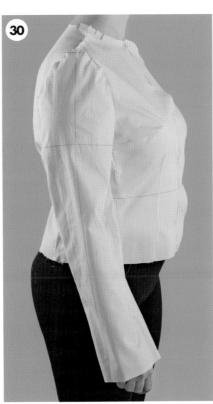

27 Move a short distance away, and again fold under the seam allowance of the sleeve.

28 Create ease through the top of the sleeve cap, as described, pinning the sleeve in place every few inches (cm). From the crease of the arm through the underarm, hold and pin the fabric flat, since there typically is no ease through this part of the sleeve.

29 Repeat the process on the other side of the sleeve.

30 Note that the sleeve HBL dips slightly in the front and that some of the sleeve excess has been pinned out along the underarm seam. Note the slight drag line at the sleeve front near the elbow.

(continued)

31 To correct the sleeve HBL dipping at the front, unpin the front of the sleeve and move the sleeve cap up a bit toward the shoulder seam. Note that shifting the sleeve cap also reduces the drag line at the elbow identified in the step above.

32 Re-pin the front sleeve, putting more ease into the upper portion of the sleeve. How to resolve the issue of a sleeve cap having too much ease relative to the armhole opening is addressed on page 174. The drag line at the sleeve front near the elbow is due to the natural bend in the client's arm when it is at rest. This sleeve does not have sufficient curvature, which you can correct if the sleeve has two seams. This is a two-piece tailored sleeve with a panel at the underarm, so it's possible to pin a wedge at the front underarm seam going to nothing at the back underarm seam. See pattern work on next page.

33 Check to see if the client can move her arms forward comfortably. If you only have one sleeve draped in, hold the other armhole in place. Note the tension across the back and at the back crease of the arm.

34 Putting more curvature in the center back bodice seam will provide more reach for the client. The pattern work is shown opposite. You can also adjust where the sleeve cap attaches to the bodice at the back armhole. Making both of these adjustments provides a good deal more reach for the client, although it also means that some excess fabric will be noticeable across the back and at the back of the arm when the client's arm is at rest. There are many situations in fitting where you must decide what is most important: to have a comfortable amount of reach or to have a picture-perfect garment.

Pattern Work Examples

See Fundamentals of Altering Patterns for basic patternmaking techniques (page 44).

Creating a New Bust Dart

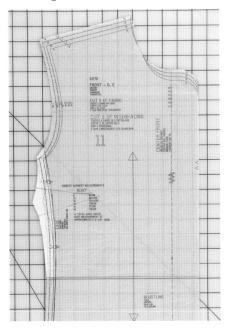

Creating a Center Back Seam

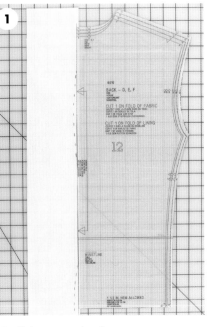

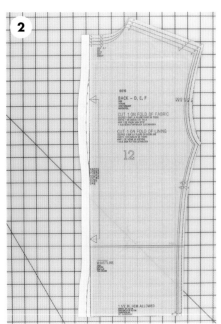

Transfer markings and create the new dart. When truing the dart legs for a newly created dart, it's often necessary to add paper along the intersecting seam in order to get a nice blend.

1 If the center back pattern was originally cut on the fold but you want to create a center back seam, the fold line represents the new seam line. In this example, we want to create shaping for the upper back and the buttocks, shown by the red tick marks, so it is necessary to make a center back seam.

2 Blend the tick marks to the center back fold line, creating the new center back seam line. Then add seam allowances, and trim away excess paper.

Creating Curvature on a Long Sleeve

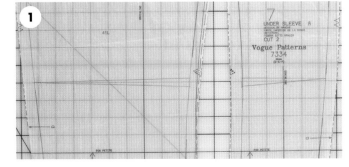

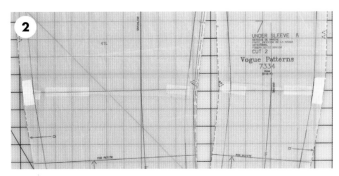

1 Mark the close-wedges from the fitting muslin. Here the close-wedges are the same amount at the underarm seam, going to nothing at the outer seam.

2 Close the wedges and redraw the grainlines, which are taken from the upper portions of the sleeve.

TUNIC WITH ARMSCYE PRINCESS LINE

Because this princess line goes from the bust to the armhole, the area above the bust is free of seams. This clean upper portion of the bodice works well for many different types of garments and fabrics.

Style/Fitting Considerations

Armscye princess lines are excellent fitting tools for the bust, since they go over or near the bust apex. And because the style line intersects the armhole, it's easy to make armhole adjustments as well. The placement and curvature of the armscye princess line between the apex and the armhole impacts the bodice visually and can make the bust appear to be larger or smaller, as seen in the illustrations on page 97.

Armscye princess lines can be difficult to sew because you are joining a convex curve to a concave curve. This is especially true for larger bust sizes and for very curved princess lines that intersect the armhole near or below the midpoint of the armhole. Raising the intersection point along the armhole makes sewing the seam easier, due to the change in curvature.

Process of Fitting the Tunic with Armscye Princess Line

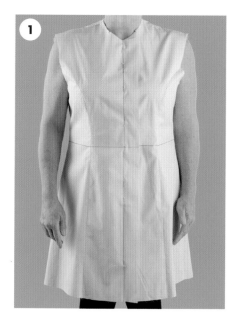

1 The tunic front. Note the slight tightness across the bust, indicated by the drag lines above the bust. Note the drag line going from the bust to the side waist, indicating the need for more bust shaping.

2 When viewing the garment from the side, note the drag line from the bust to the side waist and from the mid-back to the side waist. Also note that the HBL is low in the back. In addition, note that the back of the arm is causing the back armhole to crumple and fold.

3 The tunic back. Note a slightly low left shoulder, small vertical folds of fabric in the mid-back, slight excess at the back neck, drag lines at the sides, and folds of fabric at the back armhole near the underarm.

4 Raise the left shoulder with a small shoulder pad for the fitting process, even though this client does not make an adjustment in her clothes to make her shoulders look perfectly even. Clip the back armholes to the crease. It's important to have the armhole seam positioned at or very near the crease. Otherwise, the arm pushes down on any excess fabric that extends beyond the crease and creates unwanted folds of fabric on the bodice below the underarm. Clip the neckline where it is tight.

5 A tuck or a tuck and wedge combination will bring the HBL level. Decide where to make this adjustment on the back. It's important to know where the client has fleshy areas.

6 Make the tuck above the fleshy area, which allows the fabric to float over the fleshy area rather than accentuate it. When making a tuck or a tuck and wedge combination, let the folds of fabric tell you what to do. In this case, the tuck was continued across the side back in order to eliminate the folds of fabric identified in step 3 at the sides of the body. This tuck was resolved on the side front with a wedge going to nothing at the front princess seam.

7 The HBL is now level. The tuck on the side back still needs to be resolved because it was pinned just to the side seam. Since the bust needs more shaping, which was indicated by the drag lines identified in step 1 and again noted in step 2, a wedge needs to be pinned across the side front. This will also resolve the side back tuck. There is frequently a direct correlation between front and back tucks and wedges, as is the case with this example.

8 Before pinning the wedge, reassess the slight strain across the front at bust level. How tightly a person wears her clothes is personal preference. Both the fitter and this client felt that the area across the bust is too tight.

(continued)

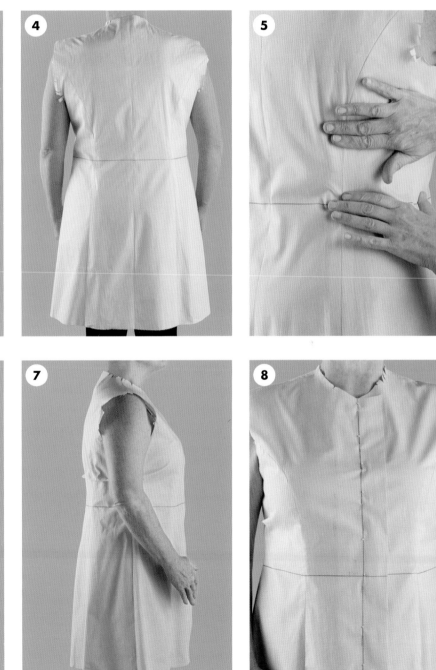

9 Release the front princess seams over the bust. Then pin the wedge across the side front as follows: Beginning where the side back tuck ended, pin out the same amount as the side back tuck, going to nothing at the front princess seam. For the correct angle of the wedge, follow the drag line formed in the fabric. Even though the drag line does not extend all the way to the front princess seam, the wedge must terminate at the princess seam in order to make the flat pattern adjustment. You needn't worry about the fabric that will be eliminated by the wedge near the princess seam, because it is such a small amount.

10 Assess the location of the front princess seam at the fullest part of the bust. To get the best fit, the princess line should lie at or just barely to the side of the apex, or the fullest part of the bust. The vertical pin on the front panel (arrow) indicates the client's apex. In this case, the princess seam extends beyond where there is any breast tissue.

11 Pin the front princess seam, increasing the amount of fabric on the side front and decreasing the amount of fabric on the front. Also change the angle and position of where the front princess seam intersects the armhole, if desired. Note the small vertical fold of fabric

at the client's right underarm. This is also shown in the following photo.

12 A close-up of the excess fabric.

13 This excess fabric is due to the client's bust shape, which is round and full on the side of the bust.

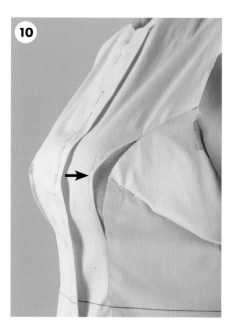

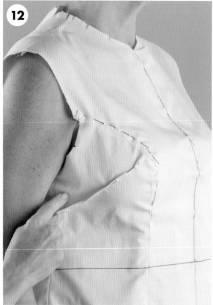

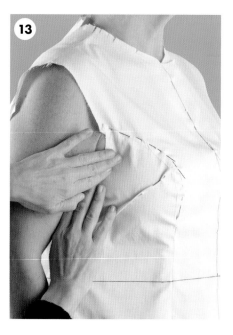

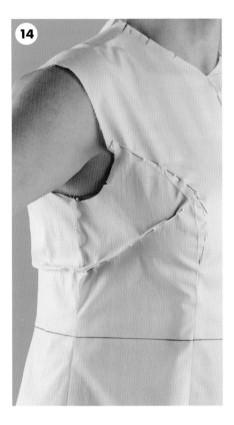

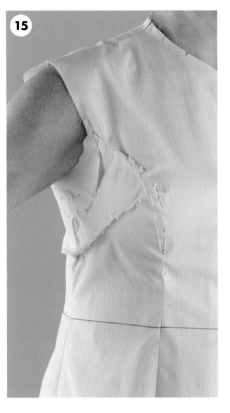

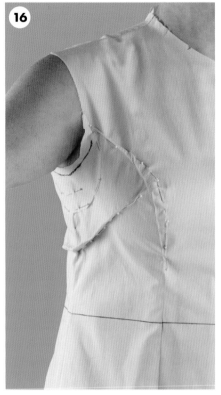

14 Sometimes you can eliminate extra fabric in this location by adjusting the princess seam where it intersects the armhole. In this case, the excess is actually in the side seam, so pin out the excess fabric there. Frequently in the fitting process, once you make the HBL level and give the bust adequate room where it needs it (at the bust), there is excess fabric at the side seam. Fitting is much more about where the space occurs than it is about total circumference. Also note that the underarm of the mock-up is much lower than the client's underarm.

15 In order to mark the proper placement of the underarm seam, pin in some extra fabric.

16 Then draw in the underarm. The underarm placement should be high, because a low underarm actually restricts movement unless the garment is quite loose and oversized. For more information about underarm placement, see pages 92.

17 To finish fitting the back, revisit the fabric folds at the mid-back identified in step 3. Pin out one side along the princess line to see if you like the results. Note the slight strain between the shoulder blades.

(continued)

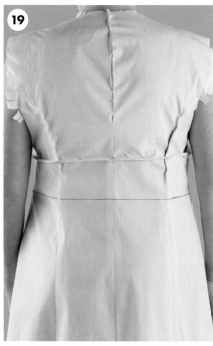

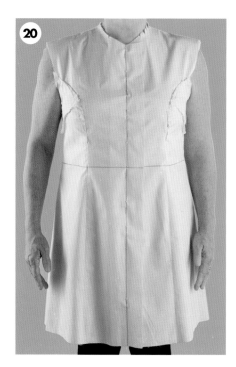

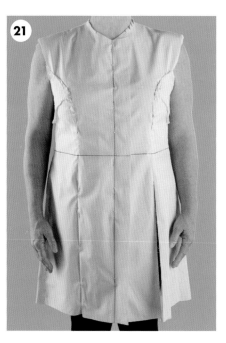

18 I like how the muslin looks with the back princess seams taken in slightly. To make the back of the garment quite comfortable, release the center back seam. Note that the center back seam at the neck is loose, which was first identified in step 3.

19 Pin the center back seam, letting it out through the mid-back to release the strain and taking it in at the neck to eliminate the excess fabric. This will result in a curved center back seam.

20 Assess the skirt portion of the tunic front. This client prefers a straighter tunic rather than such an A-line shape.

21 To take in the skirt, release the princess line from hip level through the hem to assess how the skirt wants to hang on the client. Note that on the unpinned side, the front slips underneath the side front.

Reading the fabric, this tells me that much of what needs to be taken in is on the front seam. Try pinning one side, including pinning out the side seam as well.

22 Read the back in a similar way and pin as desired.

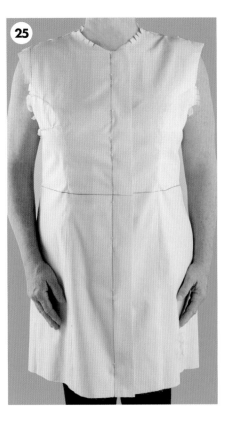

23 Assess the front bodice one final time. The slight vertical folds of fabric in the upper bodice going from the shoulders to the bust indicate that there is too much width in the front bodice. This could have been addressed earlier, but sometimes an issue like this resolves itself through the course of other fitting changes.

24 To check if the front bodice is too wide relative to the client's build, release one shoulder seam. Before I release the seam, I often pin the back shoulder area to the client's bra strap to prevent the garment from falling off. Keeping the front and back shoulder seams next to each other, slide the front shoulder seam away from the neck a small

amount, in this case about ⅜" (1 cm). Align the shoulder seams and re-pin. At the neck, you can see that ⅜" (1 cm) of the back shoulder seam shows. At the arm, ⅜" (1 cm) of the front shoulder seam extends beyond the back shoulder seam. The resulting pattern work is like any other shoulder seam repositioning; see pages 92.

25 The second mock-up front with a few fine-tuning adjustments made to the client's right side. The pattern was not adjusted for the client's narrow front prior to sewing the second mock-up, so the adjustment was made and pinned again here.

26 The second mock-up back.

BODICE WITH RAGLAN SLEEVE

A raglan sleeve differs a great deal from a set-in sleeve, because the raglan sleeve forms a portion of the bodice at the shoulder.

Style/Fitting Considerations

Raglan seams intersect the neckline, and the position of this intersection impacts the proportions of the garment. In addition, the angle and curve of the raglan seam affects the garment's proportions. Moreover, since you often make fitting changes along seams, the position and shape of the raglan seams also impacts your ability to fit the garment. Sometimes a small change to the intersection point and to the angle or curve of the seam makes the garment both more flattering and easier to fit.

Another factor to consider when deciding if a raglan style is appropriate for your build is your shoulder shape. Although many women with sloped shoulders feel that raglan sleeves accentuate the slope of their shoulders, using a raglan shoulder pad in the garment squares the shoulder line nicely.

Some raglan sleeve patterns have a seam down the middle of the sleeve, while others use a dart to provide the shaping at the shoulder where the arm connects to the torso. In a pattern, it's easy to change a dart at the shoulder to a seam down the top of the arm if that allows you to get a better fit.

Fitting Tip

Since more seams give you more fitting opportunities, consider adding seams in appropriate and logical places in order to achieve your desired fit.

Process of Fitting the Bodice with Raglan Sleeve

1 The bodice front. Clip the neckline to release tightness. Note the vertical fold of fabric formed between the neck and the bust level at center front. The garment is generally loose all over.

2 Viewed from the side, the HBL is low in the back, the shoulder seam points toward the very back of the neck, and the garment front swings away from the body at the hemline. That these three situations occur together indicates the client is shorter in the front between the bust level and the shoulder than the garment is, which causes the garment to shift or "travel" toward the back. After the back is assessed,

this is the first fitting issue to address, since it's important to get the garment to settle on the body before dealing with the other fitting issues.

3 The bodice back. Note the strain between the shoulder blades, indicated by a horizontal drag line between the back raglan seams and by the short drag lines emanating from the shoulder seam pointing toward the back raglan seam. Also note the vertical folds of fabric forming from the shoulder blades to the hem.

4 Because the garment is longer in the front upper torso than the client's body, as discussed in step 2,

shorten the front bodice between the bust level and the shoulders. With a raglan sleeve, shorten the front bodice by moving the front raglan sleeve seam farther down onto the bodice front and pin in place. This is preferable to pinning out equal amounts along the front raglan seam, which would make the distance between the front raglan seam and the shoulder seam disproportionately small. To figure out how much to shorten the front bodice, use the shoulder seam and the front HBL as your guides. The shoulder seam should be brought forward so it points to the middle of the neck, and the front HBL should be level.

5 After making the changes in step 4, I had the client wiggle and move around, and once again the garment traveled toward the back, as seen here. This tells me that I must track down an additional fitting issue.

6 To proceed with the fitting, shift the garment forward again on the client's body so that the shoulder seam is in an appropriate place and the front HBL is level. Until I identify and solve the underlying fitting issue that is causing the

garment to shift backward on the client's body, I will periodically check that the shoulder seam is where it should be. Because the garment circumference seems quite loose, assess how big it is.

(continued)

7 Pin out some of the excess fabric at the side seams. When there is so much excess fabric, it probably won't be possible to reduce the garment's circumference by reshaping at just the side seams. Note the drag line in this photograph and in step 6 going from under the bust to the side waist, indicating the need for bust shaping.

8 Because this client is small busted, drape in a dart with a small intake. A dart with too much intake will form an unattractive pouch or large bubble of fabric around the front of the bust. Note that with a small bust dart pinned in the right side of the garment, the area between the dart and the hem hangs nicely.

9 Bring the back HBL to level by pinning a tuck. Even though the back tuck is not at the same level as the side bust dart, the amount of the tuck at the back side seam equals the front dart intake. Also pin out some of the excess along the center back seam through the small of the back down to the hem, which will require adding a center back seam.

10 Note the strain across the upper back between the shoulder blades. Now that the garment is starting to fit better, this strain is even more pronounced. With situations like this, you may need to experiment to figure out if the garment needs more width or more length. Because the garment is not tight over the shoulders and because the garment wants to shift towards the back on the client's body, I suspected a length issue.

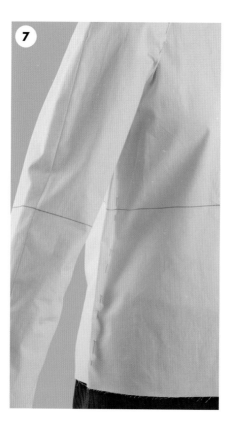

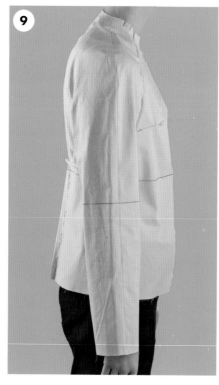

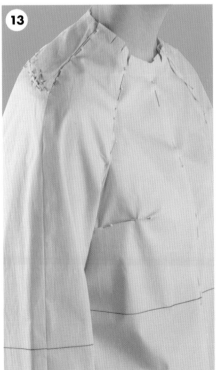

11 Cut the garment horizontally across the upper back where the strain occurs, ending at the seam at the center of the sleeve. The garment immediately spreads, indicating the need for a good deal more length in the upper back. Because the garment has raglan seams, the pattern work is straightforward: lengthen the center back pattern with an even spread and the back sleeve in a wedge spread. Also note the drag line starting about halfway between where the garment was slashed and the neck along the back raglan seam.

12 Pin in fabric where the garment spread apart. To eliminate the drag line above the spread noted in step 11, release the shoulder seam at the neck, allowing the seam to spread and the fabric in the shoulder area to relax.

13 Let out the back shoulder, and pin. The garment has finally settled on the client now that it reflects her body's proportions. Note the excess circumference in the sleeve, indicated by the vertical fold line.

14 To reduce its circumference, the sleeve can be altered on either the seam down the top of the sleeve, the seam at the underarm, or a combination of both. Pinning out the excess along the top of the sleeve causes the drag lines between the underarm and the shoulder to become more pronounced. Pinning a wedge above the elbow starting at the underarm seam and going to nothing at the center-of-the-sleeve seam on both the front and back sleeve brings the sleeve HBL to level and allows the lower portion of the sleeve to hang nicely.

(continued)

15 Reducing the sleeve's circumference by pinning out the underarm seam of the sleeve produces better results and also resolves the adjustment of taking in the bodice side seam.

16 The second mock-up front. Note that the fabric crumples at the underarm. The shoulder line also needs a little fine-tuning, pinning out the slight excess at the mid-shoulder toward the neck.

17 The second mock-up side. Note that the HBL dips at the side seam and that there is a slight drag line under the bust.

18 The second mock-up back. Note the drag lines emanating from the small of the back going up and down, indicating that the center back seam was taken in too much at the small of the back. The back underarm area needs fine-tuning, but there will be a trade-off between having enough movement and how pristine the garment looks here.

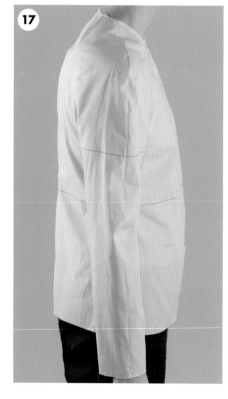

19 To bring the HBL to level, take a wedge starting at the side seam and going to nothing at the center back. To resolve the amount of this wedge at the side seam, and to bring the HBL level in the front, increase the dart intake, which will also eliminate the slight drag line under the bust. Fine-tune the dart position. Rather than re-draping the dart, you can draw a line indicating the new dart position. See pattern work for increasing and repositioning the dart on page 125.

20 When the client reaches forward, note the strain at the mid-back, at the underarm, and across the arm.

21 To provide more reach, let out the back raglan seam.

22 To resolve the front underarm issues, check whether or not the raglan seam is actually at the client's crease. The garment will look better and be more comfortable if the raglan seam is at the crease.

(continued)

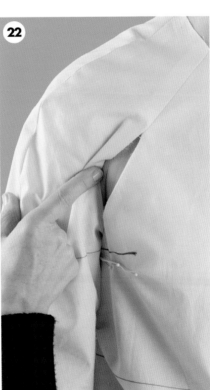

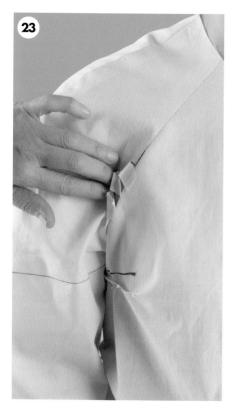

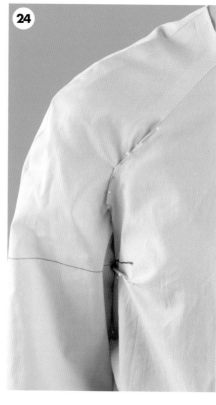

23 Locate where the client's crease is on the muslin, drawing on the muslin if it's helpful.

24 Re-pin the raglan seam, in this case letting out the front bodice and taking in the front sleeve along the raglan seam.

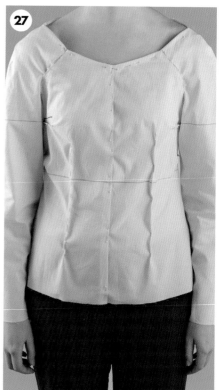

25 Stylistically, this client would prefer an open neckline. Experimenting a bit will help you find a flattering look.

26 The new neckline from the back.

27 While assessing the neckline shape, also assess the garment as a whole. Waist-fitting darts look flattering on this client, and she prefers a trimmer look.

28 Talking with the client about sleeve lengths, we wondered about what a cap sleeve would look like. Drawing where the cap sleeve would fall on her arm led us to think about creating a yoke to add more visual interest.

29 To create the final garment, I made two additional mock-ups. For the third mock-up, I incorporated the new neckline and fine-tuned the shape. I also checked the fitting changes from the second mock-up and fine-tuned where necessary.

In the fourth mock-up, the fit and the neckline were right where I wanted them, and then I marked the final yoke placement seam. For some clients, I would have made a fifth mock-up to verify the yoke placement, but in this case I did not feel it was necessary. These additional mock-ups gave me the opportunity to fine-tune both the fit and the stylistic elements, so by the time I cut into the fashion fabric, I no longer had questions about my pattern or the fit.

Pattern Work Examples

See Fundamentals of Altering Patterns for basic pattern-making techniques.

Increasing the Dart Intake and Repositioning the Dart

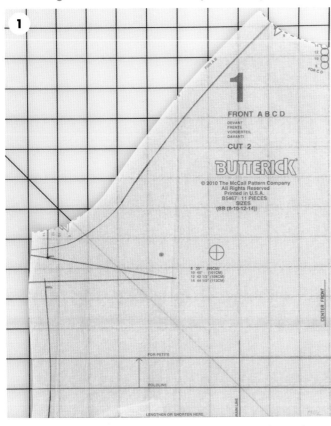

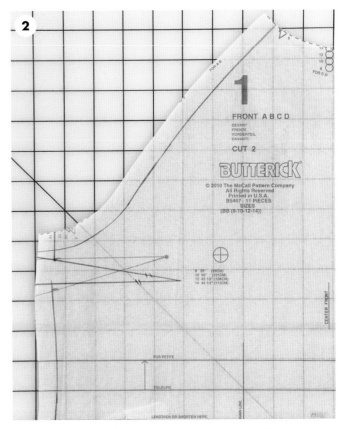

1 The new dart legs and dart point are indicated in red.

2 Connect each dart leg to the new dart point. The dart legs will need to be trued.

Fitting Solutions for Body Types and Related Pattern Alterations

Part of what makes fitting challenging is that there are hundreds upon hundreds of figure variations. Each woman's proportion is unique to her. While it's possible to make broad generalizations about figure types, I find that categorizing a person's figure is frustrating because there are as many variants as there are conformities.

When I'm fitting, I get the best results when I concentrate on manipulating the fitting muslin so that it reflects and enhances the client's figure. I usually get frustrated and have poorer results when I try to make her figure conform to generalized categories and rules.

Yet, without the generalizations and categories, we have no logical method to discuss the variations. In this chapter, I discuss fitting solutions for different areas of the body. For the upper torso, I provide examples using garments with a number of different style lines. Some style lines make fitting certain areas of the body easier. If you're having trouble getting a garment with one style line to fit, consider trying a different style line. For instance, if you are large busted and cannot get a bodice with a side bust dart to fit beautifully, try a pattern with princess seams.

When exploring how to fit a specific area of the body, keep in mind that you must fit the body as one entity, not as distinctly separate parts. How the back of a garment

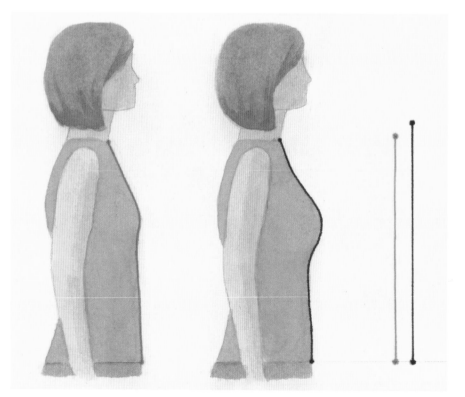

The distance from the neck to the hem is longer for a full-busted figure than it is for a small-busted figure.

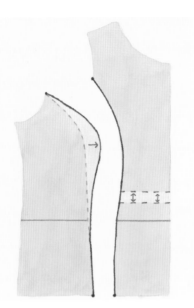

An armscye princess line pattern for a small-busted figure.

For a large-busted figure, the side front of the pattern is extended to accommodate the larger mound. Because the distance between the armscye and the hem on the side front is now longer, the adjoining front pattern must also be lengthened.

These lines show the difference in length of the two princess seams.

fits will affect the way the bust area is fitting. This section of the book provides additional tools you can use when you are in the process of fitting a garment. The previous chapter is intended to help you understand the flow of the process.

BUST

Understanding Bust Adjustments

Getting a pattern to reflect your bust size and shape is essential in order for your clothes to fit well. For many women, accommodating the bust is one of the most challenging aspects of fit and pattern work. The first step in developing the front of a bodice is to understand how bust size impacts not only the width but also the length of a garment.

To explore this topic, let's suppose that we have two women with exactly the same measurement around the rib cage directly underneath the bust. However, woman

A is large busted with a full bust measurement of 40" (101.6 cm), and woman B is small busted with a full bust measurement of 34" (86.4 cm).

The bodice front for woman A must be wider than the bodice for woman B, because the fabric needs to go over larger mounds of flesh. This concept is usually easy to grasp. What's not so apparent is that the bodice for woman A also needs to be longer, as is easily discernible in the illustration on the previous page.

Once we understand these relationships on the body, we can translate the information to the pattern.

For a small bust adjustment, the process is the same, but it goes in the other direction. The side front of the pattern would be reduced in width to accommodate a smaller mound. Then because the distance between the armscye and the hem on the side front is shorter, the adjoining front pattern must also be shortened.

Making Bust Adjustments during a Fitting and on a Pattern

There are many examples of fitting the bust in this chapter and the previous chapter. In these examples, I have not made any changes to the pattern prior to the fitting. It's my preference to manipulate the fabric on the body, because it provides me the opportunity to experiment with what is most flattering to my client.

Many people, however, prefer to make some changes to the pattern prior to cutting out the first mock-up. Making either a full bust adjustment or small bust adjustment often reduces the number of changes you'll need to make to the mock-up during the fitting. However, making too much of a bust adjustment can create additional problems that are difficult to correct during a fitting. Therefore, it's best to make these initial changes on a modest scale.

Full Bust and Small Bust Adjustments on a Pattern with a Side Bust Dart

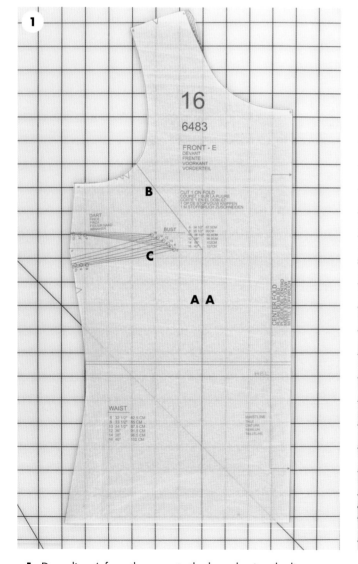

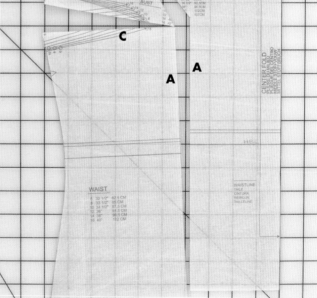

1 Draw line A from the apex to the hem, having the line parallel to the grainline and center front. Draw line B from the apex to the lower third of the armhole. Draw line C from the apex to the side seam through the middle of the dart.

2 Cut the pattern along line A to the apex, continuing to cut along line B to, but not through, the armhole. Cut along line C from the side to, but not through, the apex.

Full Bust Adjustment

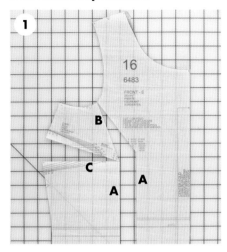

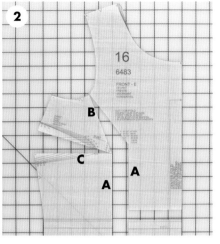

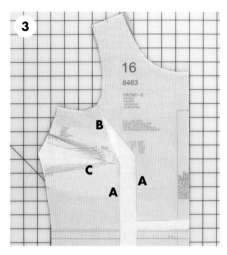

1 For a full bust adjustment, spread the pattern rotating the side sections down and to the side. As you do so, the dart will automatically open. Keep the center front aligned to a grid, and have both sides of line A parallel to a grid line. The amount you spread the pattern depends on how much of a bust adjustment you want to make. For guidelines, see next page.

2 To true the front portion of the pattern, draw a line perpendicular to the center front and the grainline just above the HBL. Cut along the line. Move this free section of the pattern down so that the pattern sections are even, keeping the grainline aligned.

3 Tape in paper where the pattern has spread. If the pattern has spread at the dart point location, place the dart point at the midpoint of the spread. Connect the dart legs to the dart point and true the dart legs.

Small Bust Adjustment

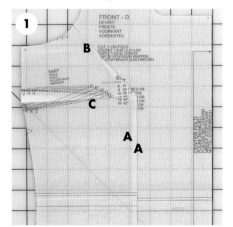

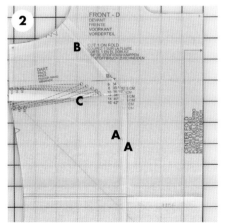

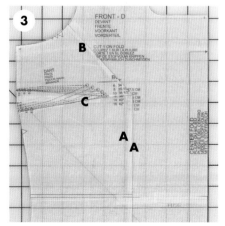

1 For a small bust adjustment, close the pattern rotating the side sections up and toward the center front. As you do so, the dart will close. Keep the center front aligned to a grid, and have line A parallel to a grid line.

2 To true the front portion of the pattern, draw a line perpendicular to the center front and the grainline just above the HBL. Cut along the line. Move this free section of the pattern up so that the pattern sections are even, keeping the grainline aligned.

3 Tape the pattern together. Redraw and true the dart legs, if necessary.

Full Bust and Small Bust Adjustments with Princess Seams

The drawing on page 97 shows a full bust adjustment for an armscye princess pattern. For a shoulder princess pattern, the concept is the same. For a small bust adjustment, reduce the amount of curvature along the side front princess seam, and shorten the front pattern above the HBL to true the adjoining princess seams.

When making either full or small bust adjustments on patterns with princess lines, the front princess seam controls the seam placement, while the side front princess seam provides the shaping for the bust.

Spread and Close Amounts

How much to spread the pattern for a full bust adjustment, or to close the pattern for a small bust adjustment, depends on your bust shape as well as the cup size for which the pattern was developed. For a pattern that has been developed for a B cup, the following chart provides general guidelines. The adjustment amount is for one side of the pattern, so the total increase or decrease across the entire front will be double the amount.

AA cup – close ⅜" (1 cm)

A cup – close ¼" (6 mm)

B cup – no change

C cup – spread ⅜" (1 cm)

D cup – spread ¾" (1.9 cm)

DD cup – spread 1¼" (3.2 cm)

Shaping the Bust with Side Bust Darts

Increasing the Dart Intake

1 There is enough fabric in this garment with side darts to accommodate the bust, but the fit is loose and shapeless. Note the drag lines going from the bust to the side waist, indicating the need for more dart intake.

2 In fact, there is also excess fabric in the side seam.

3 Increasing the side bust dart intake eliminates the drag lines noted in step 1. Small waist-fitting darts make the client look more shapely and proportionate without making the garment tight.

4 The area between the bust and the armhole can be fit more closely, if desired. Be careful not to overfit this area, which can make the bust look low and make the armhole feel tight. If fitting this area closely achieves the look you want, you can combine the dart intakes with a basic dart rotation manipulation.

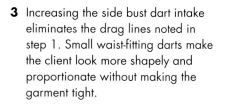

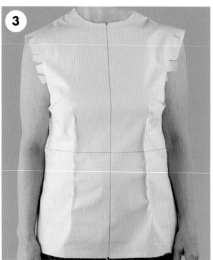

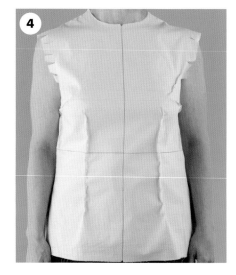

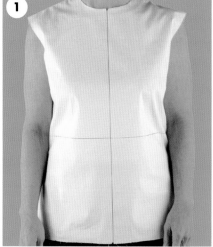

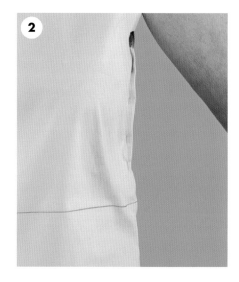

Draping in a Dart and Parallel Darts

1 There is adequate fabric across the bust, but the drag lines indicate the need for a greater dart intake.

2 When viewing the garment from the side, note the excess fabric in the armscye and the drag lines below the bust going to the waist.

3 You can proceed with the fitting in two different ways. You could pin out an armscye dart, which would then be rotated in the side bust dart in pattern work, and also increase the existing side bust dart intake.

4 Or you could drape a new dart. I usually prefer to drape the dart, because I can experiment with different dart intakes and dart positions, and I can see the results right away. In order to drape the dart, first release the upper portion of the side seam going down to just below the existing dart. Then move the excess fabric at the armscye above the bust to the side of the garment. To do this, smooth this excess fabric with your fingers, gently pushing the fabric around the side of the body and down toward where the original dart was located. Don't pull the fabric tight through the front armhole, but leave enough so that it floats over the body. To form the dart, grasp the dart intake with one hand, and pinch the fabric with the other hand where you want the dart to end.

(continued)

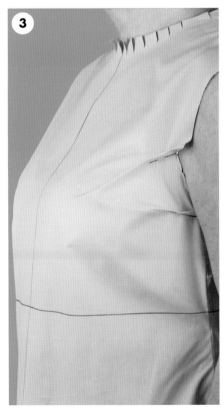

5 Fold the dart intake upward so that it is flat against the body. This is when you can experiment with the amount of dart intake, as well as the position and angle of the dart. The amount of dart intake should be sufficient to eliminate the drag lines below the bust first identified in step 2.

6 When you are happy with the dart position and the dart intake, pin the dart in place. Note the very slight vertical fold of fabric under the bust between the center front and the side seam.

7 Adding a waist-fitting dart provides a bit more shaping for the client without making the garment tight, and it eliminates the slight vertical fold of fabric identified in step 6.

8 Further assessing the client's bust shape can help you determine how best to fit the garment on her figure. This model's bust is quite rounded on the side, deep from the side to the apex, and broad from above the bust to under the bust.

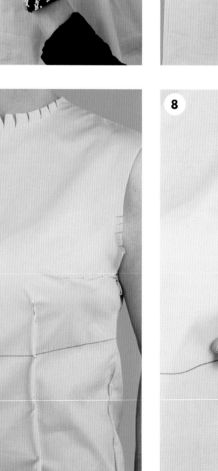

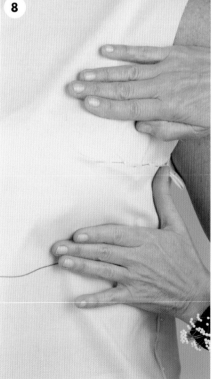

9 Parallel darts can be very flattering on fuller busted figures. This is because one of the functions of a dart is to create a pouch of space. With two darts, two pouches of space are created, one above the other. For this client, parallel darts better accommodate her bust shape, which is broad from above the bust to under the bust. To drape in parallel darts, divide the dart intake, drape one dart, and then drape the second dart. The pattern work for this is then very straightforward. Simply mark both dart points and dart legs from the muslin onto the pattern.

10 The bust darting can also be put into an armscye dart. The draping process is the same as described in step 4, except that all of the excess fabric is gently pushed to the front armhole.

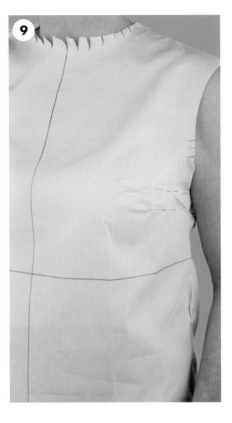

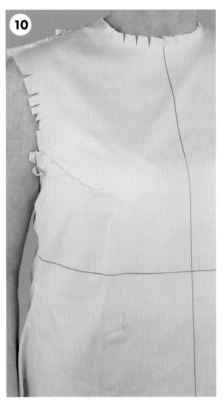

Adjusting Excess Above and Below the Bust

1 Part of fitting the bust is adjusting the garment length between the bust level and the shoulder line. Here the garment moves to the back, indicating that the client is short between the bust and shoulder.

2 Taking an even tuck in the upper portion of the garment proportions the garment to the client's body. Even though this client is small busted, note the slight drag line at the side of the bust going toward the hip.

(continued)

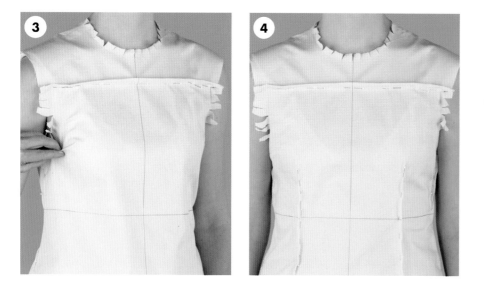

3 Increasing the dart intake slightly would eliminate the drag line but it would also cause the HBL to rise too much.

4 Waist-fitting darts also eliminate the drag line. In addition, waist-fitting darts provide enough shaping through the torso to make the client feel that the garment fits without being tight.

Shaping the Bust with Armscye Princess Seams

Letting Out Princess Seams

1 Note the strain at the apex, indicating that there isn't enough room across the bust. Also note the excess fabric at the front armhole at the top of the princess seam and below the bust.

2 Release both princess seams over the bust. The fabric spreads over the bust, indicating the amount of extra fabric needed. If the princess seam falls over or very near the apex, as in this case, make all of the fitting adjustments on the side princess seam. Remember, the front princess seam line controls the placement of the princess seam over

the apex, and the side princess seam allows for the proper shaping around the bust.

3 Pin the front princess seam, letting out the side princess seam over the full part of the bust. To eliminate the excess fabric at the front armhole, release the upper portion of the front princess seam. Let the side front slip underneath the front, and pin in place. Be careful not to overfit this area. In this case, the fit at the bust was finalized after the back HBL was adjusted, and so the wedge from the side seam going to nothing at the apex eliminates the looseness identified in step 1.

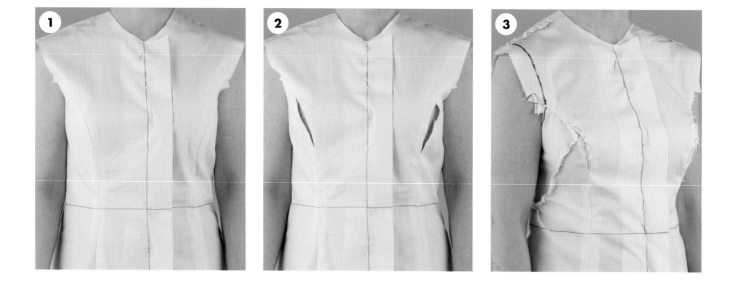

Placing Princess Seams

1 Note the excess fabric over the bust, indicating a small bust. The princess seams do not fall over or near the client's apex, marked with an "X."

2 The placement of the princess seam impacts both how comfortable the garment is to wear and how flattering it is on the body. If you place the princess seam directly over the apex, the client's torso from the waist up looks skinny through the center front and disproportionately wide on the side. Here, the front princess seam was taken in and the side front princess seam let out.

3 If you place the princess seam just to the side of the apex, the overall proportion of the torso from the waist up is better. However, the curvature of the princess seam above the bust and its intersection point with the armscye impacts the garment visually. A tight curve makes the bust look low.

4 Having the intersection point too high on the armhole accentuates the client's thinness.

5 Having the intersection between its location in step 3 and step 4 proportions the client the best. Make variations like these by adjusting the front princess seam and the side front princess seam, letting one out while taking the other in. Even though the curve of the princess seam is now in a good position, the fit through the bust area is still not flattering.

(continued)

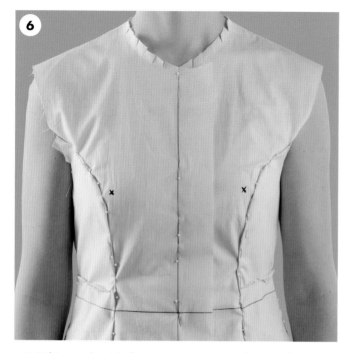

6 Taking in the side front princess seam only a small amount under the bust and through the mid-torso makes a big difference visually, bringing the entire garment into proportion with the client's figure.

7 The second mock-up. Note the slight bagginess and drag lines on the client's right side. Due to the HBL dipping at the side, a wedge was pinned, starting at the side seam and going to nothing at both the front and the back princess seam. As seen on the client's left side, this resolves both the bagginess and drag lines.

Accommodating a Prominent Chest Structure

1 Some fitting issues take a while to understand. You will start to fit what obviously needs addressing and perhaps much later in the process discover what's really going on. Fitting this armscye tunic is a good example. Here, note the tightness across the bust, the excess fabric in the front armhole, the drag lines under the bust going to the side seam (which are the result of a prominent chest structure), as well as the slight tightness across the stomach.

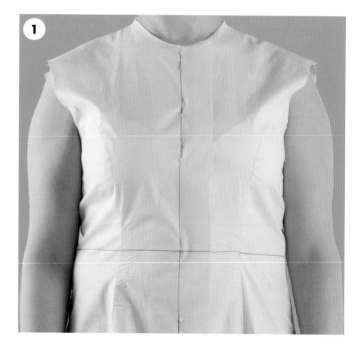

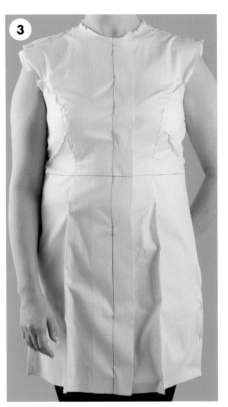

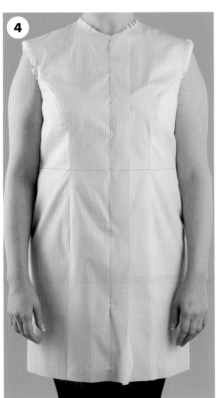

2 Let out the side princess seam to accommodate the bust. On the client's right side, adjust and pin the princess seams to remove the excess fabric at the armhole. In this case, take in both the front and the side front at the armhole.

3 Here's the first mock-up front after making the most obvious fitting changes to the back and side front. The client also prefers a straight rather than flared silhouette in the tunic skirt.

4 The second mock-up. The bust and armhole area fit much better. Note the drag lines on the side of the bodice above the HBL as well as the drag lines starting at the front princess lines just below the HBL and going toward the hip.

5 From the side, the client's figure is much more evident: prominent chest structure, sway back, and defined buttocks. The bust itself is full, but the chest structure makes the bust appear fuller. The bust cannot be fit properly without addressing all of these issues together. Getting the back to fit is an integral part of fitting the front. You will see this client being fit in this tunic in other sections (pages 112, 155).

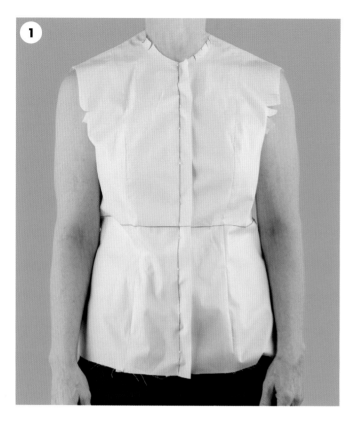

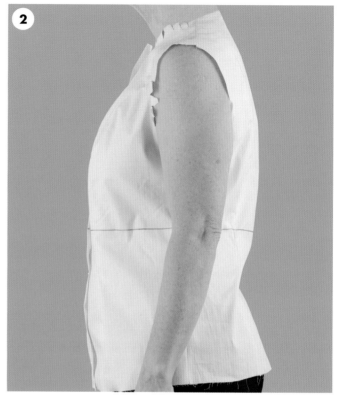

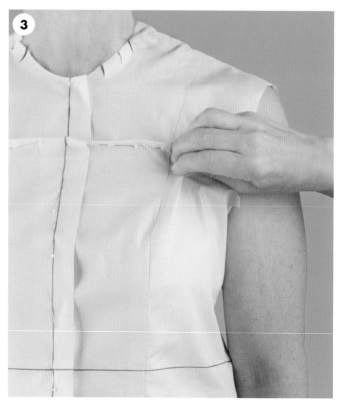

Shaping the Bust with Shoulder Princess Seams

Adjusting Excess Above and Below the Bust

1 There is adequate room across the fullest part of the bust. Note the loose fabric between the bust and the shoulder. The excess at each armhole going into the body of the garment a few inches (cm) below the neck indicates too much length in the garment.

2 Viewing the garment from the side, note the excess fabric above the client's bust, indicating that the pattern was developed for someone with an entirely different bust shape. This excess indicates too much width in the garment above the bust.

3 Take an even tuck across the entire front a few inches (cm) below the neck to eliminate the excess length. Pinching out fabric on the side front panel gives me an idea of how much extra width there is and where I want to remove the excess.

4 Pin out the excess width above the bust. In this case, all of the excess was removed from the side panel, but there might be situations where you want to remove some of the excess from each side of the princess seam.

5 Part of fitting the bust is to fit below the bust. Pinning out some of the excess fabric from under the bust to the hem makes the garment more fitted. Assess which seams you want to remove the excess from. How fitted or loose to make the garment is purely personal preference.

6 An alternate way to get a more shapely and fitted garment is to add a waist-fitting dart, which creates a different effect from removing the excess fabric along the princess seam, as you can see here.

7 For a more relaxed fit through the hip while still getting some shape under the bust, end the waist-fitting darts higher up.

(continued)

8 The waist dart from the side.

9 Sometimes it's encouraging during a fitting to get a sense of how the fitting muslin will translate into a "real" garment. Often a flattering neckline such as this gently rounded V-neckline does the trick.

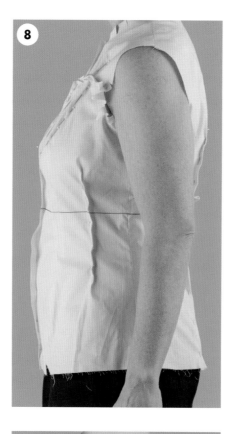

Making Sure the Garment Settles

1 Sometimes fitting the bust area must involve fitting another portion of the body. This is always the case if you cannot get the garment to settle on the body. The front neckline, even though it has been clipped, seems to be choking the client. In addition, the drag lines emanating from the front of the neckline and going to either side of the bust indicate strain on the front neckline. This usually occurs because the garment is moving to the back of the body. Note that the HBL is dipping very slightly in the front, indicating too much length somewhere in the front bodice.

2 Viewing the garment from the side, note that the shoulder seam of the muslin is quite far back on the client's body, that there is excess fabric at the center back neck, and

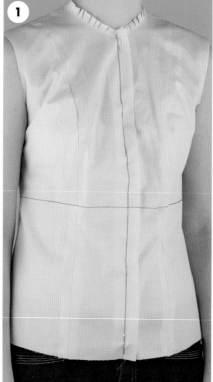

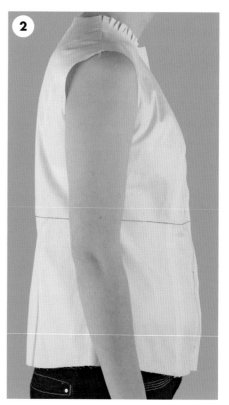

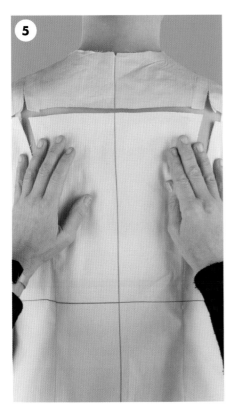

that the front HBL is lower than the back HBL. All of these things indicate too much length in the upper front bodice. However, also note the prominent shoulder blades.

3 Viewing the garment from the back, note the strain between the shoulder blades, indicated by how tight the fabric looks as well as the bubble of fabric in the middle of the upper back.

4 Clip the back armholes to eliminate strain there. Releasing the back princess seams helps to alleviate the strain, but you can still detect some remaining strain in the back between the shoulder blades. Also note the slight fold of fabric on the side back at the bottom of where the shoulder seam has been released. This fold fabric suggests that there is insufficient back length in the center of the garment.

5 To see if the back length is too short, make a horizontal cut all the way across the center back and to the approximate armhole seam on the side back, making the cut at the point where you detected the most strain. The fabric immediately spreads apart, letting the back neckline move upward.

6 Pin in extra fabric underneath the back spread, and pin the back princess seams letting out as much fabric as is needed. Pattern work is shown on page 166.

(continued)

7 Now that the back length is correct, make an even tuck all the way across the garment front to correct the front length. Clip the front armholes to eliminate strain there. The front neckline is finally relaxing on the client.

8 Viewed from the side, the HBL is still low in the front.

9 To raise the front HBL, the front needs to be shortened a bit more. You could increase the amount of the even tuck at the upper front bodice. This, however, makes the area over the bust look worse compared to how it appeared in step 7.

10 Taking a second even tuck above the HBL and below the bust produces better results. Now that all length issues have been addressed, you can start to fit the bust.

11 Since there is so much excess fabric, rather than pinning out the excess fabric over the bust, release the front princess seam. You can see that a significant amount of the side front has slipped underneath the center front princess seam.

12 The front pinned over the bust. The muslin finally reflects the client's bustline.

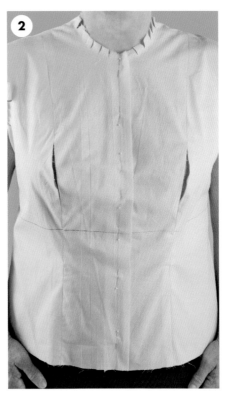

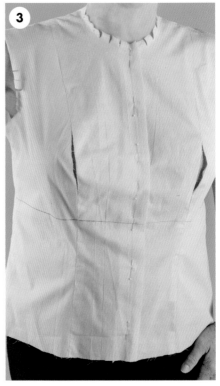

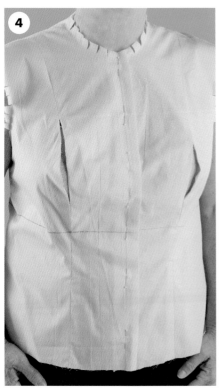

Tracking Down Strain

1 Note the drag lines from the bust up toward the neck and below the bust.

2 From fitting this client before, I know that to eliminate the drag line under the bust caused by the roundness of her side bust, an additional waist-fitting dart may be necessary. To eliminate the drag line above the bust, check for tightness across the full bust by releasing the front princess seams over the apex. The fabric spreads a little bit over the apex, but only slightly. The strain lines pointing toward the neck are still there, now starting at the top of where the fabric was released.

3 Since strain usually indicates tightness, check the muslin for other signs of tightness. There is actually a bit of excess fabric at the top of the side seam, so there appears to be enough room in the garment front.

4 To track down what is causing the strain between the front princess seam and the neck, release the princess seam a bit higher. Just as happened in step 2, the strain moved to the top of where the seam was released.

(continued)

5 After releasing the front princess seam even higher, a bubble of excess fabric forms along the front princess seam at the top of where the seam was released.

6 With the front princess seam released to the shoulder, the same type of bubble forms at the top of where the seam was released.

7 Since I know that the side front princess seam and the front princess seam are the same length, the bubble of fabric is puzzling. I cannot pin a wedge, pinning out the bubble and going to nothing at the neck, because then the front princess seam will be short in comparison to the side front. To figure out how to resolve this issue, release the front princess panel along the shoulder seam. This allows the center front princess panel to rotate and finally relax, totally eliminating the strain line.

8 Let out the side front princess seam to fill in the gap produced in step 7. Re-pin the shoulder seam and the front princess seam. Interestingly, there is no width adjustment necessary in the princess seam except right over the apex where the side front is let out a very small amount. Pin in a waist-fitting dart to fit the roundness on the side of the bust. And pin out the excess fabric on the side seam, if desired.

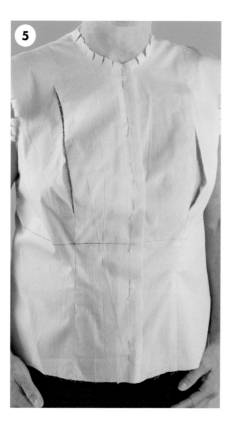

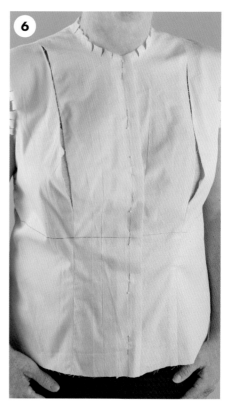

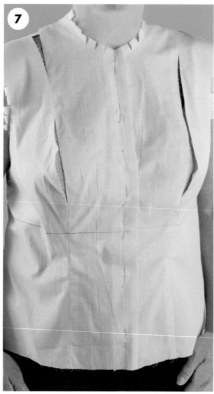

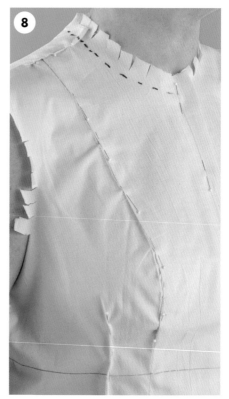

Shaping the Bust with a Side Panel

Draping In and Placing a Dart

1 There is enough room to accommodate the bust, but the garment is boxy and has little shape. Note the slight drag lines above and below the bust.

2 The mock-up viewed from the side. As discussed on page 102, garments with a side panel usually fit better if a bust dart is added. Raising the center back HBL so it is level with the center front HBL is often a good way to determine the amount of bust shaping that is needed, since the front side panel seams must be the same length. Sometimes you get better results if these amounts are not equal, but frequently they are indeed the same.

3 Release the front side panel seam.

4 When draping the dart, experiment to find a dart placement that's pleasing to the eye. This dart is angled, which sometimes makes the waist appear smaller.

(continued)

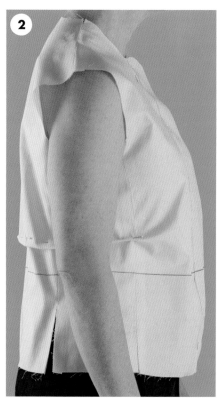
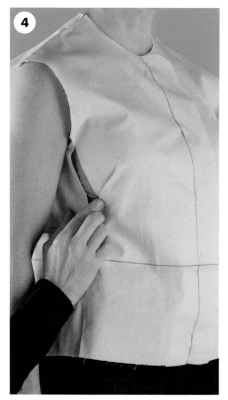

5 This dart is straight, which to my eye makes the bust look more prominent.

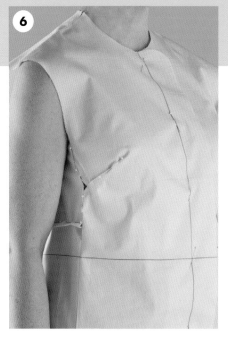

6 Drape in the preferred dart, and re-pin the side front panel seam, incorporating any fitting that is required. In this case, the front needed to be let out above the dart.

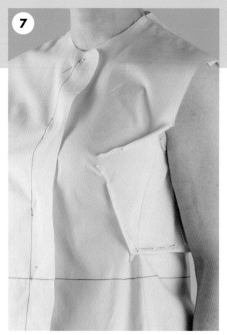

7 The garment can be fit much more closely to the body. In this case, the armscye dart would be rotated to the side dart in pattern work.

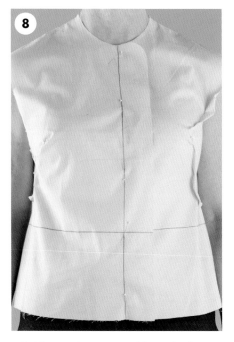

8 The mock-up viewed from the front with each side fit differently. The client's right side preserves the boxy look of the jacket while still getting some shaping, while the client's left side produces a much more fitted look.

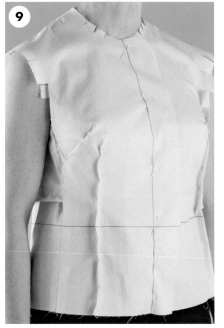

9 To reduce the excess fabric under the bust, pin waist-fitting darts.

10 The second mock-up. The fitting is progressing nicely. Increasing the bust dart will eliminate the drag line under the bust going to the side seam. The garment reflects the client's figure without being closely fitted.

Adjusting Dart Intake and Eliminating Excess Circumference

1 As we know from fitting this client before, she's short between the bust and the shoulder, which causes excess fabric above her bust.

2 Taking an even tuck in the upper bodice and getting the length correct is the first step to fitting her bust.

3 After adjusting the muslin for her back length and allowing the garment to settle, assess the muslin for her bust. There is a lot of excess fabric, and the drag line from the bust to the side waist indicates the need for some bust shaping even though she's small busted.

4 Viewing the garment from the front, the drag lines noted in step 3 are evident. Now that the front and back HBL are level, there is more excess circumference at the bust than was evident in step 2. Because the garment fits well between the bust level and the shoulders, I chose to proceed with fitting this muslin rather than starting over with a smaller size.

5 Assess how much extra circumference there is.

(continued)

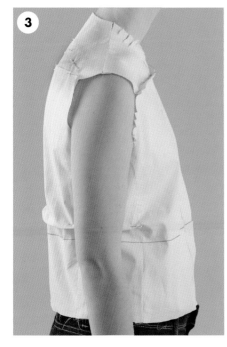

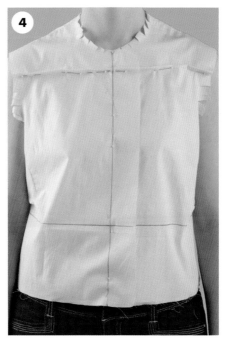

6 Assess how much dart intake is needed. The HBL stays level with a small intake. Also, this amount of dart intake defines the bust shape.

7 With a greater dart intake, the HBL gets raised, and note how the space created by the dart overwhelms the client's bust.

8 Drape in the dart and take in the side seam. Because the dart shortens the length of the front side panel seam, a close-wedge was pinned, starting at the front side panel seam and going to nothing at the back side panel seam.

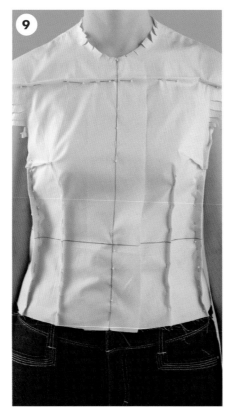

9 Waist-fitting darts further define the bust and waist.

10 The second mock-up with a few minor adjustments made.

Shaping the Bust with a Raglan Sleeve Garment

Adding a Side Bust Dart and Adjusting the Back Length

1 There is slight strain across the bust, but not enough that I would go up a pattern size, especially considering how loose in general the garment is. Note the drag lines going from under the bust to the side seam and the hemline flaring away from the body, both indicating the need for bust shaping.

2 Viewing the garment from the side, it's quite apparent that the back will need to be adjusted in conjunction with fitting the front.

3 Drape a side bust dart, which also makes the garment hang straight so that the hemline no longer flares away from the body. I find this dart angle distracting due to the angle of the raglan seam.

4 This dart angle is less obtrusive. There are still slight drag lines under the bust, which can be eliminated either by increasing the side bust dart intake or draping a waist-fitting dart.

5 To fit the back, pin a large close-wedge starting at the center back to bring the HBL to a level position. At the side seam, the back close-wedge will equal the intake of the front bust dart. Pinning out a little excess fabric along the center back, which means creating a center back seam, starts to bring the garment into proportion to the client's figure. Now that the back and front are better balanced, I would revisit the front dart.

Creating a Princess Seam

1 There is enough room across the bust, but the garment is loose both above and below the bust. The drag lines below the bust going to the side seam indicate the need for bust shaping.

2 Pin a bust dart to eliminate the drag lines identified in step 1, and bring the back HBL to a level position.

3 To give some shape to the garment, I started by pinning waist-fitting darts. As I fit the area just below the bust and up toward the apex, I discovered that with the side bust dart supplying room for the bust, there was slight excess over the apex. Experimenting, I pinned out the excess over the apex and continued pinning out the excess above the bust. I liked the effect of the waist-fitting dart going up toward the raglan seam, and so I turned the waist-fitting dart into a princess seam. The pattern work for this is shown below. In addition to the princess seam, the garment needed further fine-tuning.

Pattern Work Examples

See Fundamentals of Altering Patterns for basic patternmaking techniques (page 44).

Truing an Armscye Princess Seam at the Armhole

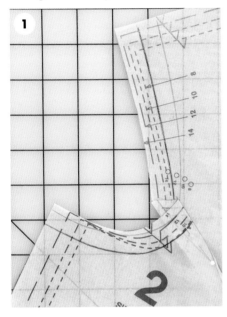

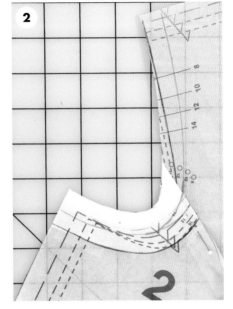

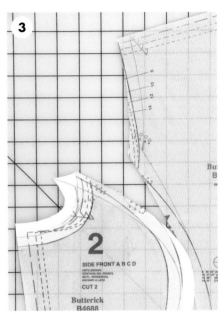

1 With the new princess seam lines drawn on the pattern, the armhole seams may no longer match when stacked, as in this example.

2 To resolve this discrepancy, blend the armhole seam, shown in green. Adjust the seam allowance and cut along the new cut line.

3 The trued pattern pieces.

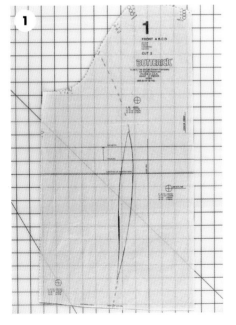

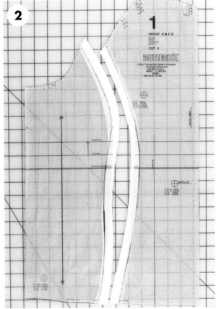

Creating a Princess Seam from Waist-Fitting Darts

1 The pattern with waist-fitting darts and tick marks indicating the placement of the princess seam. The two sides of the waist-fitting dart will become the new princess seams for the front and side front respectively.

2 Blend the princess seam to the waist-fitting dart, incorporating any additional shaping pinned on the muslin. Cut along the new princess seam and through the middle of the waist-fitting dart, creating the front and side front pattern pieces. Add seam allowance to each seam line, and cut along the new cut line.

BACK

In fitting the back, it is important to accommodate the length, width, and curvature of the back as well as to address how the garment lies on the body at the armhole, shoulder, and neck. Fitting the back is complicated because often these elements impact one another, in which case it becomes difficult to separate one problem from another. However, by reading the fabric and staying aware of the HBL level, fitting solutions become apparent.

Fitting the Back with a Basic Bodice

Narrow Back

1 Note the excess fabric, particularly through the small of the back just above the waist.

2 Also note that the HBL is dipping in the back.

3 Raise the HBL in the back with either an even tuck or a close-wedge. To fit the small of the back on a figure with a defined waist, it's usually best to distribute the vertical excess between the center back seam and the waist-fitting darts. See pages 89 and 90 for more in-depth information. Also note the excess at the back armhole.

4 Assess how much excess there is in the back armhole. It can be helpful to think of this excess as a dart, which can be moved into either a shoulder dart or a neck dart. Because of the waist-fitting darts, I think shoulder darts would look better.

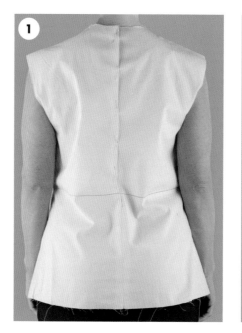

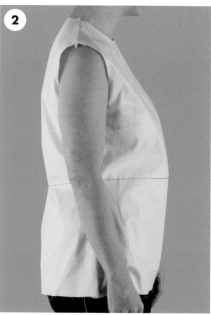

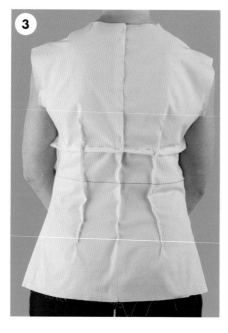

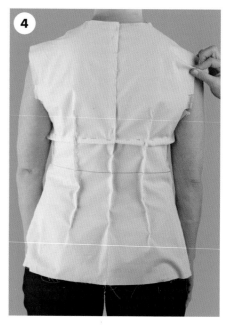

5 To create a shoulder dart with the excess fabric, first release the shoulder seam. Then smooth the fabric of the muslin armhole across the back of the arm. As you move the fabric to eliminate the excess at the armhole, a fold of fabric will form along the shoulder.

6 Pin the newly formed dart in place.

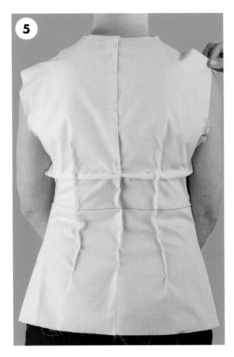

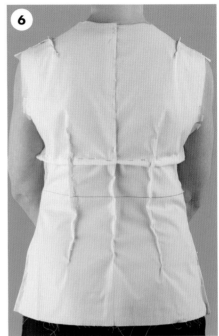

Broad Back

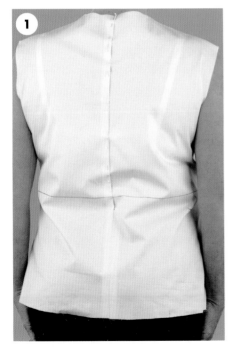

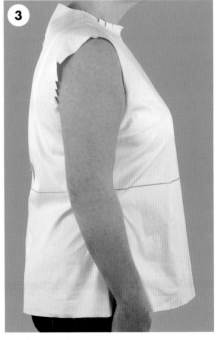

1 The back bodice. Note the excess fabric at the back neck, the tightness through the armhole, and the excess fabric through the small of the back.

2 Clip the back armholes to the back crease.

3 When viewing the garment from the side, it's apparent that the HBL is dipping in the back. Note the strain on the fabric over the hip.

(continued)

4 Making a tuck across the back raises the HBL, which allows the fabric of the lower back to relax. Now there is actually excess fabric in the lower back of the muslin. Also note the excess fabric at the back neck.

5 Running your hand gently across the client's back can help you identify the bone and muscle structures, which influence how you fit. Here you can see that the middle of the upper back is hollow and the client has well-defined shoulder blades.

6 Eliminate the excess fabric in the neck by forming either a neck dart or a shoulder dart. To form the neck dart, simply pin out the excess fabric, so that the dart points to the most prominent part of the shoulder blade, as shown on the client's left side. To form a shoulder dart, release the shoulder seam. As you form a shoulder dart with your fingers, the excess fabric at the neck will disappear. Make the shoulder dart intake the amount needed to make the back neck fabric lie flat. Choose which dart placement to use based on how well the dart makes the garment fit, how flattering the dart placement looks on the body, and how compatible the dart placement is with the rest of the garment. Also assess the fit in the small of the back.

7 To eliminate the excess fabric at the small of the back, pin waist-fitting darts if you want a garment that is more form fitting.

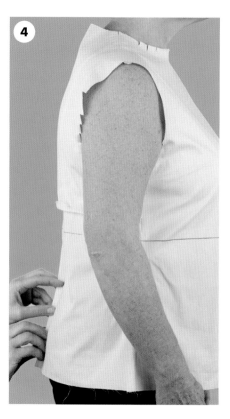

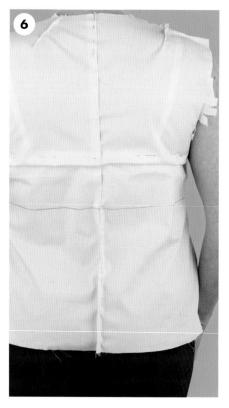

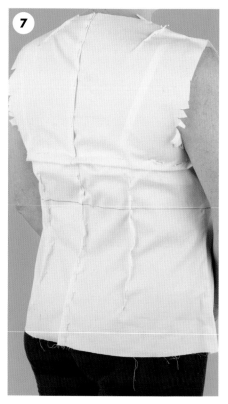

Long Back and Rounded Upper Back

1 Even though a garment might have sufficient overall length, it's important for the garment to be long enough in the right places. Here, the HBL is dipping slightly in the back. Note the roundness of the upper back from the shoulder blade up to the shoulder line. Also note the forward neck, which is usually indicative of a rounded back.

2 Pin a tuck to bring the HBL to a level position. Note the strain across the upper back between the shoulder blades as well as from the shoulder blade up to the shoulder line.

3 Making a horizontal cut where the most strain occurs will allow the fabric to spread open if more length is needed. In this case, the upper portion of the muslin moved higher on the client's neck. This is a very similar adjustment used to fit a dowager's rounded upper back, which is described in the following example. The pattern work for this alteration, including the resulting neck darts, is shown on page 166.

4 Pin in extra fabric where the mock-up spread. The center back seam can also be let out if more width across the back improves the fit or makes the garment more comfortable. To fit the small of the back, drape waist-fitting darts.

(continued)

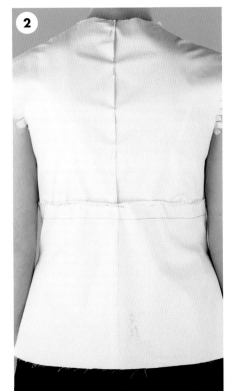

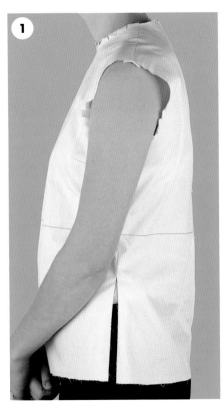

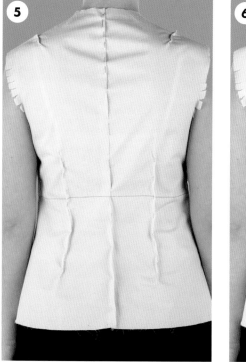

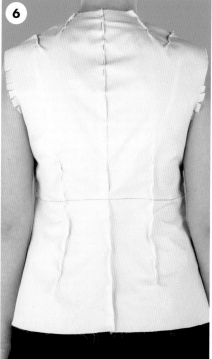

5 The second mock-up with a few fine-tuning adjustments made. Note both the strain between the shoulder blades in the hollow of the upper back and the slight looseness in the fabric at the back neck.

6 Pinning neck darts improves the fit and reduces the strain between the shoulder blades. Since it looks odd to have both shoulder and neck darts, I would transfer the shoulder dart intake into the neck darts.

Dowager's Rounded Back

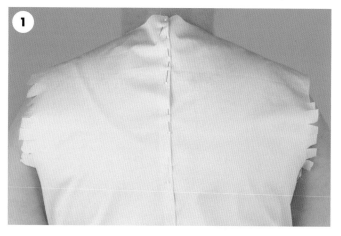

1 Note the excess fabric at the back neck resulting from the rounded upper back.

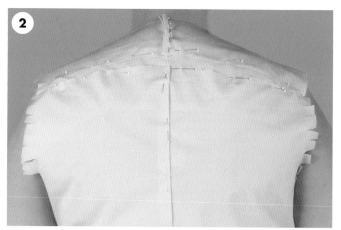

2 Make a horizontal cut across the upper back where the rounding of the back begins. This allows the upper portion of the garment to move higher on the client's neck. In this case, the center back seam can then be shaped to follow the curve of the upper back and neck. Neck darts usually provide the best fit. This example is shown on a basic blouse, but the alteration can be done on any style of garment. For related pattern work, see page 166.

Fitting the Back with Armscye Princess Seams

Sway Back and Very Erect Posture

1 Viewed from the side, the poof of fabric at the mid-back indicates excess back length compared to the client's build. Note the client's sway back and very erect posture, which often occur together.

2 The folds of fabric viewed from the back. These folds usually form around and accentuate any fleshy areas. The drag line below the HBL from the side going to the buttock indicate that there might not be enough circumference in the garment at the hip. It may help to release the seam over the tight part of the buttock; however, bringing the HBL to a level position often alleviates the tightness over the hip and buttock.

3 Experiment to find the best location to take a tuck or close-wedge to bring the HBL to a level position. Taking a tuck just above the HBL produces better results to my eye. This length alteration must be resolved on the adjoining pattern pieces as well.

4 Viewed from the side: a tuck across the center back, a close-wedge on the side back, with the close-wedge continuing into bust shaping at the front.

(continued)

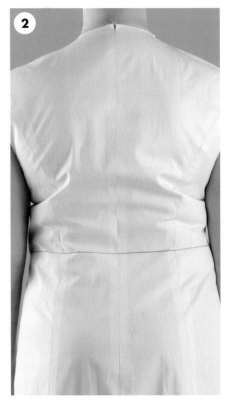

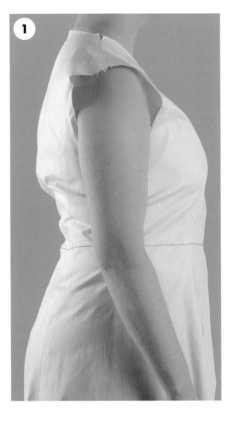

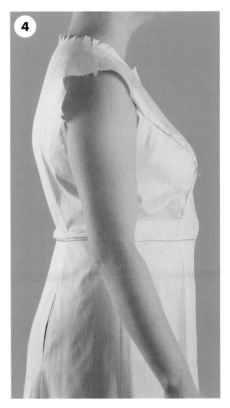

5 Note the gaping at the back armhole. Also note the folds of fabric on the side back between the armhole and the HBL. Because these two problem areas occur directly above and below one another, it's likely that getting a good fit in both areas will be interconnected. Experiment to find the best solution.

6 You could take out all of the excess along the shoulder seam, which to my eye accentuates the client's sloping shoulders.

7 You could use a shoulder pad, or you could use a combination of shoulder pads and adjusting the shoulder seam, as seen here. Although these adjustments address the excess in the back armhole itself, none of the solutions address the way the fabric is collapsing and folding a few inches (cm) above the HBL on the sides.

8 The folds below the armhole can be addressed in different ways. On the client's right, I have pinned a close-wedge in the side back panel, starting at the armhole and going to nothing at the princess seam. This alleviates the problem to some degree. On the client's left, I have released the shoulder seam. Then, starting where the large fold of fabric is underneath the arm on the side, I have smoothed the fabric upward with my hand. When draping the fabric in this way, let the fabric guide you and tell you what needs to happen. Here, as I pushed the excess fabric upward and smoothed it across the back armhole, the excess fabric got transferred to the mid-shoulder, naturally forming a dart.

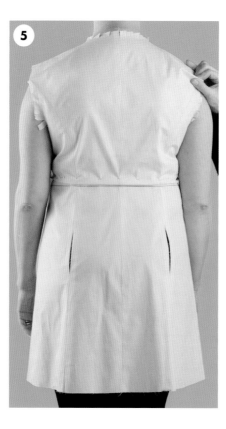

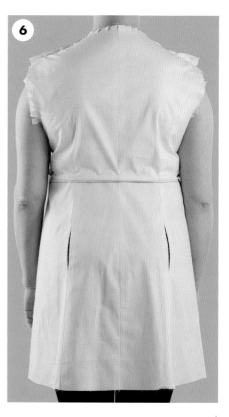

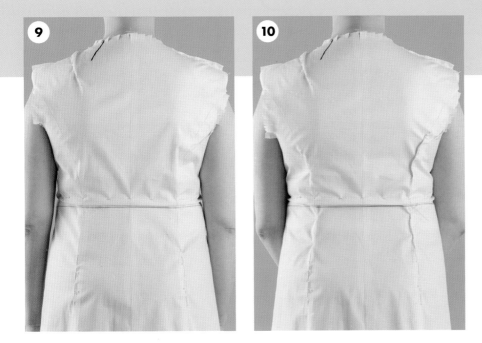

9 Pin the dart. If you do not like the look of a shoulder dart in conjunction with the armscye princess seams, you could move the dart into the neckline by either draping or pattern manipulation.

10 Now that the overall proportion of the back length is better, adjust the back princess seams, taking in excess and letting out at the fullest part of the hip. In order to fine-tune the garment, I made three more mock-ups.

Prominent Shoulder Blades and Gaping Armholes

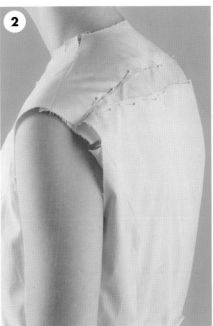

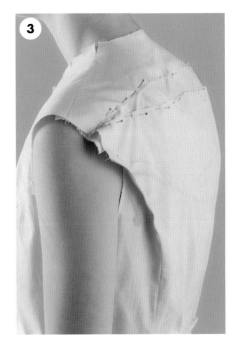

1 With prominent shoulder blades, there is often excess fabric in the back armholes, as seen here. Note the vertical folds of fabric in the mid-back, indicating too much width in the garment.

2 As described on page 120, this client's rounded upper back requires lengthening the upper back of the garment. Note the gaping armhole and excess fabric on the side back. Prior to fitting the armhole and side back, bring the HBL to a level position. I have also pinned out the excess fabric below the HBL along the princess seams.

3 The excess at the back armhole occurs where the princess seam intersects the armhole. Although pinning out the excess fabric equally on both sides of the princess seam improves the fit, it creates awkward pattern-making problems, discussed on page 166.

(continued)

4 Pinning out the excess on just the side back panel also improves the fit, but it also results in difficult pattern-making problems similar to the ones described in the previous step.

5 Taking a close-wedge in the side panel starting at the armhole and going to nothing at the princess seam produces a better fit, and the pattern work is very straightforward.

6 The second mock-up back, with adjustments to the shoulder darts, which form in the pattern work when lengthening the upper back in step 2.

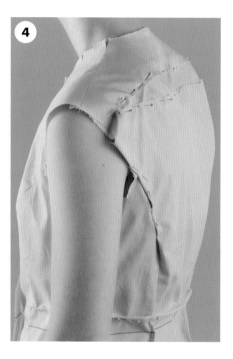

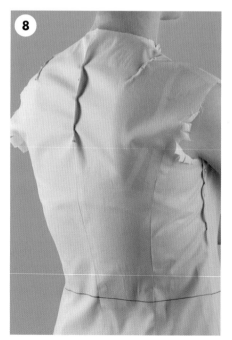

7 Note the client's hollow upper back, which often occurs between prominent shoulder blades.

8 Do not overfit a hollow back, which will restrict the client's ability to reach her arms forward when there is a sleeve in the garment. The fabric needs to float over the hollow in the back as shown in step 7.

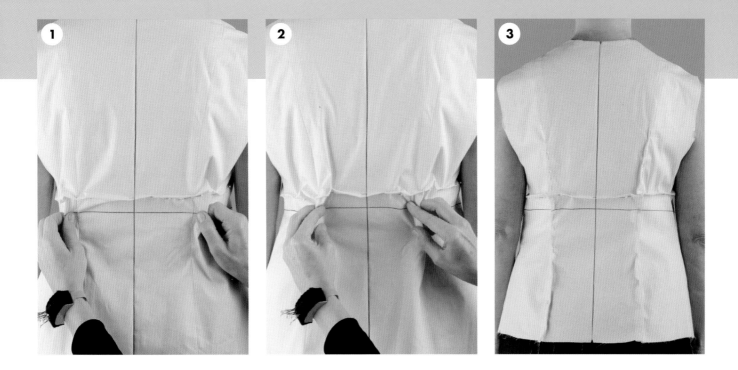

Fitting the Back with Shoulder Princess Seams

Back Proportion with Placement of Princess Seams

1 Experiment where to remove the excess fabric, which affects the placement of the princess seams. Taking all of the excess fabric from the side princess seam makes the sides of the body look disproportionately small in relation to the center back.

2 Taking all of the excess fabric from the center back princess seam makes the center of the back look disproportionately small.

3 Taking the excess fabric equally from each side of the princess seam produces the proportion that is best to my eye.

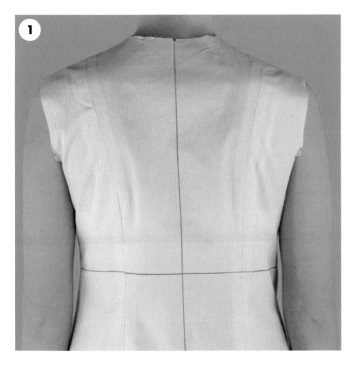

Wide Upper Back and Narrow Small of the Back

1 Note that the cut edge of the fabric at the back armhole is approximately where the back armhole seam would fall, indicating that the garment isn't wide enough across the back. Also note the slight strain between the shoulder blades.

(continued)

2 Releasing the back princess seams allows the garment to relax over the shoulder blades and spread open. At the lower end of where the fabric has been released, the slight fold of fabric on the side back panel indicates that the center back portion of the garment needs more length. Also note the slight drag line going from the side back princess line to the side seam.

3 Slash the back and add length.

4 Let out and pin the princess seams where they opened. A close-wedge starting at the side seam and going to nothing at the side back princess seam eliminates the drag line identified in step 2. This close-wedge length adjustment at the side seam is resolved on the front side panel in addressing bust shaping.

5 Note the excess fabric through the small of the back. How closely you fit this area is personal preference. As shown in other examples, the excess fabric can be pinned out equally on both princess seams or on just one side of the princess seam.

Fitting the Back with a Side Panel

Gaping Back Armholes and Defined Waist

1 Note the overall looseness of the garment and the gaping at the back armhole. The back panel seams were released because the lower edge of the garment was too tight over the hip.

2 Viewed from the side.

3 The tuck brought the HBL to a level position in conjunction with fitting the front. Assess the excess in the back armhole.

4 Pinning out along the shoulder seam only partially removes the excess fabric in the back armhole. Clip the back armhole at the back crease as needed as you fit the back armhole.

5 All of the excess fabric can be rotated to a shoulder dart (see page 72.

(continued)

6 The excess can also be rotated to a neck dart.

7 With the style of the jacket, neck darts look best to my eye at this stage of the fitting. Note the excess fabric through the mid-back.

8 Experiment with where to remove the excess. You could make a center back seam and provide shaping there.

9 Or you could remove the excess at the back panel seam.

10 Or you could use waist-fitting darts to remove the excess. Assess how the jacket looks with both waist-fitting darts and neck darts.

11 With the waist-fitting darts, I prefer the look of shoulder darts.

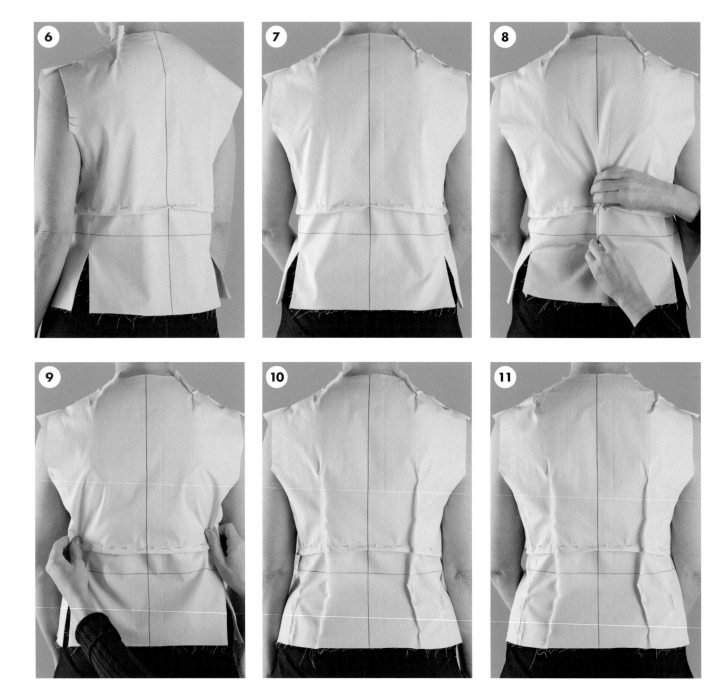

Fitting the Back
with Raglan Sleeves

Narrow Back and Defined Waist

1 Note the excess fabric through the back, indicated by the vertical folds of fabric. Also note the drag lines at the shoulder seam, which will be taken care of when fitting the shoulder line and perhaps the front of the garment.

2 Bring the HBL to a level position in conjunction with fitting the front. A center back seam is the most efficient tool to fit the small of the back. Here, pin out some of the excess fabric along the center back in order to start shaping the small of the back. See page 111 for creating a center back seam from a fold line.

3 Since the back of the garment is so loose, waist-fitting darts are a good tool to remove some of the excess fabric. If you pinned out all of the excess at the center back, you'd create new drag lines since there is a great deal of excess fabric. As I pinned this waist-fitting dart from the HBL upward, I let my fingers assess the amount of fabric to take in. Letting the fabric guide me in this way, I liked the effect of taking the dart all the way to the raglan seam. With only one side pinned, you can see that the waist-fitting dart lets the client's figure appear under the fabric.

4 With both waist-fitting darts pinned in, the garment nicely reflects the client's figure. Reduce the dart intake if you want a looser fit. A similar waist-fitting dart was used on the front of the bodice (see page 124). In the next mock-up, I turned these waist-fitting darts on both the front and the back into princess seams, creating an interesting design element.

Pattern Work Examples

See Fundamentals of Altering Patterns for basic pattern-making techniques.

Adjusting Length for Curved Upper Back or Dowager's Back

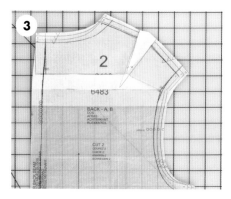
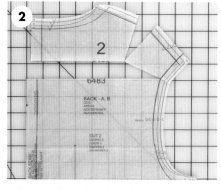

1 In order to lengthen the middle of the pattern but not alter the armholes, you must create either a shoulder or neckline dart. For a dowager's back, a neck dart improves the overall fit. Here is the back pattern with the horizontal cut line and shoulder dart placement indicated in red.

2 Cut along the slash line to, but not through, the armhole seam. Also cut the shoulder dart from the shoulder seam to, but not through, the slash line, creating a hinge. As you spread the pattern to create more back length, the shoulder dart will open up.

3 Tape in paper, blend seams, and add seam allowances. Draw in the dart and true the dart legs.

SIDES

Side seams should hang straight and plumb, and they should fall approximately in the middle of the body when viewed from the side. If a side seam is curved, the strain may be due to another fitting issue, such as a full bust or full buttocks. Often, once the bust and buttocks are fit properly, the side seam will be in the correct position.

Some people like to have the side seam positioned slightly toward the back of the body, because then the side seam is less visible when the garment is viewed from the front. Another factor to consider is the visual proportion that the side seam creates.

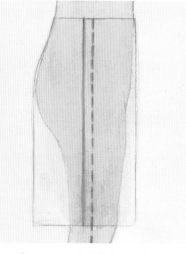

For a figure with full buttocks, having the side seam positioned in the middle of the side of the body (dashed line) accentuates the fullness of the buttocks. Moving the side seam slightly to back (solid line) makes the body look more balanced and proportionate.

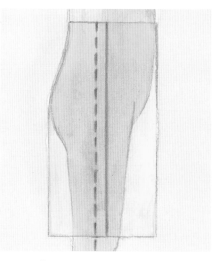

For a figure with a large stomach, having the side seam positioned in the middle of the side of the body (dashed line) accentuates the fullness of the stomach. Moving the side seam slightly to the front (solid line) makes the body look more balanced and proportionate.

Excess in the Side Seam

1 Note the excess pinned out on the side seam. You could leave the muslin pinned like this, but the pins make it difficult to assess the side seam.

2 Release the lower portion of the seam, allowing one side of the fabric to lie flat. In this example, I let the front fabric relax.

3 Using the amount pinned out in step 1 as a guide, fold under the back fabric.

4 Adjust the amount turned under in the previous step, if necessary, and pin in place.

5 Now it's quite easy to assess the side seam. Adjust if necessary to make the seam straight and plumb.

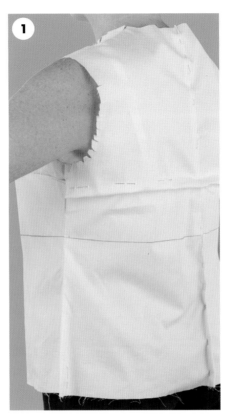

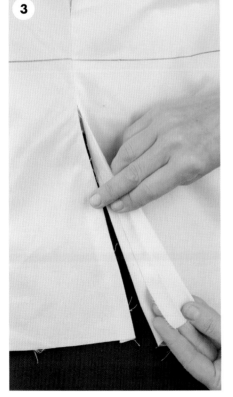

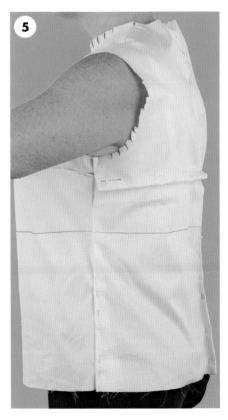

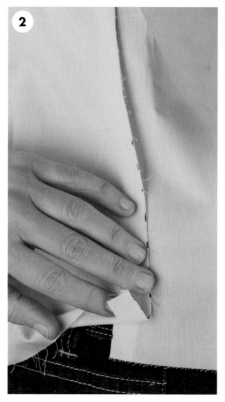

Side Seam Skewing to the Back

1 Assess the side seam; the dashed lines are on the side seam in order to make it easier to see the seam line. Note that the side seam is relatively straight but rather than being plumb, it is in the middle of the body at the underarm but toward the back of the body at the hem. This indicates that near the hem, there is too much fabric in the front.

2 Release the side seam, lift the back, and let the front fabric relax. Note that the front naturally slips underneath the back. Letting the fabric guide you, lay the back on top of the front and pin in place.

Overfitting the Side Seam

1 Be careful not to overfit along the side seam. Assessed from the front, it seemed appropriate to pin out the excess fabric over the hip.

2 From the side, however, you can see that small drag lines are forming going from the side hip to the buttock and from the side hip to the stomach. This is a good example of how small the difference between looseness and tightness can be in a garment. Another factor to consider, of course, is how the client wants the garment to fit and feel on her body.

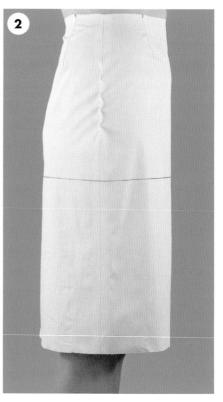

SHOULDER LINE AND NECK

The position of the shoulder seam is important because it affects the fit, the comfort, and the visual proportions of the garment. But determining where the shoulder line is on the body isn't always as straightforward as it sounds, because our necks connect to our torsos in a variety of ways, as do our heads to our necks. Therefore, the placement of the shoulder line is a subjective decision to a large degree. Some people like the shoulder seam to be slightly to the back of the garment so that it's not as visible when the garment is viewed from the front.

There are a small number of examples in this section because fitting the neck and shoulder line often takes place in conjunction with fitting the bodice front and back.

Shoulder Line

Determining Shoulder Line Placement

1 The black tape is laid across the muslin's shoulder line to make the shoulder line easier to sight along. Even though the front bodice has been shortened, the shoulder line falls toward the back of the client's neck.

2 Moving the shoulder line forward at the neck better proportions the client's frame.

Shoulder Line Place on a Raglan Garment

1 Fitting the shoulder line of a raglan sleeve garment must be done in conjunction with fitting the raglan seams. In this example, the front and back raglan seams have been adjusted to follow the crease of the client's arm. Note the excess fabric along the shoulder line. Also note that the shoulder seam is too far back.

2 Release the shoulder seam and let the front shoulder seam slide under the back shoulder seam.

(continued)

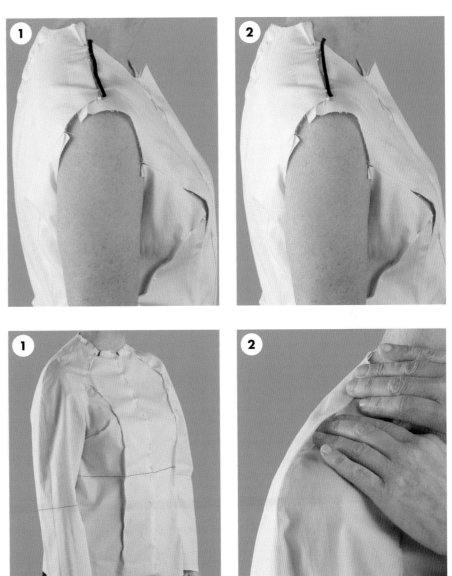

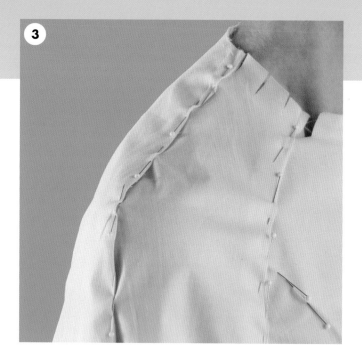

3 Pin the shoulder seam in place. Now that the shoulder line has been established near the neck, it can be fine-tuned over the ball of the shoulder and down the arm. Because the client has a slightly forward shoulder, it's more important to blend this seam nicely down the top of the arm rather than making sure that it goes over the middle of the ball of the shoulder.

Necks

Too Tight Necklines

1 Here the neckline is so tight that it chokes the client, and the center fronts cannot be pinned together.

2 Clipping the neckline allows the fabric to open enough to pin together the center front.

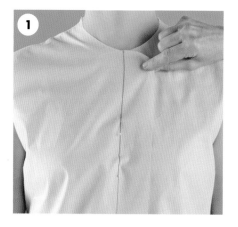

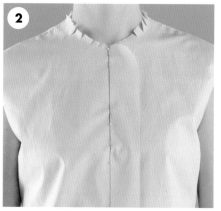

Visualizing Garment Necklines

At the end of fitting a mock-up, I like to begin visualizing the garment with some stylistic elements, which often occur at the front neckline. This muslin was fitted with the center front pinned up to the neck (see pages 145). However, letting the fronts lie open as they would in a finished garment let's you see a more realistic and flattering view of the garment.

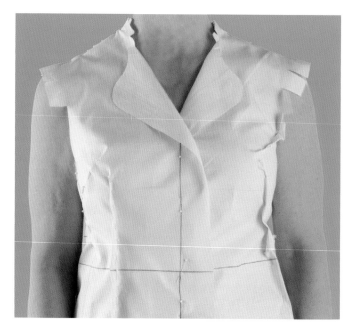

Neck and Shoulder Line

1 Note the excess fabric at the back neck.

2 Pin out the excess fabric, following the shape of the client's body.

3 After adjusting the shoulder seam to get a better fit, I found it easiest in this fitting to draw in the placement for the new shoulder line rather than manipulating the fabric

to reflect both the fitting adjustment and the shoulder line placement. It's okay to indicate the shoulder line in either way.

4 The second mock-up. Fine-tune the base of the neck, following the natural curve of the client's neck. I find it helpful to lightly run several fingers along the client's neck to help me find what feels like the base of the neck.

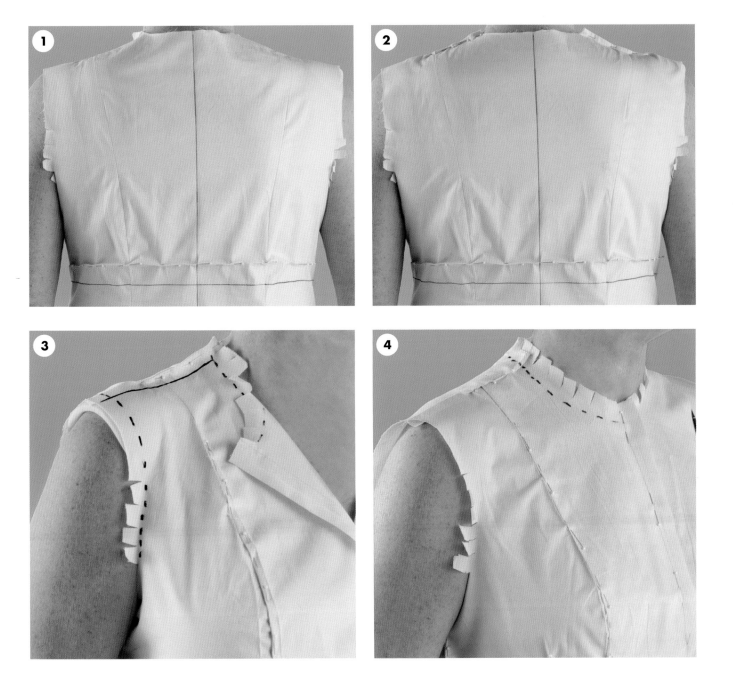

SET-IN SLEEVES

Developing a well-fitting garment with set-in sleeves that looks nice and is comfortable can be challenging. Not only must the sleeve fit the arm, but the sleeve must also go into the armhole opening cleanly and smoothly, which is often where problems arise. Understanding the variables associated with the upper portion of the sleeve and with the armhole opening sheds light on the complicated relationship between the sleeve and the armhole opening.

The Upper Portion of the Sleeve

Let's start by looking at the upper portion of the sleeve.

On a traditional set-in sleeve, the sleeve cap length is a bit longer than the armhole opening of the bodice, and the excess fabric is eased in along the upper portion of the sleeve. This ease plays an important role, because it produces a slight amount of cupping at the top of the sleeve. This cupping causes the top of the sleeve to sit slightly away from the arm. This in turn makes the sleeve look nicer, and it also makes the sleeve more comfortable, because there is more space for the arm to move within the sleeve. Determining how much ease to include in the sleeve cap depends on a number of factors, such as the amount of cupping you want in the sleeve cap, the type of fashion fabric you will be using, and the size of the arm and shoulder. Approximately ¾" (1.9 cm) of ease is a good starting place.

The circumference of the sleeve at the bicep must accommodate the arm's girth. For a sleeve to be comfortable, the sleeve needs to be about 2" (5.1 cm) larger than the bicep measurement of the arm. For a thin

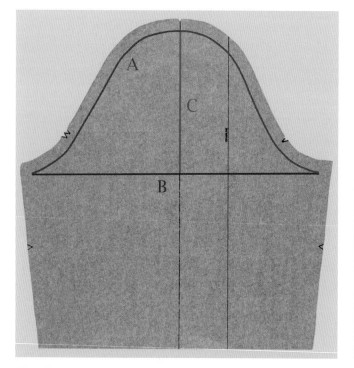

The three variables of the upper portion of a sleeve are the sleeve cap length (line A), the bicep (line B), and the cap height (line C).

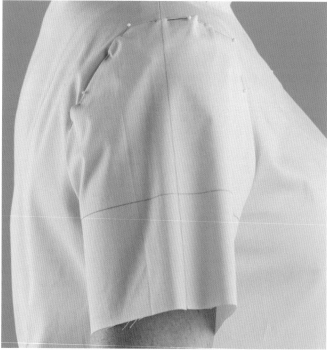

When there is not enough cap height, drag lines form on either side of the sleeve.

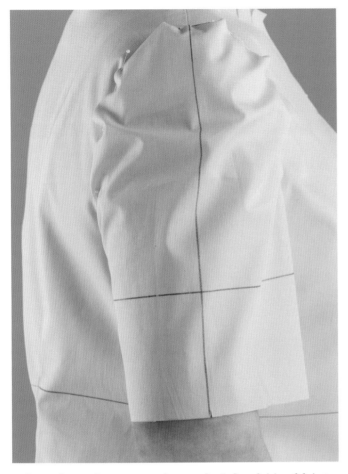

When there is too much cap height, folds of fabric form in the middle of the sleeve.

Also as seen in the fitting examples, the placement of the armhole seam at the shoulder visually impacts the client's overall proportions. While the traditional placement is at the hinge of the shoulder, this is not always the most flattering on the figure. Having this seam in just the right place can make the hip, the bust, and the shoulder width look more proportionate.

Where the armhole seam falls at the underarm is also important. If the armhole seam is too low, it actually restricts rotational movement and the ability to reach the arms forward. Having a high armhole provides more rotational movement and ability to reach.

Because you do not want the armhole to be loose and gaping, and because you do want the armhole to be relatively high under the arm, the result of individualized fitting is often a smaller armhole opening than many commercial patterns provide. The reason many commercial patterns have larger armhole openings is partly because the pattern company understandably wants to provide the consumer with a pattern that goes together nicely. There certainly are many good fitting elements in commercial patterns. But when it comes to sleeves and armhole openings, the fit is often quite generalized in order to simplify otherwise complex pattern-making issues.

arm, you might need slightly less than 2" (5.1 cm), and for a heavy arm, you will probably need more than 2" (5.1 cm).

The cap height plays an important role in how the sleeve looks. If the cap height is too short, drag lines form; if the cap height is too long, folds of fabric form.

The Armhole Opening

In fitting the bodices, I show many examples of getting the armhole opening to reflect the client's figure. The armhole should not be too tight and restrictive, nor should it be too loose and gaping.

My Approach to Sleeves and Armhole Openings

Rather than fitting the sleeve and the armhole in conjunction with one another and making one dependent on factors associated with the other, I initially approach the sleeve and armhole separately. First, I fit the bodice without a sleeve, which allows me to get a beautifully fitting armhole. Then I fit the sleeve semi-attached to the armhole, which allows me to get a beautifully fitting sleeve.

To determine how the two elements go together, I compare the sleeve cap length to the armhole opening and assess the results as follows.

(continued)

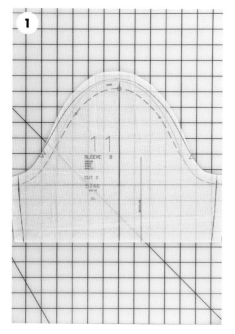

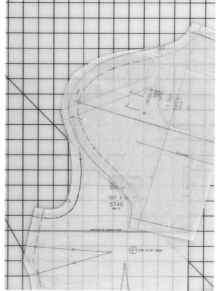

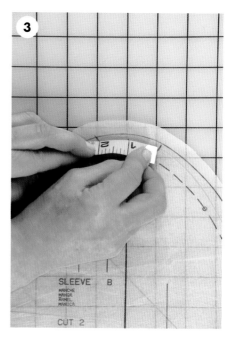

1 Draw a line parallel to the grainline at the center of the sleeve.

2 Compare the front bodice armhole seam to the front sleeve cap seam (marked in pink) by walking the two seams, starting at the underarm and having the sleeve on top of the bodice. When you come to the shoulder seam, mark the sleeve cap. Repeat the process for the back bodice and back sleeve.

3 Measure the distance between the two marks on the sleeve cap. Walking the sleeve to the bodice in this way tells you not only how much total ease there is, but also how much ease there is on the front of the sleeve and on the back of the sleeve.

If there is a reasonable amount of ease, the sleeve needs no adjustment. If there is too much ease for the garment to be sewn well, I must further assess the situation. For instance, if there is a total of 1⅛" (2.9 cm) ease, and I prefer to have ¾" (1.9 cm) of ease, I have an excess of ⅜" (1 cm) of ease. If there is plenty of room in the bicep, I might reduce the sleeve cap length at each underarm seam of the sleeve by ³⁄₁₆" (0.19 cm). Or, if the underarm of the bodice was very high, I might lower it by ¼" (6 mm) and reduce the sleeve cap length at each underarm seam by the remaining amount needed (lowering the underarm of the bodice by ¼" [6 mm] will not necessarily increase the armhole opening by ¼" [6 mm]). If I am able to make minor alterations to the sleeve or to the armhole without sacrificing the fit I want, then I'm happy to make these adjustments.

If, however, the alterations would cause me to adjust either the sleeve or the armhole in a deleterious way, then I prefer to use an alternate sleeve design. Developing a two-piece sleeve with a seam down the center of it allows you to make many changes to the sleeve so that it will fit into a smaller armhole without sacrificing the fit of the sleeve—and in fact, this sleeve often lets you get an even better fit on the arm. Following are step-by-step instructions for making this type of two-piece sleeve.

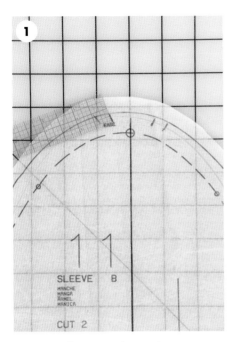

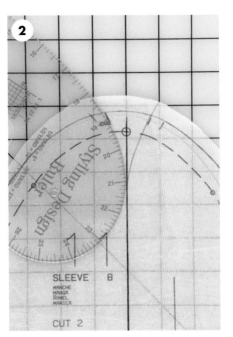

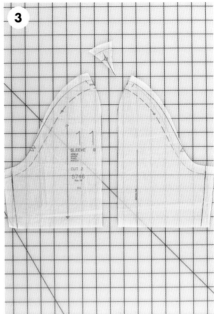

1 First, determine the total amount of ease you want and divide the amount in half, since one-half of the ease will be put on the front of the sleeve cap and one-half will be put on the back of the sleeve cap. In this example, I want a total of ¾" (1.9 cm) of ease, so I will mark ⅜" (1 cm) of ease to both the front and the back of the sleeve.

2 Blend each of these marks to the center line. I usually make the blend to the center line fairly high up on the sleeve cap, because when you fit a muslin of the new sleeve, it's easy to pin out any excess fabric and shape this upper area of the center-of-the-sleeve seam to a pleasing curve.

3 Cut the pattern along the new seam, discarding the excess paper in the middle of the upper portion of the sleeve cap. Add the grainline on the other side of the sleeve. Walk the new seams. True if necessary. Add paper, and add the seam allowance.

Getting More "Reach"

To be comfortable in our garments with sleeves and to be able to go about our daily activities, we need good freedom of movement. As mentioned above, keeping the armhole high provides more rotational movement of the arm than with a low armhole. However, the armhole should not cut into the skin. Trimming out the excess seam allowance in the lower portion of the armhole once the sleeve has been sewn to the garment can make a considerable difference in the sleeve's comfort and the amount of reach.

You can improve the ability to reach forward by adding to the center back seam through the upper back of the bodice. If there is not a center back seam in the garment

already, you can create one. Another way to get more reach is to let out the back armhole, as shown on page 110. Both of these adjustments involve a trade-off, because they will likely result in a bit of excess fabric at the back of the garment when the arm is at rest, but you will definitely have more reach.

An overall larger sleeve also allows you to move your arms more freely. To enlarge a sleeve, you can cut down the middle of the sleeve and make either an open-wedge or an even spread. When I do this, I often view the extra fabric in the sleeve cap length as a means to making a stylistic statement, using interesting tucks, pleats, or gathers to control the extra ease in the sleeve cap.

Increasing the Bicep with a Fitting Compromise

Increasing the bicep also improves your ability to reach, but some pattern manipulations to do this impact the sleeve more than others. To increase the bicep of a sleeve that has only one seam without increasing the sleeve cap length, you must spread the sleeve horizontally. However, this leads to a shortened cap height.

I personally never use this pattern adjustment because shortening the sleeve cap height creates drag lines across the sleeve. However, you need to decide which trade-offs are acceptable to you and which are not.

Increasing the Bicep without Shortening the Cap Height

A two-piece sleeve with the seam down the center is a nice solution for creating more reach, because it allows you to easily increase the bicep circumference without shortening the cap height or sacrificing fit. It also allows you to increase the circumference of the sleeve wherever the client needs it the most. The pattern work for this is simple.

More Seams Mean More Fitting Opportunities

A three-piece sleeve, which usually has one center seam as well as one seam on each side of an underarm panel, is one of the best sleeve designs to use when fitting due to the number of seams where fitting adjustments can be made. If the idea of multiple seams in a sleeve seems odd, the reason might simply be because the majority of patterns provide a sleeve with only one seam at the underarm. If more seams means that you can get a better fit, why not use such a sleeve?

Utilizing a Sleeve That Fits

One of the best things about having a sleeve that fits your arm is that you can use it in other garments that have a similar armhole shape and fit. For instance, if you develop a blouse sleeve that fits and is comfortable, you'll be able to use it—perhaps with only very minor adjustments—in most of your blouses. If you develop a sleeve for a jacket, you'll be able to use it in most of your jackets. Fine-tuning a sleeve may be a lengthy process, but it has its advantages.

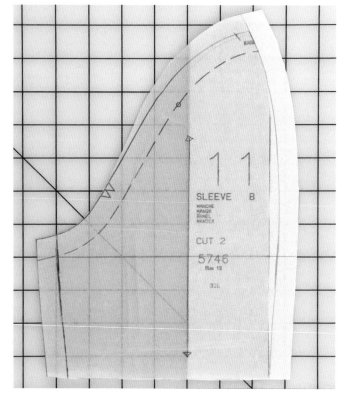

Add paper along the seam at the center of the sleeve. Redraw the center seam, arcing it out beyond the original seam and then blending it back to the original seam. While I have given just one example of where to add fullness on the sleeve, you can increase the girth of the sleeve wherever it would be most beneficial. Repeat for the other side of the sleeve; then walk and true the seams.

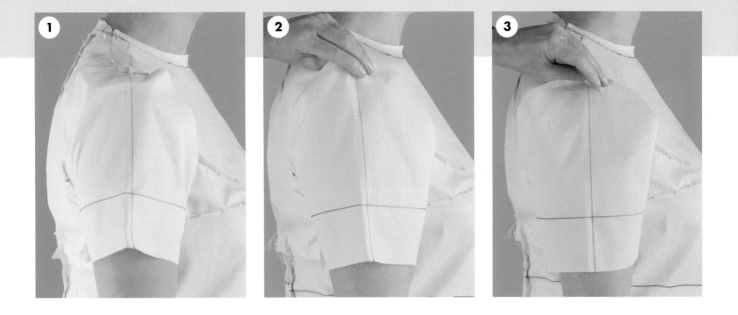

Fitting Examples

Eliminating Drag Lines That Indicate Insufficient Cap Height

1 Note the drag lines on either side of the sleeve. On a short sleeve like this, the hem flares away from the arm. Also note that the HBL is not level.

2 As I move the sleeve cap lower down on the arm, the drag lines become less pronounced.

3 With the sleeve HBL level, there are no drag lines at all.

Adding Cap Height

1 Another way to begin a sleeve fitting is to bring the HBL to a level position. Here it is clear that the there is insufficient cap height on the front of the sleeve.

2 The back is a bit better, but there is still a gap indicating insufficient cap height.

(continued)

3 Measuring with a ruler lets you accurately gauge how much more cap height to add to the pattern. To see a pattern with cap height added, see page 181.

4 The second mock-up with the center of the sleeve drawn to match the shoulder seam. This sleeve still looks a bit tight all over. Because of the extra cap height required, a two-piece sleeve with the seam in the center of the sleeve will almost certainly be necessary; this seam will be the perfect place to provide more girth in the sleeve.

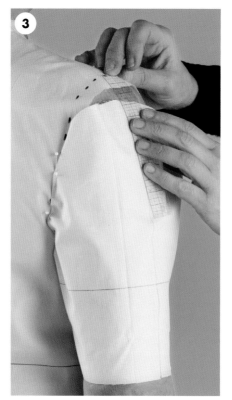
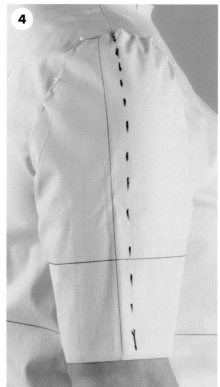

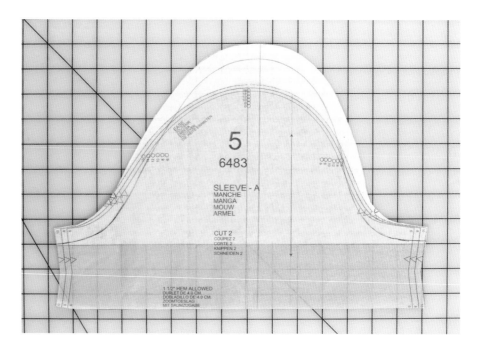

The final sleeve pattern with the center of the sleeve repositioned and the front of the sleeve reshaped for a forward shoulder.

Forward Shoulder

1 In order to have equal amounts of ease on the front and the back of the arm, the center of the sleeve is toward the back of the bodice shoulder seam.

2 Draw the new center line on the sleeve muslin and transfer this to the pattern. This is a typical adjustment for a figure with a forward shoulder. Pin the front and back of the sleeve to the bodice armhole, distributing ease in the upper sleeve cap as shown on page 107.

3 In the previous photograph and here, you can see that there is not quite enough sleeve cap height to accommodate the client's forward shoulder. Indicate on the muslin how much more is needed in this area and transfer the information to the pattern. The final pattern for this sleeve is shown on page 181.

4 The second mock-up viewed from the side. Note that with a forward shoulder, the back of the sleeve cap is often flatter in the back. Do not fit the back of the sleeve cap too closely, because it will restrict movement and also visually accentuate the client's forward shoulder.

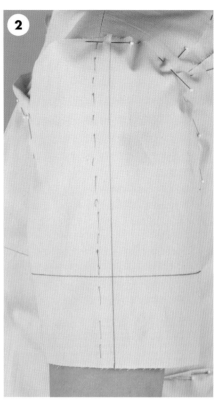

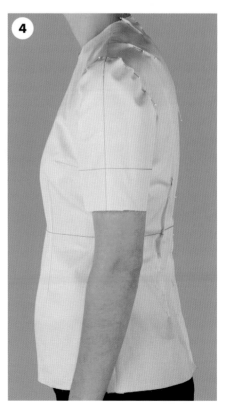

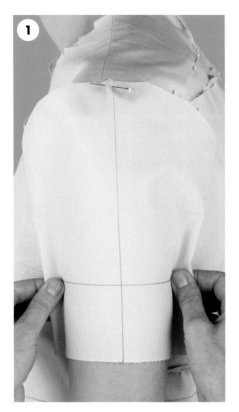

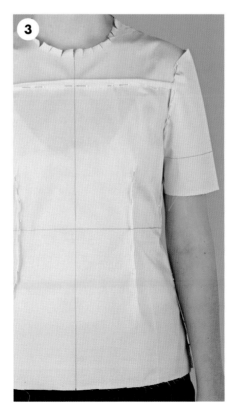

Fitting a Long Sleeve

I often fit a short sleeve and then lengthen it to make a long sleeve. When fitting a long sleeve, in addition to getting the sleeve cap to fit well, you must also get the sleeve to follow the natural curvature of the client's arm.

1 Here, the sleeve follows the client's arm without many wrinkles, but the HBL is not level.

2 I prefer to fit the sleeve with the HBL at the bicep in a level position. Note that the sleeve then crumples at the front of the arm, because there is no built-in curvature to the sleeve.

3 To build curvature into the sleeve, it must have at least two seams, so any kind of two-piece or three-piece sleeve works well. In this fitting example, I know that I will be developing a two-piece sleeve with a seam down the center of the sleeve in order to control the amount of ease in the sleeve cap. Therefore, I will make the following adjustment, knowing that the line drawn at the center of the sleeve will become a seam. Pin a close-wedge where the fabric crumples, starting at the underarm sleeve seam going to nothing at the center of the sleeve; the close-wedge is on both the front and the back of the sleeve. The pattern work is similar to that shown on page 111.

4 The second mock-up of the sleeve with a seam down the center of the sleeve. Continue to fine-tune the sleeve to follow the arm's curvature and to proportion the width of the sleeve all the way down the arm. This sleeve needs a bit more cap height to bring the HBL to a level position. I often will make quite a number of mock-ups in order to get a sleeve to fit perfectly.

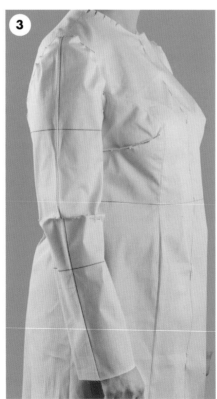

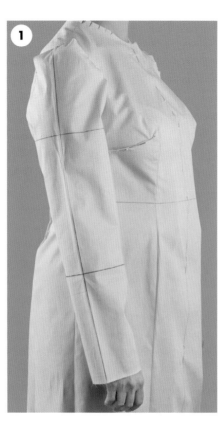

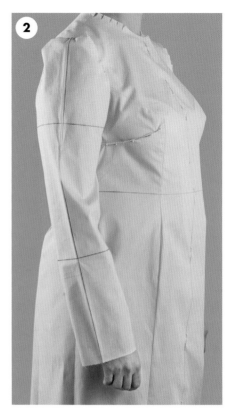

Proportioning the Front and Back of the Sleeve

1 Sleeves should have about the same amount of room at the bicep on the front of the sleeve as on the back of the sleeve. Here, the sleeve touches the back of the arm and all of the room is in the front of the sleeve.

2 Moving the center of the sleeve toward the back rotates the sleeve, moving some of the room from the front of the sleeve toward the back of the arm. For this client, in order to get enough room in the sleeve at the back of the arm, I also needed to reposition the underarm seam of the sleeve. To do this on the muslin, I unpinned the sleeve at the underarm and moved the underarm seam of the sleeve about ⅝" (1.6 cm) toward the back of her arm; then I pinned the sleeve in place again at the underarm. Because the underarm seam of the sleeve and the side seam of the bodice traditionally match, the seam on the sleeve will need to be moved.

3 The second mock-up sleeve viewed from the front with fine-tuning adjustments along the lower portion of the arm. In order to control the amount of ease in the sleeve cap length, this sleeve has a seam down the center.

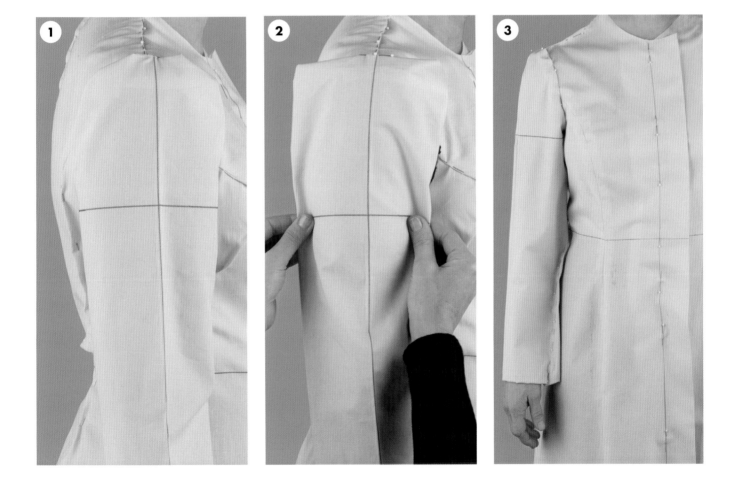

RAGLAN SLEEVES

Fitting a raglan sleeve is entirely different from fitting a set-in sleeve, because the raglan sleeve forms part of the bodice across the upper portion of the garment and across the shoulder. See fitting the bodice front, back, and shoulder line for more information on fitting these areas of raglan garments.

Fitting the Front and Back Crease and a Long Sleeve

1 Note the strain at the ball of the shoulder.

2 Letting out the back shoulder seam improves the fit. Fitting a prominent shoulder ball without any small strain lines is difficult with a raglan sleeve. However, these small strain lines are usually less noticeable in the fashion fabric.

3 Note that the front raglan seam does not fall at the crease of the arm.

4 Also note how low the armhole of the muslin is. My scissors indicate where the underarm seam should fall on the client's body.

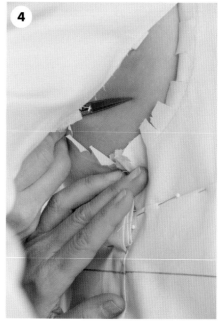
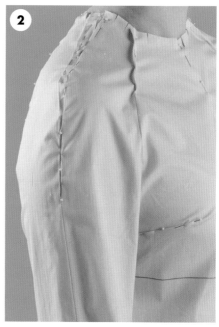
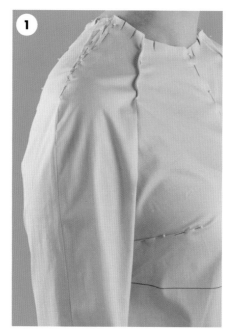
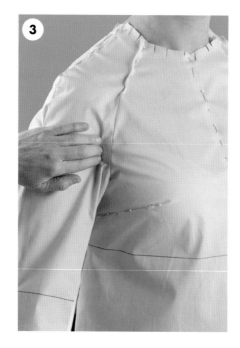

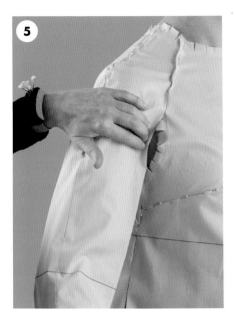

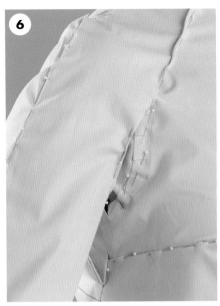

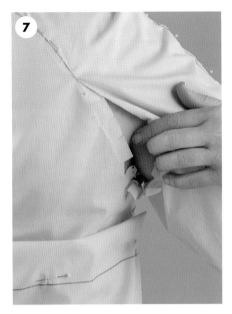

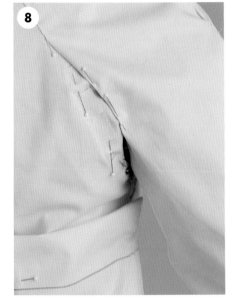

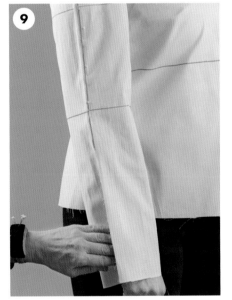

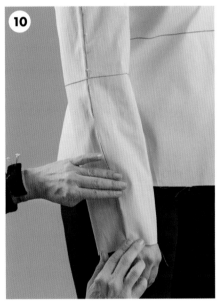

5 Here I have clipped and folded under the front of the raglan sleeve to the crease, showing how much fabric needs to be added to the front bodice in the armhole area.

6 Extra fabric pinned in. The fold line of the raglan sleeve indicates the new seam line.

7 Similarly, the back raglan seam does not fall at the back crease.

8 Extra fabric pinned in. The fold line of the raglan sleeve indicates the new seam line.

9 To fit the lower portion of the sleeve, release the sleeve seam along the top of the arm and allow the fabric to relax. My hand indicates how much fabric on the sleeve back is sliding underneath the sleeve front.

10 Fold under the front of the sleeve so that the placement of the seam is pleasing.

(continued)

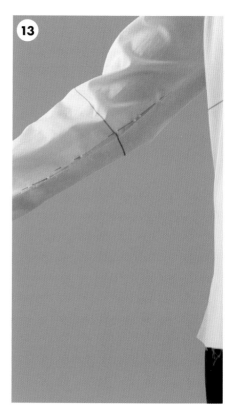

11 The seam along the outer sleeve seam pinned in place.

12 Have the client bend her elbow to check that there is enough room in the sleeve to be comfortable. Here the client said it feels slightly tight.

13 Because I liked the way the seam along the top of the arm looked, I chose to let out the underarm seam to provide more room through the area of the elbow.

Fitting the Back and Back Crease

1 Note the slight strain across the mid back.

2 To determine where the strain is coming from, release the center back seam and the princess seams that were created for this client.

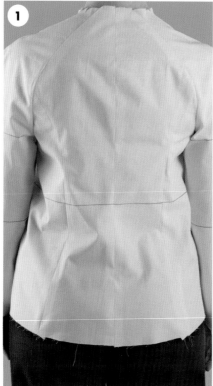

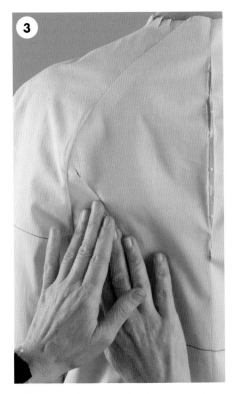

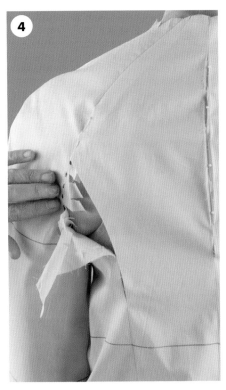

3 Let out the center back seam and pin in place. Smoothing the fabric of the back princess seam, a bubble forms where the princess seam intersects the back raglan seam. This indicates that the problem probably lies in the back raglan seam.

4 Releasing the back raglan seam lets me see that the raglan seam does not lie along the back crease of the arm, which has been indicated with a black dashed line.

5 Let the fabric guide you as you smooth and pin the fabric in place.

WAIST AND HIPS

This section focuses on fitting skirts through the waist and hip. Numerous examples of fitting the waist and hip areas on bodices are found in the sections on fitting the bust and the back.

Deciding how snugly or loosely to fit the waist of a skirt is largely dependent on personal preference. Some people like a skirt waist to be tight, while others like 1" (2.5 cm) or more of ease. In either case, the decision is usually based on comfort. When fitting the hip, the client often bases her preference on how much she wants to show her figure.

In my experience, a woman tends to be more willing to show her figure when her clothing fits well, because well-fitting clothing makes her body look proportionate. This is true for bodices as well as skirts and pants.

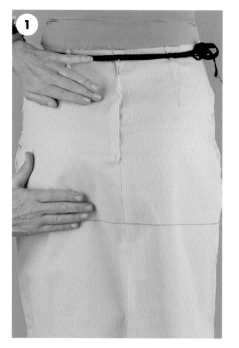

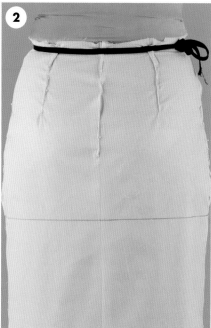

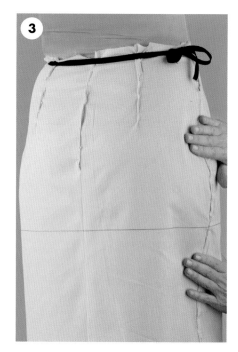

Small Waist and Defined Buttocks

1 Back darts on a skirt should point toward the fullest part of the buttock, except in the case of a high shelf hip, shown in the last example of this section. Cupping the buttocks with your hands can help you identify the fullest part of the buttock.

2 Pin the darts so that the dart point is slightly above the fullest part of the buttock.

3 Avoid overfitting fleshy areas. Running your hands lightly over the client's body will often help you identify fleshy areas your eyes do not at first see. Due to weight fluctuations, which commonly occur and experienced fitters become accustomed to, the side seams of this mock-up had to be let out for the fitting to proceed.

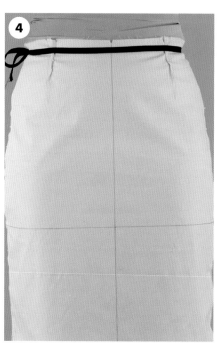

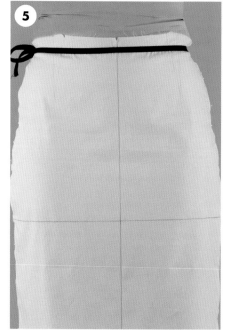

4 Front darts on skirts and pants sometimes look good; other times they accentuate the roundness of the stomach.

5 This client and I both agreed that the flat front made her stomach look flatter. To eliminate the dart in the pattern, simply remove the dart intake equivalent from the side seam.

Flat Buttock and Wide Hips

1 This client has very flat buttocks.

2 And she has wide hips.

3 Although there is a significant difference between the client's hip and waist measurement, it's important to keep the dart intake relatively small since she also has flat buttocks. To reduce the amount of fabric at the waist, take in the side seams and the center back seam. This leaves a fairly small dart intake.

4 Having a traditional dart placement pointing toward the fullest part of the buttock is okay, though not flattering.

(continued)

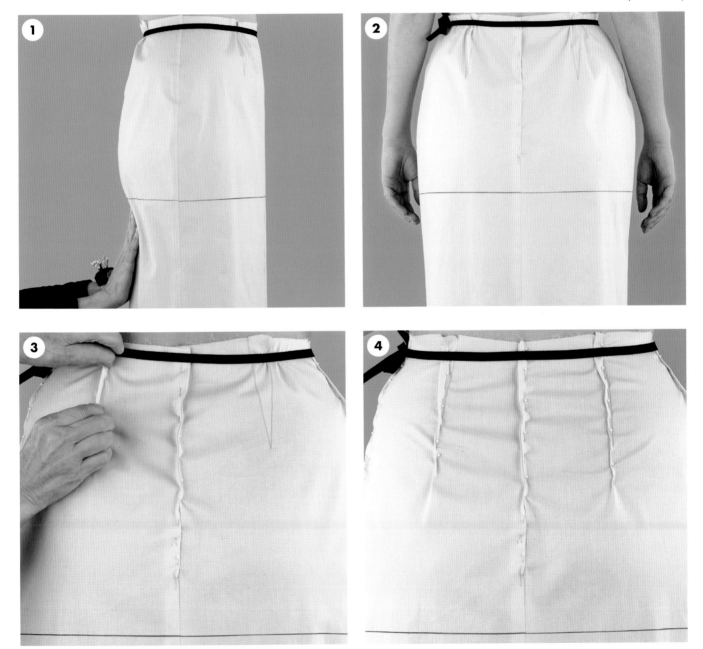

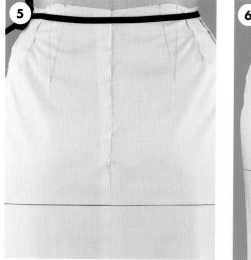

5 Moving the darts toward the side back contour her high shelf hip. The drag lines pointing toward the buttocks indicate that splitting the dart intake between her high shelf hip and the buttock would probably produce the best results.

6 This client and I both like the way front darts look on her figure.

High or Low Hips

1 Having the HBL in a level position and the elastic at the client's waist makes it easy to see that she has a high right hip.

2 Drape in the waist darts as you normally would and mark the waist carefully. You will need to develop a full pattern since the right and left sides are not symmetrical. The pattern work for this adjustment is shown at the end of the section. Be careful not to overfit the side of the body with the low hip, because it is often smaller than the high hip side and fitting too closely can make the client's body appear more uneven.

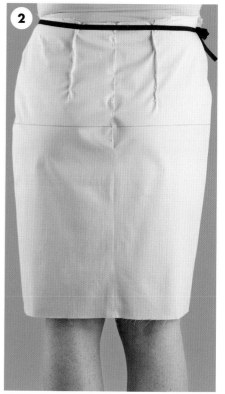

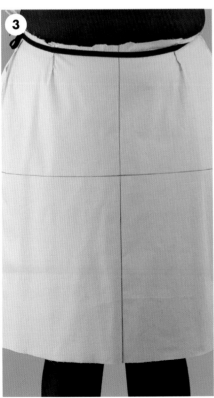

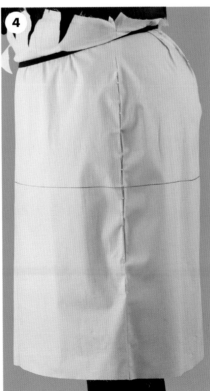

Tilted Waist and Round, High Buttocks

1 A tilted waist usually occurs with a prominent stomach, sometimes with a tilted pelvic structure also being a contributing factor. Work with the client to position the elastic, and then make sure that the elastic is snug enough to hold the skirt in place. Cut the mock-up front above the elastic wherever it is tight, allowing the fabric to relax on the body. Concentrate on bringing the HBL to a level position, and check it frequently during the fitting.

2 With large and round buttocks, experiment with dart placement and the number of darts. Three darts often produce a better fit than two.

3 Front darts frequently are unattractive because they accentuate the hollow area beneath the stomach. Sometimes the front dart intake can be removed at the side seams, thereby eliminating the front darts.

4 In this example, the back of the skirt kept creeping upward, as indicated by the slightly high back HBL and the vertical folds of fabric beneath the buttock, even though I pulled the skirt back downward into place several times. When a garment creeps up in this way, it's a sure sign that the garment is too tight somewhere, usually over the largest portion of the body. For this reason, I let out the side seams to allow more room across the buttocks.

(continued)

5 The second mock-up. Note the strain over the fullest part of the buttocks, indicated by the small drag lines on the back side above the buttocks and pointing toward the waist. This indicates that there is not enough room in the skirt to accommodate the buttocks, even though there is excess fabric at the hip on the side seams.

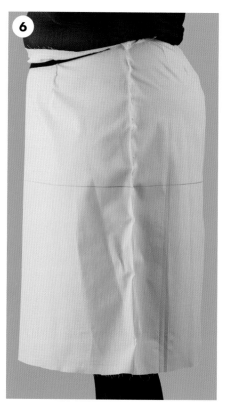

6 Here you can clearly see the strain and that it is being caused by the tightness of the fabric at the fullest part of the buttock.

7 In order to provide the fabric where it was needed, which is over the fullest part of the buttock, I created princess lines. The princess lines provide an attractive stylistic element (see page 218 for more information on creating style lines). But more importantly, they provide a fitting solution, because I was able to shape the princess seams over the buttocks, providing as much room as was needed.

8 The third mock-up. With enough room for the buttocks provided by the back princess seams, I was able to take in the side seams a bit more. I was also able to incorporate all of the necessary front darting in the princess seams.

Pattern Work Examples

See Fundamentals of Altering Patterns for basic patternmaking techniques (page 44).

Complete Skirt Pattern for High and Low Hips

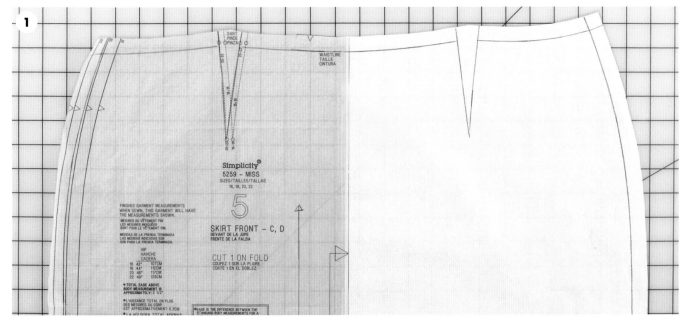

1 The waist of the front skirt pattern. Note that on the grid board, the left side of the skirt (as the skirt would be worn) is higher than the right side.

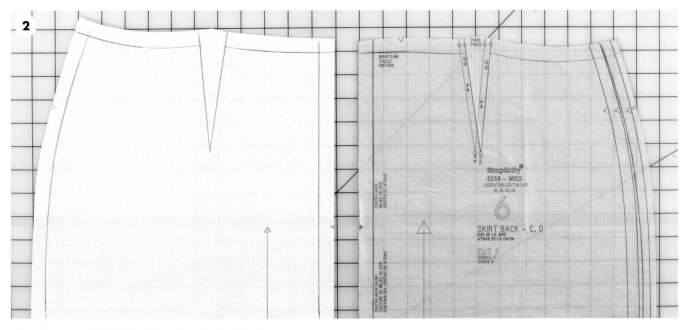

2 The waist of both the left and right skirt back patterns.

Fitting Pants

Pants can be troublesome to fit because of the different variables you need to take into consideration: the rise from the crotch level to the waist, the shape and depth of the pelvic structure, and the size and the shape of the waist, stomach, buttock, and upper thigh. Bowed legs, knock knees, and other leg variations are additional fitting issues.

There are also many styles of pants, which can be broken down into three general categories based on the width of the pants leg at the upper thigh in conjunction with where the pants crotch is in relation to the body. For trousers **(A)**, the pants rise is long enough so that the crotch of the pants does not touch the body, and the leg is wide enough so that it hangs off the buttock. For slacks **(B)**, the crotch of the pants barely touches the body and the leg is narrow enough so that there is just a little cupping under the buttock. For

jeans **(C)**, the crotch of the pants is quite close to the body and there is a great deal of cupping under the buttock.

For the fitting examples here, I use a slacks silhouette, which is not as stylized as either a jean or a trouser and which nicely illustrates many typical pants fitting issues. Learning to recognize these issues and how to correct them will help you to develop a method for fitting all types and styles of pants.

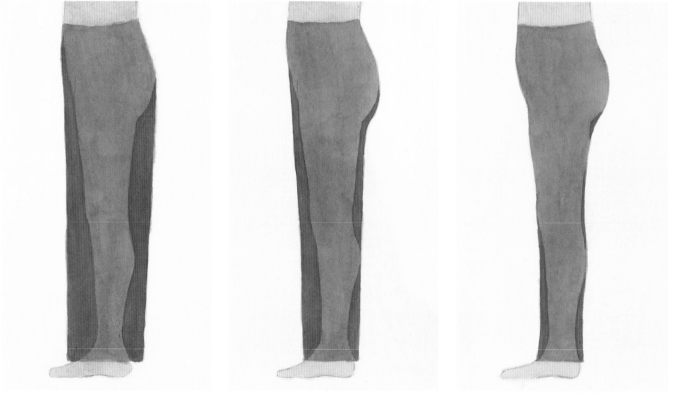

(A) Trouser silhouette.   **(B)** Slacks silhouette.   **(C)** Jeans silhouette.

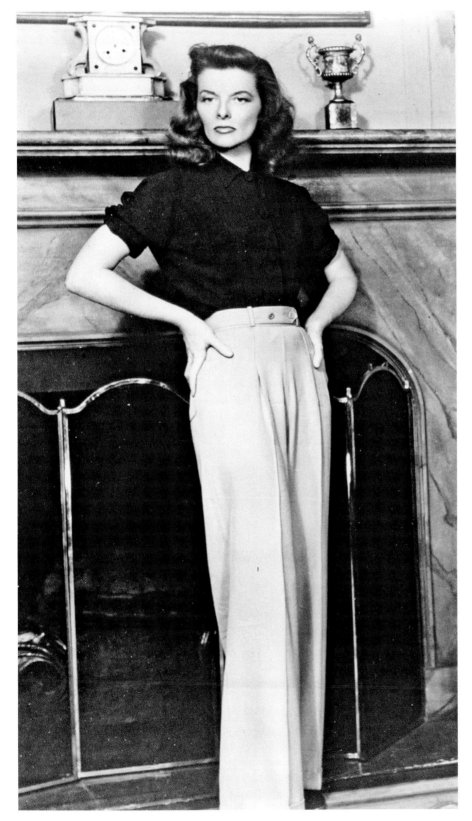

UNDERSTANDING BODY MASS AND PANTS VOLUME

The most difficult area of pants to fit is the lower torso. Learning how the body mass sits within the space created by the pants makes the fitting process and the resulting pattern work easier, especially since some fitting corrections for pants seem counterintuitive.

When fitting pants, think of the body as a box. You have three dimensions to deal with: (1) the height, which is the distance from the waist to the bottom of the torso; (2) the width, which is the distance from one side of the body to the other; and (3) the depth, which is the distance from the front to the back of the body. This last dimension, the body's depth, is further complicated because you must consider the particular shape of the pelvic bone structure as well as the flesh of the stomach and the buttocks.

When fitting pants, you must get the shape of the pattern's crotch curve to reflect the shape of the body's crotch—the pelvic structure plus stomach and buttocks. Many pants patterns have a relatively flat crotch curve **(A)**.

However, if we could slice our bodies in half and view them from the side, we would see that our buttocks are lower than the front of the pelvis. To see this for yourself, stand with your side to a mirror and place one hand cupping the front of the body and the other hand cupping the buttocks **(B)**.

Another indicator that the back crotch curve needs to be lowered is when there is too much inseam length on the pants relative to the body **(C)**.

The crotch curve of the pants also needs to reflect the shape of the lower front pelvis **(D)**.

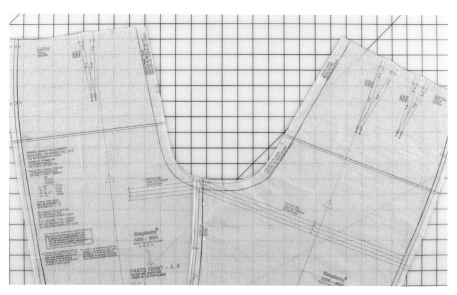

(A) A typical pants pattern with a flat crotch curve.

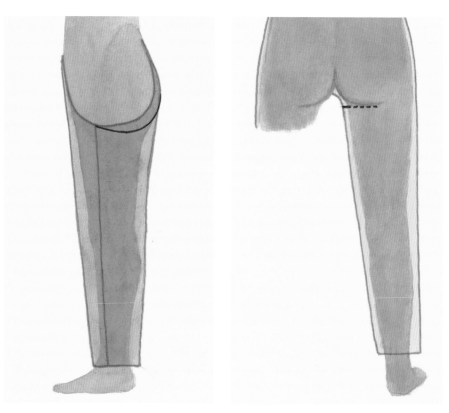

(B) The purple line shows the body's buttock shape and position relative to the flat crotch shape of many pants patterns. In a fitting, this is indicated by the pants fabric cutting into the buttocks, as is shown on page 204.

(C) When the crotch curve of the pattern is too high in the back, there is often excessive length at the intersection of the inseam and the crotch seam.

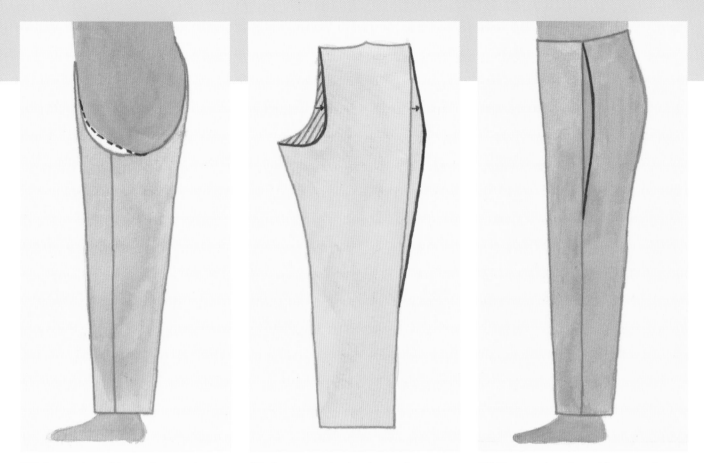

(D) For a sloped lower front pelvis, change the crotch curve of the pattern to reflect the body's shape.

(E) Scooping the back crotch curve provides more space for the buttock to sit within the pants. However, in order not to make the pants too small in total circumference, add the amount of the scoop to the back outseam directly across from the scoop, and blend up to the waist and down to toward the knee. The long blend toward the knee prevents a bubble or "jodhpur" effect from developing at the side seam.

(F) This is what the addition to the outseam looks like when viewing the pants from the side. This visual perspective also emphasizes that if the buttocks are larger, extra room is needed on the pants back.

In conjunction with getting the angle of the crotch curve correct, pants must also provide enough depth—the amount of space the body needs from the front of the lower torso to the back of the buttocks. To accommodate fleshy buttocks, the fitting and pattern solution is to "scoop" the crotch, which provides more space for the buttock to sit within. Because scooping the crotch reduces the width of the pants back, you'll need to adjust the outseam in order not to reduce the total width of the pants **(E, F)**.

Scooping the back crotch on the pattern is also effective for fitting a body that has a deep pelvic structure front to back. Pants usually are more flattering if the front crotch curve is a good deal shorter than the back crotch curve, which is logical since there is more depth in the buttocks than the front pelvic structure.

Getting pants to fit can be challenging. It typically takes me four to ten mock-ups to develop and then fine-tune a pair of pants. Part of what makes the process difficult is achieving the right balance between how the pants look on the body and how the pants feel on the body. While you don't want to settle for a messy and unflattering fit, you also want to be comfortable when wearing the pants. And there are often trade-offs involved.

One set of trade-offs between looks and comfort is due to the change in our bodies between standing and sitting. When you sit, the back of the body from the waist to the knee is much longer than when you are standing, and the front of the body from the waist to the knee is much shorter.

To accommodate this change of length in the back, the fit in the upper thigh, under the buttock, and through the crotch must be a bit loose. If you want these areas to fit quite snugly, the trade-off is that under the buttocks you will have some horizontal wrinkles of fabric, which provides the extra fabric needed so you can sit down. To see this for yourself, take a pair of jeans with these fabric folds under the buttocks; then firmly grasp these fabric folds under one buttock with one hand and try to sit down.

The front of the body becomes shorter when you sit, resulting in one or more horizontal folds of fabric below the stomach. A very large horizontal fold tells me that I probably still have too much front crotch length. But I know that there needs to be some amount of excess fabric. To see this for yourself, firmly grasp the fold or folds in one hand while sitting and try to stand up.

You certainly can fit a pair of trim-looking pants where the front is perfectly smooth and there isn't a hint of extra fabric under the buttocks. But the result is what I call "cocktail party" pants—they look perfect when you're standing, but you won't be able to sit down.

Experiment with Small Changes when Fine-Tuning the Fit

When you're fine-tuning the fit of pants, experiment to find out how to get the results you want. Fine-tuning the crotch area is a good example. Sometimes letting out the back inseam at the crotch just ¼" (6 mm) improves the fit and makes the pants more comfortable when sitting. But you might get even better results by letting out the back inseam and taking in the front inseam the same amount. Or you might try scooping the back crotch another ¼" (6 mm) and then experiment with small changes at the inseams. The only way to tell is to make the changes and assess the fit with each change.

When making these types of changes, it's not necessary to make a new mock-up each time. Rather, make a change, try the pants on, and make a few notes about what the change accomplished. Then try a different alteration, again taking notes so you can track what the result was for each fitting change. If one set of changes definitely does not improve the fit, then rule that out and concentrate on the other possibilities.

When you think you've gotten the fit right, make a pair of pants and wear the garment. I think of this version as my wearable mock-up. Actually wearing the pants and going through your normal activities will tell you much more about the fit and comfort of the garment than standing in front of the mirror. There are often one or two small adjustments that will make the pants even better. To me, working on wearable mock-ups is essential to get the pants absolutely perfect.

Waistbands versus Waist Facings

As is the case for skirts, you can put either a waistband or a waist facing on pants. Which to use is largely personal preference. Occasionally you need to take fitting considerations into account when making the decision. For instance, some women with a large difference between their hip and waist measurements find that a waistband works best because it anchors the pants to the torso more securely. In this case, the width of the waistband is largely a stylistic consideration, although many women find a narrow waistband that is ½" to ⅝" (1.3 to 1.6 cm) wide to be more comfortable than the standard waistbands that are 1¼" to 1½" (3.2 to 1.3) wide.

Helpful Fitting Aids

The horizontal balance line, which should be drawn on the pattern and the muslin at hip level, helps you fit the crotch length. Use the HBL to determine where on the body to lengthen or shorten the crotch seam. Not only should the crotch seam provide adequate overall length for the lower torso, it should also be proportionate to the lower torso.

The "break point" on pants is where the center front and center back crotch seams turn and curve to go underneath the body. It is important to establish a break point when fitting the crotch seam in order to get the rise proportionate to the client's lower torso.

The "crease line" is the middle of the pant leg. See page 209 for instructions on how to establish the crease line on the pattern. The crease line is parallel to the grainline and can be used for the grainline as well. Transfer the crease line to at least one leg of the fitting muslin. The crease line should hang as straight as possible. A curved crease line indicates that there is a fitting problem that needs to be solved. This is shown in the fitting examples.

THE PROCESS OF FITTING PANTS

One of the biggest challenges of fitting pants is to get the crotch curve and lower torso of the pants to reflect the client's body. Because this is a sensitive area of the body, clients often feel more protected if they wear two pairs of underpants or underpants and tights during the fitting process. In my experience, the level of trust between the fitter and the client is the biggest factor in how smoothly and productive a pants fitting proceeds. A fitter can develop trust with her client in many ways, but especially by telling the client what she would like to check on the pants and why. Some clients will feel more comfortable slipping the pants off so that you can make a change, and then put them back on for further fitting. Other clients will feel comfortable having you do more adjustments while the pants are on the body.

Total Crotch Length and Relative Crotch Length

One of primary concerns when fitting pants is getting the crotch length correct. Rather than concentrating on the total crotch length, think about the crotch length in relative terms using the HBL as the starting point. With the HBL level, there must be adequate fabric from the HBL up to the front waist and from the HBL up to the back waist. There must also be adequate fabric from the HBL down and around the crotch and back to the HBL on the other side of the body.

Fitting Pants

1 Tie elastic around the waist, as is done when fitting a skirt. Check the length of the pants. While you might like to wear your pants with the fabric breaking over the foot or shoe, this distorts the fit of the pants leg. Note that there is a bubble of fabric at the front crotch.

2 Pin the hem so that the pants hang freely above the foot and shoe. Note that the pants are a bit tight through the front upper thigh, as seen by the drag lines going from the front thigh to the side seam. The HBL looks fairly level from the side.

3 From the back, the HBL dips sharply at the center back, indicating that there is not enough crotch length to accommodate the depth of the pelvic structure plus the buttocks. There seems to be enough total crotch length because the fabric does not dip at either the center front or the center back waist. And in fact, the bubble at the crotch front indicates too much length there. But the crotch length is not in the correct place. Also note that there are drag lines through the upper back thigh.

4 Before addressing other issues, bring the HBL to a level position. To do this, release the stitching along the crotch seam for about 2" (5.1 cm) on either side of the inseam. Also release the inseam on both legs down about 7" to 8" (17.8 to 20.3 cm). Having the crotch area of the pants released allows you to take a wedge above the HBL, which starts to bring the HBL to level. In a first mock-up, I'm concerned about getting the relative crotch length more or less in proportion to the client's body mass. In subsequent mock-ups, I can fine-tune this. Also note that there are drag lines through the upper back thigh, and how tight the pants are below the HBL at the full buttock.

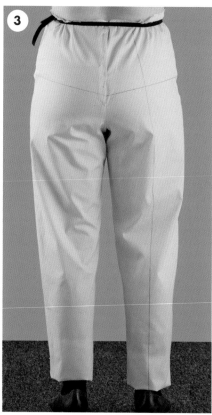

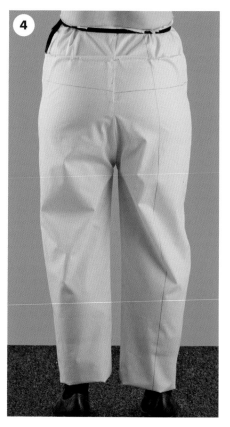

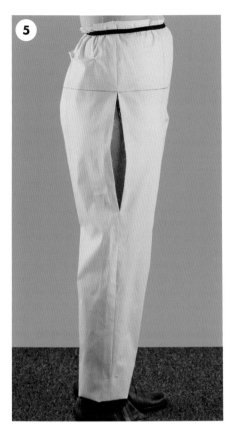

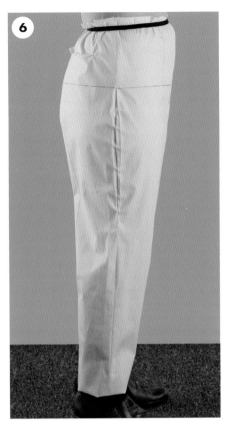

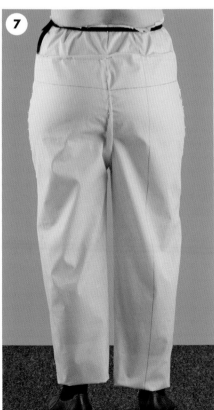

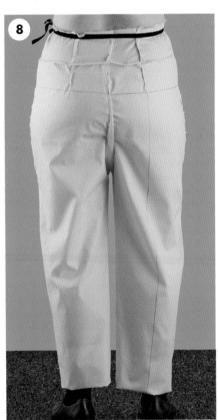

5 Release the side seams to address the tightness identified in the previous step. The spread of the fabric indicates how much to add at the side seam. Some of the addition will be on the back outseam to accommodate the full buttock and full high upper thigh, but some will also be on the front outseam to accommodate the full forward thigh.

6 Pin both side seams, adjusting the amount let out on both the front and back to keep the side seam as straight as possible.

7 To eliminate the drag lines through the thigh area, scoop the crotch by pinning out the excess fabric. Scooping the crotch also makes the crease line of the pants in the middle of the leg start to hang straight. In fact, paying attention to the crease line and getting it to hang straight is an effective guide for how much to scoop the crotch.

8 Pin the back darts to begin to get an idea of the fit at the waist.

(continued)

9 Similarly, pin the front darts. Pinning the darts in this first mock-up isn't necessary, but I like to get an idea of how the pant is fitting at the waist. Assess how much the inseams have spread apart in order to complete the necessary pattern work before taking the first mock-up off the client. Have the client stand with her legs spread a small amount. (If she spreads her legs a lot, her stance will cause the inseams to spread too much.)Put your hands around the client's upper thigh so that your middle fingers are touching. You will be able to feel where the front inseam is on one hand, and where the back inseam is on the other hand. Slip your thumbs between your hands and the pants fabric. On each hand, press your thumb against your fingers where

the inseam touches the hand. Bring your hands away from the client's body while continuing to press your thumbs against the hand. The distance between the end of the middle finger and your thumb is the amount that must be added to the respective inseam. In this example, I would add the amount indicated on my left hand to the front inseam, and the amount indicated on my right hand to the back inseam.

10 The second mock-up. How roomy you want the pants crotch to be is personal preference. Here the fit in the front crotch is loose, and some people prefer a tighter fit.

11 To make the front crotch fit more snugly so that the crotch seam follows the body's contour, have the

client put the pants on with the pants turned inside out. With the crotch seam allowance pointing away from the body, it's easy to pin the pants following the body's contours. For comparison purposes, the original stitching line is colored black and the pins represent the new crotch seam line. While this is similar to scooping the back crotch curve, the amount taken off the crotch curve will not be added to the front side seam, so the front circumference of the pant is reduced—causing the pants to fit more snugly. This adjustment alters the fit of the front crotch without substantially changing the length of the front crotch. You could also take in the front inseam of the pants, but this would change the total crotch length to a greater extent.

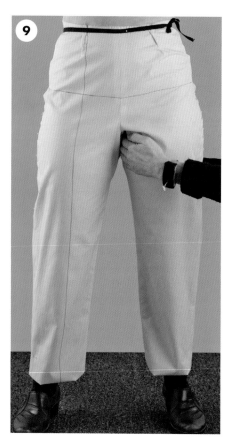

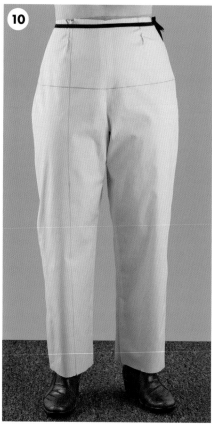

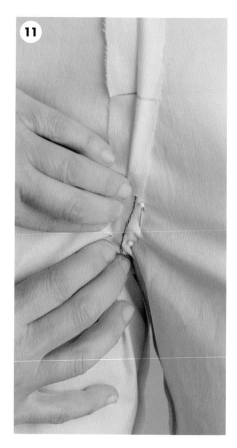

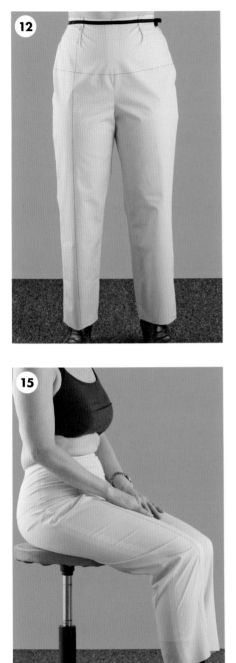

13 Taking a wedge between the waist and the HBL raises the HBL to level. To my eye, this also improves the look of this snugly fit pants front.

14 The fourth mock-up front. The slight drag lines between the center front seam and the front thigh is a result of the crotch seam being fit more snugly. To accommodate the client's muscular forward thigh without sacrificing the snug fit in the front crotch, the pant could be let out along the front outseam.

15 The tightness in the upper leg when the client sits also indicates that letting out the outseam would provide a more comfortable fit.

16 Viewed from the side, the fit is coming along nicely. The HBL is level, and the side seam is hanging straight. Note the slight crumpling along the back under the buttock.

(continued)

12 The third mock-up. It's easy to see that the front crotch is fitting more snugly. As a result, there are slight drag lines emanating from where the front crotch was taken in to the stomach and to the front thighs, which is the trade-off for snug fit through the front. Note that the HBL is dipping slightly at the center front.

17 Now that the front crotch is fitting better, revisit the back and the back crotch. Distribute the excess pinned out at the center back among the darts. Because the client has a round buttock, a larger dart intake is appropriate. To get the fabric to hang straight off the back buttock, scoop the back crotch curve and add to the back side seam, as described on page 211. Also, make another wedge above the HBL to bring the HBL to level and add to the back inseam.

BODY TYPE EXAMPLES

Insufficient Rise

The rise is the vertical distance from the crotch level to the waist. As is the case with skirts, with pants you'll be able to work efficiently and get the best fit if the garment is anchored at the waist. After the fit is complete, lowering the waistline placement is a stylistic decision.

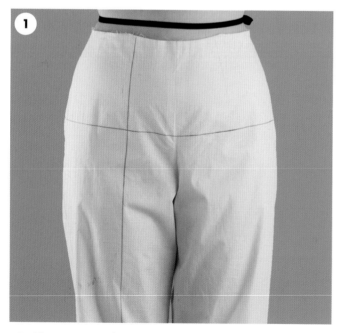

1 The rise is too short.

2 Slash the pants on the HBL and add fabric. It's best to measure and draw a consistent amount on the fabric so that the addition is precise.

Fitting Flat Buttocks

1 A good example of flat buttocks.

2 Note the amount of excess fabric at the waist, due to the small waist and wide hips.

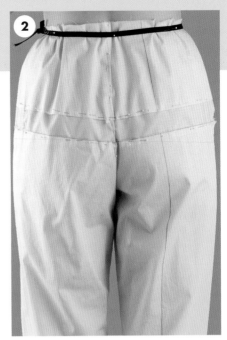

3 Keep the amount of intake on the back darts relatively small when fitting flat buttocks, since larger darts create a larger amount of space in the seat of the pants. To reduce the amount of fabric at the waist so that the dart intake is small, pin out along the center back seam and the side seams. Here, the typical adjustments for raising the HBL and scooping the crotch have also been made.

4 The second mock-up. Experiment with the dart placement and length. Even though the long dart on the left points toward the client's buttock, the result is unflattering. The two small darts on the right fit this client's high shelf hip nicely. Further reducing the amount of fabric at the center back and side seams makes the dart intake smaller, producing a better fit for the flat buttocks. Note the drag lines in the upper thigh. These "smile" lines indicate that the crotch needs more scooping.

5 Further fine-tune the HBL level by making another wedge. Scooping the back crotch a bit more eliminates the drag lines identified in step 4 and also makes the crease line hang nicely. Note that the back crotch is now cutting into the buttocks, indicating the need for more back crotch length. Provide this additional crotch length by adding to the back inseam.

(continued)

6 The third mock-up. The back crotch is still cutting into the buttocks a bit. The small folds of fabric under the buttock suggest that the back crotch curve needs to be lowered. This is a similar situation as sometimes occurs when fitting the back armhole of a bodice and the arm pushes down on the garment creating folds of fabric (see page 87). The correction for both situations is similar, but it's easier to see what needs to be done on a sleeve because you can slash the excess fabric to the crease. For pants, it helps to have the client put the pants on inside out.

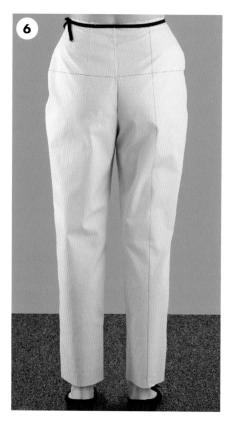

7 The pants turned inside out. The original seam at the back crotch curve is drawn in black.

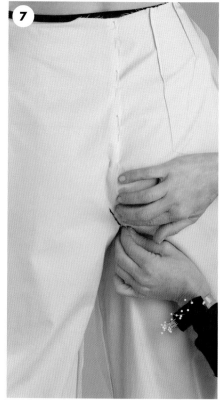

8 Here you can see that the original break point of the crotch curve is too high for the body. The dashed black line indicates where the buttocks end and the break point needs to be.

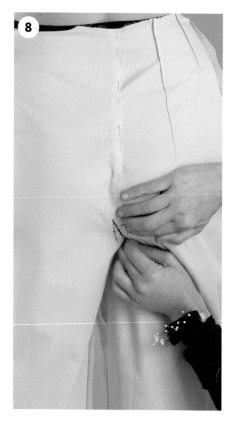

9 To see how this correction looks, sew the new crotch curve (the dashed black line), clip the curve, and have the client slip the pants back on. The back crotch curve is fitting better. The small drag line on the right side indicates that a little more fine-tuning is in order. I'd try different combinations of scooping and lowering the back crotch curve, and perhaps letting out the back inseam a very small amount. Having the client wear the pant at this point would also give you helpful feedback.

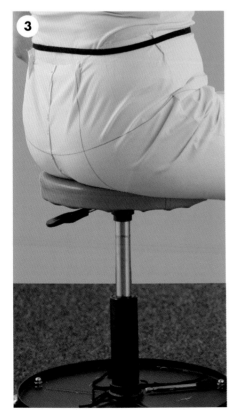

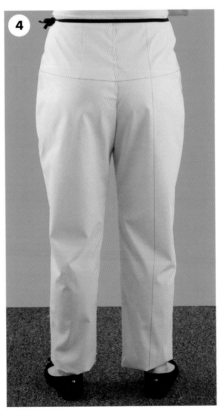

Fitting Deep Buttocks

1 Buttocks come in all shapes and sizes. If the buttock is deep but not wide, the fitting challenge is to provide enough depth to the pants without getting too much width. Here, the protrusion of the buttock is causing the HBL to dip in the back. Note the drag lines under the buttock in the thigh area, indicating the need to scoop the back crotch curve. The back crotch is also pulling into the buttocks, indicating the need for more crotch length.

2 Scooping the back crotch almost eliminates the drag lines under the buttocks at the upper thigh. It also allows the HBL to move upward. To alleviate the center back seam from cutting into the buttocks, let out the back inseam at the crotch. This will allow the crotch of the pants to move farther out on the body, which will also let the HBL rise a bit. Note that the center back waist is dipping.

3 When the client sits, the back waist drops significantly, which also indicates the need for more back crotch length. Pants often dip a bit in the back when you sit. However, I try to keep this amount to no more than ¾" (1.9 cm), and less if possible.

4 The second mock-up back. The back crotch below the HBL needs just a little fine-tuning. As usual, some experimenting is in order. Scooping the crotch to lower the curve will give the buttocks a bit more space to sit within. The pants also look tight just below the HBL at the center back. Due to the angle of the center back seam, this seam can actually be let out, which will provide more space for the deeper buttock. I would avoid letting out the side seams any more if possible, since the side of the pant already is a bit loose.

Fitting Very Full Buttocks and Tilted Waist

Figures with very full buttocks often have a tilted waist as well, so I describe fitting these two figure variations together. The elastic tied at the waist is always an important fitting tool, because the elastic will naturally seek the smallest part of the torso. This then provides you with a visual aid as well as a marking guide.

1 For a tilted waist, the back rise will be significantly longer than the front rise. If there is strain at the upper edge of the front waist, clipping along the upper edge will allow the fabric to spread and enable you to accurately establish the front waist. With very full buttocks, you must accommodate both the depth of the buttock and the height of the buttock. Note that there is strain across the hip and that there is insufficient back rise.

2 Release the side seams to allow the fabric across the hip to relax. Note that the pant length has been pinned up to allow the pant to hang without breaking on the foot or shoe.

3 Because more room is needed in the back of the pants to accommodate the full buttock, it's likely you'll need to let out the back outseam more than the front outseam. When pinning this seam, the outseam should be as straight and plumb as possible.

4 Viewed from the back, the HBL is dipping at the center back, indicating the need for more crotch length below the HBL.

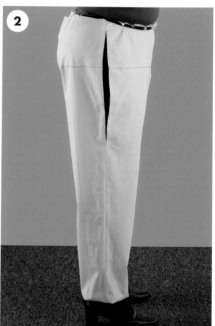

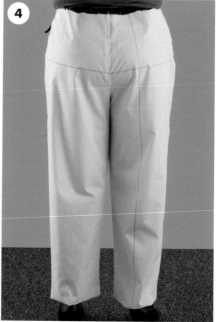

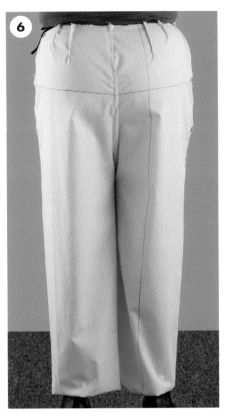

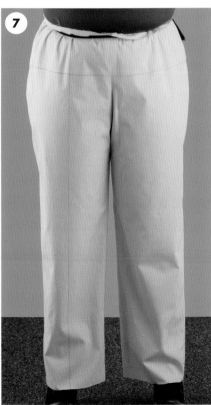

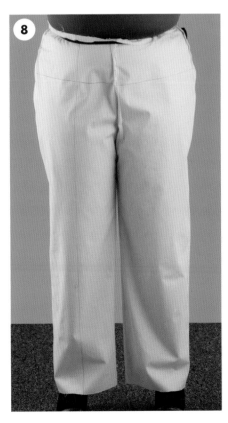

5 Release the stitching at the crotch and inseam, as described in the pants fitting process above. This allows the HBL to rise to an almost level position and the back waist of the pants to come close to the client's waist. Pin the darts. For very full buttocks, the total dart intake will be quite large. Split the intake between as many darts as needed in order to get a flattering fit. Pay attention to where the buttock is full. For this client, the longer darts point toward and accommodate the fullest part of the buttock, and the short darts accommodate the roundness of the side hip. For very full buttocks, it's not uncommon to have three darts on each side of the back pants. Note also the drag lines at the center back and that the crease line is quite crooked.

6 Take in the center back seam; this scoops the crotch, which gives the client more room front-to-back and also brings the crease line closer to being straight. Assess the amount to add to the front and back inseams, as described above in the process of fitting pants, and make a new mock-up.

7 In the second mock-up, assess the fit of the front now that the waist is in a better position. Note that there is a lot of excess fabric across the front at the waist, which would require a large amount of dart intake. Also note that the front crease line is pretty straight.

8 To eliminate some of the excess fabric at the front waist, take in the side seams and the center front. This will mean that the center front waist is angled, which in this case improves the fit. However, on a figure with a round stomach, overfitting the center front seam can make the stomach appear larger.

(continued)

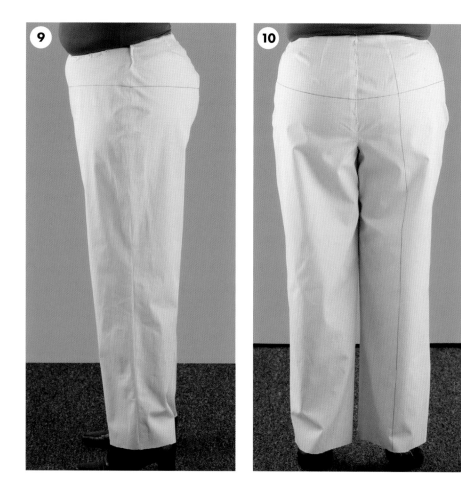

9 The third mock-up viewed from the side. With minor adjustments, the waist fits nicely, reflecting the client's tilted waist. The amount of cupping under the buttocks is the client's preference.

10 The third mock-up viewed from the back. The drag lines under the buttock indicate the need for more scooping in the back crotch curve. Because the back of the pants is snug now, I'd also make the customary addition to the back outseam. The strain at the base of the buttocks indicates that the back crotch needs to be lengthened. Fine-tuning the fit will involve experimenting with combinations of letting out the back inseam, scooping the back crotch curve, and adding to the back outseam. Lengthening the back crotch will help the HBL to level out a bit more, although it's common for the back HBL to dip slightly when the pants cup like this under the buttocks.

Fitting a Rounded Stomach

1 For a rounded stomach, be careful not to overfit the area below the stomach and through the crotch too snugly. Doing so will accentuate the roundness of the stomach in slacks-style pants. Getting the front crotch length correct will improve the overall look of the pants. The excess fabric at the front of the crotch indicates that the front crotch is just a little too long.

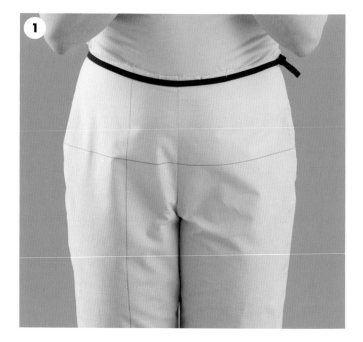

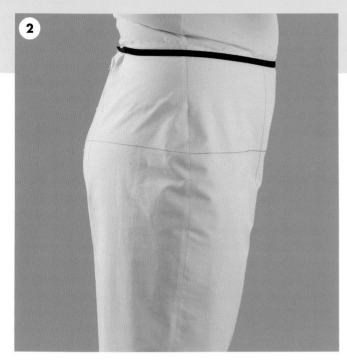

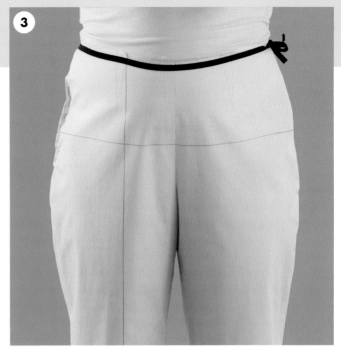

2 From the side, you can see that the fabric "floats" over the hollow space to either side of the stomach that is created by the stomach's protrusion. Unless I am fitting jeans, I prefer not to overfit this area of the body.

3 The second mock-up front. The fit is looking pretty good. If you have a dip on the side of the body above the thigh, do not overfit this area. On the client's right, the excess fabric has been pinned out, which actually accentuates the dip. The fabric needs to float over this dip, as shown on the client's left.

TYPICAL PANTS PATTERN ALTERATIONS

See Fundamentals of Altering Patterns for basic patternmaking techniques (page 44).

Adding the Crease Line on a Pant Leg

1 Measure the width of the pant leg at the hem between the two seam lines and mark the mid-point.

2 Align the pant pattern so that the grainline follows the grid, and draw a vertical line up the pant leg. The crease line can also be used as a grainline.

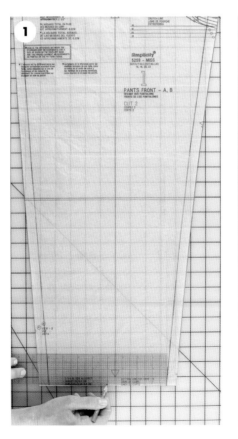

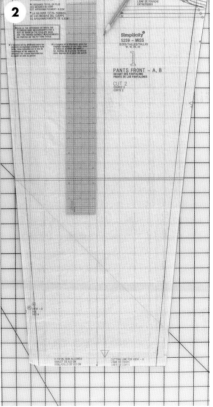

Altering the Waistline

Alterations to the waistline are made to the pattern in a normal manner: transfer tick marks from the waistline as marked on the muslin, blend the new seam line, add seam allowances, and cut on the new cut line.

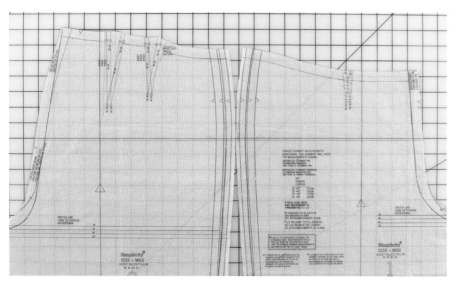

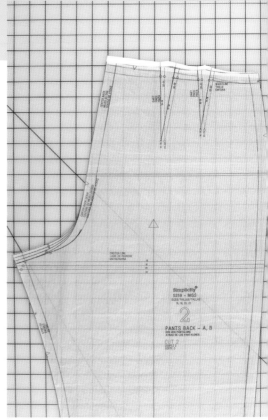

If the client has a tilted waistline, you'll need to lower the front waist. Here are front and back patterns typical for a tilted waist.

Often it is necessary to raise the back waist as you see here, especially if there is not enough fabric at the back waist when the client sits.

Lowering the Crotch Curve

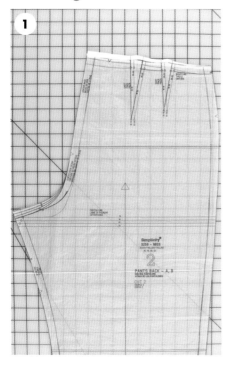

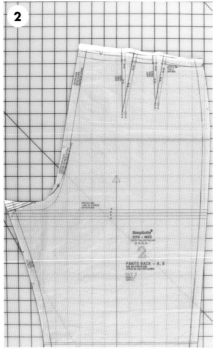

1 If the client's pelvic structure is lower than the pant pattern allows for, you'll need to lower the crotch curve.

2 The finished pattern. Note that lowering the crotch curve is different from scooping, which is shown in step 3 of the next section. The difference, however, is subtle: lowering the crotch curve provides more room in the length of the crotch; scooping provides more room in the front-to-back depth of the crotch.

A Typical Wedge-and-Scoop Alteration

Because most pant patterns do not provide enough scooping in the back crotch to accommodate a woman's pelvic structure, it is common to see the HBL dip in the center back as the back of the pants moves downward to accommodate the need for more space in the buttock area. Here are the typical pattern adjustments to correct this.

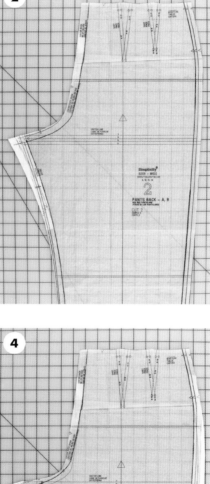

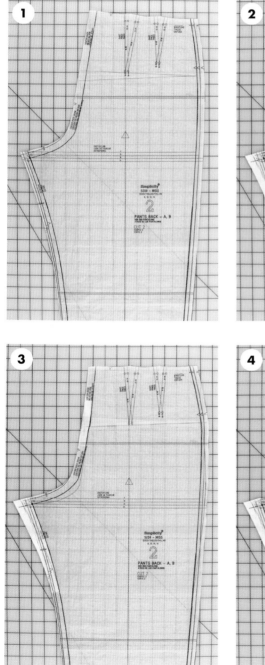

1 Draw in adjustment lines for the close-wedge, which brought the HBL to a level position. In this example, the wedge raises the center back by ¾" (1.9 cm) and goes to nothing at the outseam.

2 Add the same amount that was removed by the close-wedge to the back inseam, so as not to reduce the overall length of the crotch curve. Add even more to the back inseam than the wedge amount if, during the fitting, the released inseams spread more than the wedge amount.

3 Scoop the crotch by blending a new seam line. In order not to reduce the width of the pant back across the buttocks, add the amount of the scoop to the back outseam, making a long blend up to the waist and down toward the knee.

4 The finished pattern.

GOING TO
THE NEXT LEVEL

Only a few more steps are necessary before you are ready to sew a garment from your altered pattern. So far you have only worked on the major pattern pieces, so now you need to adjust the smaller pieces like waistbands and facings. Once you have completed the alterations to all the pieces, your pattern can be used to create new garments from different fabrics and with different style details, confident that the fit will be perfect every time.

Correcting Pattern Elements Affected by Fitting Changes

When fitting a mock-up, we concentrate on fitting the core components of the garment, such as a skirt front and skirt back. In addition to these core pattern pieces, there are usually auxiliary pattern pieces. On a skirt, for example, there is probably a waistband or waist facing and perhaps a lining pattern. On a bodice with long sleeves, there might be neck and front facings, a collar, and a cuff. During the course of fitting the core garment, changes that improve the fit often affect these auxiliary garment components, in which case these pattern pieces also need to be altered.

WAISTBANDS

Straight Waistbands

For a garment with a straight waistband, if you alter the waist in any way, you'll also need to alter the waistband. First, decide if you want any ease in the garment relative to the waistband. A small amount of ease, perhaps ⅜" to ½" (1 to 1.3 cm) total across the front, gives the skirt or pants a very slight roundness over the stomach, which some women prefer over having the skirt waist seam and waistband the same length. This is a personal decision.

Alter the existing waistband pattern by first walking it to the garment back and front, lengthening or shortening the waistband as necessary. If you prefer to draft the waistband, the length of the waistband will be the length of the waist on the pattern, less any amount of ease you want to incorporate into the garment. Alternatively, you can first develop a waistband that is comfortable and then walk it to the garment's

core pattern pieces, making any adjustments to them as necessary. In either case, it's a good idea to have a waistband on the final fitting muslin, or at the point in the garment development when you want to begin finalizing the waist.

Shaped Waistbands

Garments with shaped or contour waistbands should be fit with the waistband attached to the fitting muslin, since it is an integral part of the garment. Be sure to walk and true the seam, joining the shaped waistband to the rest of the garment.

FACINGS

Neck, front, and waist facings often require adjustments, since the perimeter of a garment is frequently altered during the fitting process.

Altering a Facing Pattern

If there are minor changes, simply make the same change to the facing

as was made on the garment. For example, if a back neck dart was used to improve the fit of the garment, the resulting change in the neck facing would be as follows:

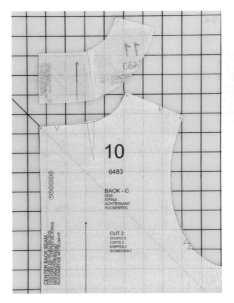

Lay the back neck facing on top of the back pattern and draw the dart onto the facing pattern. Rather than having a dart in the facing, make a close-wedge adjustment: cut along one of the dart legs, align the dart legs, and tape in place. Here are the pattern and the corrected neck facing.

Drafting a New Facing Pattern

If extensive pattern changes have been made to the core pattern piece, it's often easiest to draft a new facing pattern.

To make a facing pattern, first lay paper over the altered core pattern piece where the facing occurs. Trace the outer perimeter of the core pattern and cut away the excess paper.

Then decide how deep you want the facing to be. Use the same measurement as the original facing, or change the facing depth if you feel it will enhance your garment to have a narrower or deeper facing. Measure and mark the new facing depth, blend with a fashion ruler, and cut along this cut line. Page 216 below includes a step-by-step description of how to develop a facing pattern in conjunction with developing a lining pattern.

Most of the time, facings are developed directly from the pattern as described here. If the fashion fabric is quite bulky and thick, it's best to make the facing slightly smaller than the garment itself. This allows for the turn of the cloth, since the inner layer of fabric will need to be slightly smaller than the outer layer of fabric. How much smaller to make the facing in comparison to the garment depends on the style of the garment, the thickness of the garment fashion fabric, and the thickness of the facing fabric. Cutting off 1/16" to 1/8" (1.6 to 3 mm) from the outer edges of the facing is a good starting place.

COLLARS

On garments with collars, if you alter the neckline of the pattern, you also need to alter the collar pattern. If the neckline is altered substantially, be sure to make a mock-up of the collar because it may need more extensive adjustments to maintain the intended degree of collar roll.

The object of the collar alteration is to adjust the length of the neck seam on the collar pattern so that it is the same length as the neck seam of the garment pattern. It's important to alter the neck seam on the collar in the same place that the neck seam of the garment was changed. For instance, if the center back seam of the garment was altered, adjust the neck seam of the collar at the center back. If the neck seam of the garment changed along the shoulder line, then make the change on the neck seam of the collar where it intersects with the shoulder seam.

To pick up the exact location of a neckline alteration onto the collar, walk the neck seam of the collar pattern along the neck seam of the garment. Start walking the patterns on the portion of the garment where no changes have occurred. For instance, if only the center back of the garment was adjusted, start walking the patterns at center front, making the change at center back. If the front neckline of the garment was lowered, and there was also a change along the shoulder line, start walking the patterns at the center

back, making one change at the shoulder point and another change at the center front.

The following two examples provide the theory behind this type of pattern adjustment, which should help you understand how to make many different collar alterations.

Shortened Neckline

1   In this example, the back neckline of the garment was shortened while creating a neck dart. Walk the patterns with the collar on top, and mark the collar pattern at the first dart leg on the garment neckline. Continue walking the patterns, and mark the collar pattern at the second dart leg on the garment. Continue to walk the pattern to the center back if you wish to check the accuracy of the pattern.

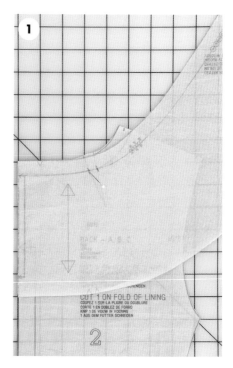

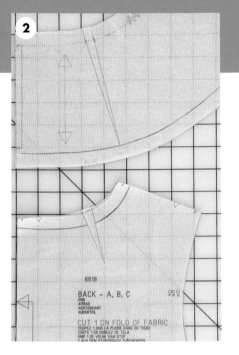

2 On the collar pattern, use a straightedge ruler and draw a line from the first dart leg mark to the seam line at the opposite side of the collar. Then draw a line from the second dart leg to the same point on the opposite seam line, and make a close-wedge between these two lines.

Lengthened Neckline

In this example, the front neckline of the garment was lowered, lengthening the neck seam. Walk the neckline seam of the collar pattern to the front neckline seam, starting at the neck match point. Pin the collar in place when you come to the end of the collar.

Note that this alteration is a starting point for correcting the collar. You will need to make a mock-up of the adjusted collar in order to fine-tune its shaping.

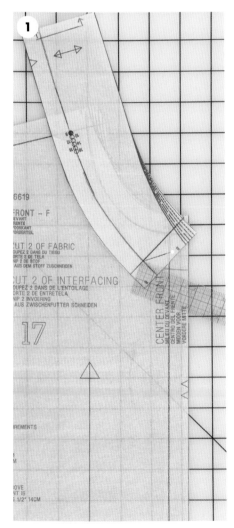

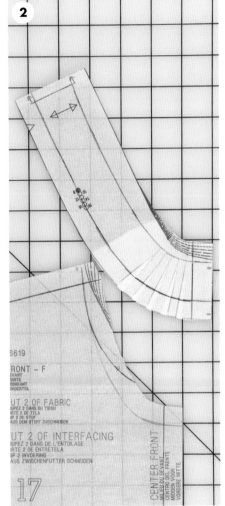

1 Measure the distance between the two differing center front points. This is the amount that the collar needs to be lengthened, which will be done with a number of open-wedge adjustments.

2 Draw several lines on the collar between the neck edge and the outer seam of the collar. Each of these lines indicates the location of an open-wedge adjustment. You will get better results with several smaller wedges than one larger one. Since most of the lowering of the neckline took place near the center front of the garment, the placement for the wedge adjustments has been made toward the front edge of the collar. Cut and spread the collar over additional paper. To spread the wedges, it is helpful to stick pins through each wedge segment into the grid board below, holding them in place until enough length has been added to the collar and then taping them to the added paper. Lastly, blend the new seam line and cut line, and trim away the excess paper.

LININGS

Always make the same adjustments to lining patterns as you make to garment patterns. If there are extensive pattern alterations to the garment, it is often easiest to develop a new lining pattern. Most basic linings are the same as the garment, with just two adjustments: the lining is shorter, taking into consideration the hem allowance for the garment; and the lining omits the area of the garment facing. For most garments, there is no need to make a size adjustment to the lining pattern for the turn of the cloth, but if you are working with thick and bulky fabric, then follow the same principles as for facings.

In the following example, I make a lining pattern for a skirt back as well as the facing pattern. This illustrates the theory of how many linings are developed, so that you can apply this theory to other situations.

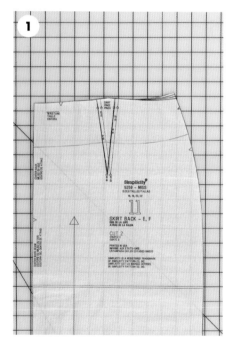

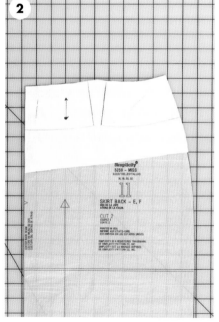

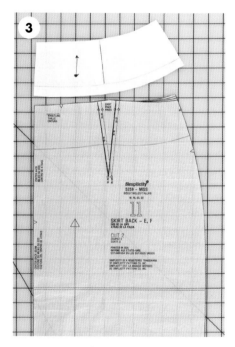

1 On the skirt garment pattern, draw the lining/facing seam line where the facing and lining will connect.

2 To develop the facing pattern, lay paper over the upper portion of the skirt and pin in place. Draw and cut along the outer perimeter of the skirt at the waist, back seam, and side seam. Draw the lining/facing seam and the waist dart, tracing them from the skirt pattern. Draw the grainline arrow, taking it from the skirt.

3 Unpin the facing pattern. Cut and close the waist dart, add the seam allowance to the lining/facing seam, and cut away the excess paper. Here is the finished facing pattern.

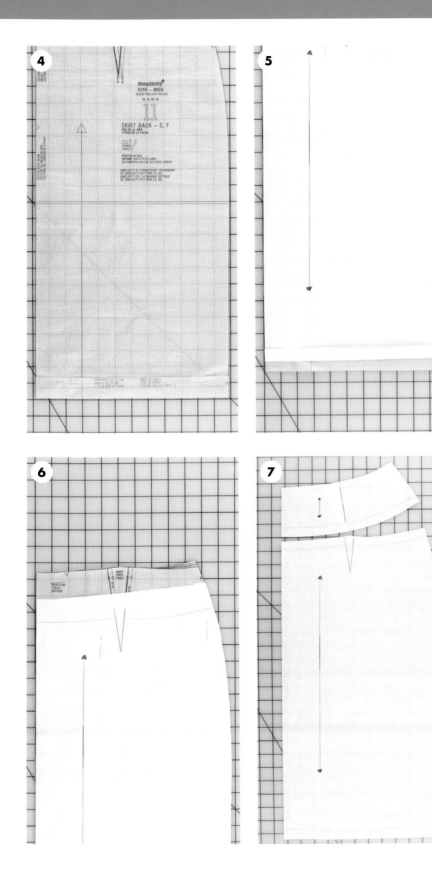

4 To develop the lining pattern, fold the garment pattern along its hemline and pin in place. Decide how much distance you want between the lining hem and the garment hem. In this example, I will make the lining hem 5/8" (1.6 cm) shorter than the garment. Measure 5/8" (1.6 cm) up from the garment hem and draw a line indicating the finished lining hem (indicated in blue).

5 Lay paper over the lower portion of the skirt and pin in place. Draw and cut along the skirt side and back. Decide how much hem allowance you want on the lining. Measure down from the lining hemline this amount and draw the cut line. Cut away the excess paper. Here I have folded the lining back along its hemline so that the garment pattern and lining pattern are stacked.

6 To finish the lining pattern, draw the lining/facing seam, the dart, and the grainline arrow, tracing them from the skirt pattern.

7 Unpin the lining pattern. Add the seam allowance to the lining/facing seam, true the dart legs, and cut away the excess paper. Here are the finished facing and lining patterns.

Get Creative

For many sewers, developing and improving their fitting and pattern-making skills naturally sparks their creativity. This is because they are no longer limited to just what the pattern companies have to offer. Rather, commercial patterns become a wonderful jumping-off point—a place to get started that lets you implement your own ideas and cultivate your own sense of style and design.

USING STYLE LINES TO CREATE PLEASING PROPORTIONS

One aspect of fitting is to create pleasing proportions on the client's body by means of how the garment is fit and through the use of style lines. This is touched on repeatedly throughout the fitting photos. Here are a few more examples.

Skirt Proportions

1 This straight skirt accentuates the client's rectangular figure.

2 Pegging the skirt so that it is narrower at the hem helps to visually elongate the figure and give her some shape, although pegging it too much will accentuate her hips.

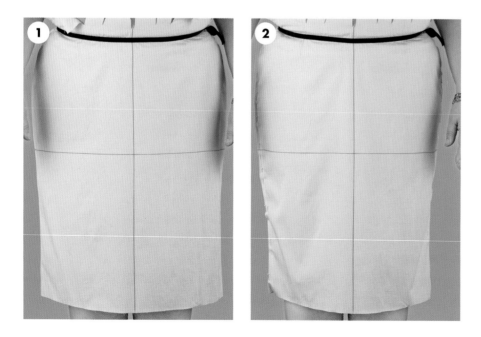

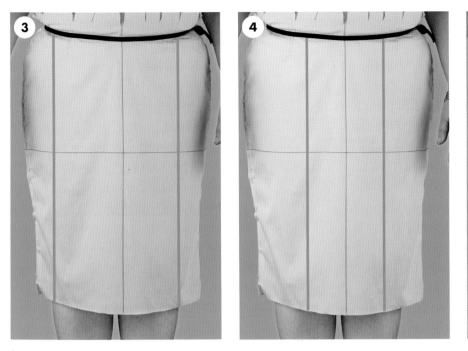

3 Developing princess seams for the skirt also proportions the body, breaking the expanse of fabric at the hip. However, the position of the princess lines impacts the overall effect a great deal. Here, the princess seams are too far apart, making the body look wide.

4 If the princess seams are too close together, the hips appear to be larger.

5 To my eye, this placement of the princess seams is flattering.

6 The same is true on the skirt back. Without any princess seams, the figure looks quite boxy and the buttocks are visually prominent.

(continued)

7 If the princess seams are too far apart, the buttocks appear to be larger.

8 If the princess seams are too close together, the hips appear to be larger.

9 To my eye, this placement of the princess seams proportions the client's back nicely.

DART EQUIVALENTS

Sewing a dart to its endpoint is just one way to resolve a dart intake. Tucks and gathers can all be implemented as dart equivalents rather than sewing a dart. As long as this kind of dart equivalent has the same intake, the pattern pieces will still walk and be true. We are accustomed to seeing darts in certain places on a garment, but using tucks or gathers can add a splash of creativity.

COLLAR VARIATIONS

Changing the shape of the outer edge of a collar is easy to do and allows you to impart to a garment your own sense of style.

Mandarin Collars

A mandarin collar can be as subdued or dramatic as you want. Rather than making a mandarin collar the same height all the way around, consider making it higher in the back, sloping gently to the front. It can overlap at the center front, meet at the center front, or end before the center front to create an interesting space at the neckline. The ends can be rounded, or squared, or treated in any way your imagination desires. For example, you can develop a Mandarin with a wing collar variation.

I think it's easiest to develop the fold-back wing by manipulating and experimenting in paper. Cut off the seam allowance of the upper edge and front edge of the Mandarin collar. Tape in paper where you will develop the wing collar.

(continued)

Experiment with all sorts of interesting angles and cuts. I find playing in paper this way very relaxing and fun.

1 Fold the paper along the front/upper edge to get a pleasing angle for where the wing will fold back. Draw a potential shape for the wing, which is the portion of the collar that folds back. Cut along lines that you think might work and assess what you have created.

2 Here is my pattern with the wing unfolded. To finish the pattern, add seam allowances to the upper and front edges of the pattern and cut along the cut line.

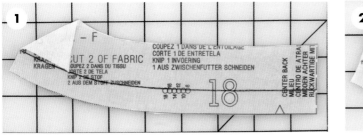

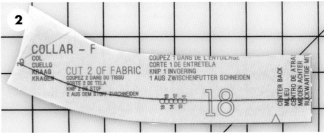

Rolled Collars

The front of a rolled collar is usually pointed or rounded, but the possibilities are endless. Playing in paper is an easy way to get your imagination working.

To do this, trace the collar onto additional paper, leaving plenty of paper along the outer perimeter. Let your imagination loose, and see what you come up with. Undulating curves **(A)**, a scalloped edge, a fold-back point that will be held in place with a button, or perhaps even a layered look.

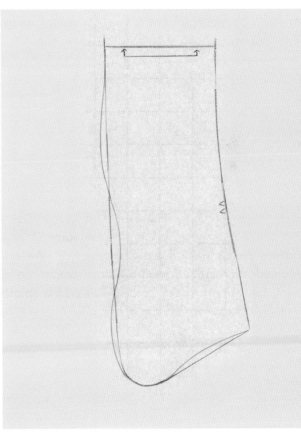

(A) A pattern I made for a collar with an undulating curve.

CUFFS AND SLEEVE HEMS

Cuffs and sleeve hems provide another opportunity to add some flare or enhance a design theme used throughout a garment. For instance, if a collar has rounded edges, you can mimic this curve in the cuff or sleeve hem.

Cuffs can be any size you want, from a very narrow band to a deep expanse covering most of the forearm. Buttons set off a cuff or sleeve hem detail very nicely, as shown on page 212.

Cuffs can turn back or extend down from the sleeve, depending on the effect you want. It's easy to create interesting shaping at the lower edge of a cuff using your ruler and a little imagination. For instance, the overlapping side of a cuff can be squared off or rounded. Or you could design a pretty scalloped edge.

While there are times we want the hem of a sleeve to be unnoticeable, the lower edge of a sleeve provides great design opportunities. For a sleeve that's a bit loose at the wrist, form a tuck and hold it in place with a snap or decorative button. Sometimes solving a problem leads your mind to other design possibilities. If you purposefully enlarged the lower edge of a sleeve on a pattern, you could then use one or more pleats to control the excess fabric, thereby creating a stylistic element for the garment.

Two-piece sleeves with a seam down the center of the sleeve provide wonderful design opportunities that are interesting on any length of sleeve. You can utilize the center seam for design purposes, such as rounding the edges or creating a small triangular fold-back similar to how the wing collar was created.

Small details such as these are often what elevates a garment from being quite good to looking exceptional. These details do not have to take center stage and be the focus of the garment. Often, extremely subtle details used with restraint are what make a garment look beautiful. And when interesting details are supported with good fit and well-executed pattern work, you will indeed be taking your creativity to the next level.

About the Author

Making clothing for her private clientele for more than twenty-five years, Sarah specializes in fit, innovative pattern design, and quality garment construction. Sarah has been a longtime and active member of the Association of Sewing and Design Professionals and was the overall winner of the 2008 THREADS/ ASDP "Fluid Fabrics" challenge. She has written more than twenty articles for THREADS magazine and has contributed to numerous other publications, including "Secrets for Sewing Knits" in PatternReview.com's *1,000 Clever Sewing Shortcuts & Tips*.

Dedicated to promoting the craft of garment-making, Sarah teaches from her studio in Maryland, online at PatternReview.com, and as a guest lecturer at venues around the United States. She currently offers classes for sewing enthusiasts and sewing professionals on fitting and patternmaking, working with knit fabrics, all levels of sewing techniques, and garment design.